The Star-Ledger
Munchmobile
Jersey Eats

BY
PETER GENOVESE

EDITED BY ENRIQUE LAVIN

ACKNOWLEDGMENTS

There are a lot of people who make The Star-Ledger Munchmobile go, and it's time to thank them. Let's start with the photographers over the years, who have been not only consummate professionals but good road buddies: Frank Conlon, Joe Epstein, Tony Kurdzuk, Ed Murray, Bill Perlman, Mia Song and, for the last five years, Tim Farrell.

In the Features Department, Susan Olds and Enrique Lavin preside over all things Munch, including editing this book. Anne-Marie Cottone has lent her sharp editing eye to the weekly report, while Bill Ramsay and the Features Copy Desk have ensured it was copy edited and proofread. Extra thanks to Tracy Politowicz for edits in this book. Heather Rohan is our Munch photo editor, while Donna Gialanella oversaw the photography in this book. And we can't forget former Features editor Rosemary Parrillo.

Our amazing page designers, including Pablo Colon, Elise Levine, Mark Morrissey and Rob Russo, worked on the Friday Munch reports; while graphic artists/illustrators Andre Malok and Drew Sheneman worked on the van design, and artist Andrew Garcia-Phillips designed the nifty online map.

Let's not forget the folks over at nj.com, who have been instrumental in creating the Munchmobile's strong online presence. And a special thanks to Bob Provost and Doug Hutton in our Marketing Department.

And, of course, Jim Willse, the Big Dog's creator and guiding light, and Mark DiIonno, captain of the Big Dog in that landmark first year.

Finally, this book would not have been possible without Frederick Kaimann and the Listings Desk, who called all 900-plus original stops to verify if they were still open. Helping the cause were Rhea Bernard, Diego Cupolo, Dan DePasquale, Sean Ewing, Michael Fensom, Yvonne Lardizabal, Thomas Levy, Gregory C. Washington and Christina Wheeler.

Thank you very Munch!

PREFACE

How many times has this happened to you? You're on the road, either alone or with the family, and you're ready to eat. You see a couple of places, but you're not so sure... they could be terrific, they could be terrible.

Do you take a gamble? Do you go for a little adventure?

If you're like most people, probably not. You play it safe. You go for the security of the brand name — McDonald's, Burger King, whatever — and you hate yourself for not trying something different.

The Munchmobile is here to change all that. We're going to give you a consumer's guide to breaking the chain-food habit.

With those words, the Munchmobile was launched 10 years ago, and the basic idea is still the same.

New Jersey is a place where people shouldn't settle for chain-store food.

We are, after all, the inventors and authenticators of the traveling meal experience. From the stage-route taverns of Colonial times, to the ubiquitous Jersey diner of the 1950s.

Before the Parkway and Turnpike, and their leased rest stops, and before the corporate, plastic-roofing of American eateries, the state highways and downtowns of New Jersey were home to thousands of mom-and-pop breakfast-and-lunch joints, owner-operated hot dog, hamburger and ice cream stands. Many were gone. Many were not. It was the mission of the Munchmobile to explore and discover the places of great local reputation, and tell the world.

And we did. Through the newspaper, and nj.com, and News 12 New Jersey. A band of us — me, the writer (and driver); photographer Bill Perlman; News 12 reporter Melinda Murphy and cameraman Bill Schlosser; and Elizabeth Willse, who wrote a blog for nj.com, although they didn't call it blogging then.

Taking suggestions from readers, we went out to find the best of simple, highway and downtown staples. Hot dogs, and the Jersey-centric Italian hot dog. Diner breakfasts. Burgers and pizza. Deli sandwiches, including the Jersey-centric Sloppy Joe.

We traveled the state in a van with a big hot dog mounted on top, the same one the Munchmobile carries today. From Day One, which started at the former Lido Diner on Route 22 in Springfield, the Big Dog was a hit.

It inspired glee. There is no other way to say it. People crowded the truck wherever we went. Kids on school buses would giggle and wave. Other drivers would point and wave.

We gave out T-shirts and trinkets. The suggestion letters and e-mails poured in. We took guest Munchers, notably Hot Dog John and Pipe Band Irv. We ate, and ate, and ate.

And despite having to once consume five Italian hot dogs in one day, it was the most fun I ever had in this business.

Mark DiIonno

FOREWORD

My uncle, Felice DeGregorio, ran an Italian restaurant called Felix's, in Greenwich Village in New York City. I worked there on and off as a bartender and waiter, and it was there that I had an important epiphany about restaurants: It's not the food people remember, it's the experience of the food.

Think about it. You don't remember how that Taylor ham-and-egg sandwich tasted at the Lido Diner in 1988. What you remember is eating that sandwich there with your friends, maybe after a big game, maybe with the person you later married.

The Munchmobile was born as a way to bring Star-Ledger readers together around the shared experience of food. Not haute cuisine, but the kind of food that is served by the roadside. Pizzas and Italian hot dogs and fried clams — Jersey food. The noshing we recall with fondness (and maybe a touch of heartburn).

This book collects 10 years of Munching, from one end of the state to the other. It is a celebration of the never-ending quest for the perfect lemon ice and hamburger and onion ring, and an updated guide to where those essentials might be found. Put it in your car and hit the road — and if you find an even better place to grab a bagel, let us know.

Enjoy.

Jim Willse

TABLE OF CONTENTS

INTRODUCTION

In the first story about the Munchmobile, in June 1998, then-Features Editor Mark DiIonno announced the birth of The Star-Ledger's roving roadside food patrol, vowing "to find the best fast-food places around, and we don't mean Mickey Dee's."

In that first year, Mark and his crew, including photographer William Perlman and News 12 New Jersey reporter Melinda Murphy, visited 60 hot dog and burger joints, diners, ice cream stands and other restaurants in search of the state's best eats.

The following year, when yours truly had taken over the wheel of the Munchmobile, the crew visited 74 places; in 2000, the number was 111.

The Big Dog was off and running.

"When my husband and I first noticed your series, we thought it was a nice piece of fluff," Christina and Dan Bilinksi wrote in August 1998. "Now we're hooked."

It didn't take long for other readers to get hooked on the Big Dog's exploits.

"The Big Dog is the coolest of all food reviews," Bob Zwigard wrote in 2000. "'It shows great appreciation for the many diverse types of culture in New Jersey. The meat and potatoes of the Big Dog is how it goes into the deep roots of New Jersey. It's not about glitz and glam. It's about the taste of New Jersey."

The Munchmobile is about New Jersey, period. Our weekly outings are really road trips with food. We cover the state; last summer we hit all 21 counties for the first time — in two days, no less, on a madcap end-of-year eating spree around the state. Sound easy? You try it!

Our typical Saturday trip is lots of fun, but it's hard work. Really! At least for me; I don't get to take a nap in the back, like many Munchers do on the 14-16 hour trips. Throw in driving 200-300 miles, shooting video, interviewing people and live-blogging on the Munchmobile Blog, and you have one busy day.

It all hits you the next morning; good luck trying to get up before noon!

Of course, there are always the Munchers who

giddily e-mail me the next morning and announce, "Wow, I was so hungry this morning — I ate a big breakfast!"

Whatever.

There is the matter of all that eating. People say, "You don't actually eat all that food, do you?" Well, yes we do; your typical Muncher is a good eater; they know what they're getting into — and no matter how stuffed they may be, if you put good food in front of them, it will disappear!

"My mom said, 'You're not going to eat everything.' I said, 'Watch me,' " Michelle Rossi said during our pork roll trip in July 2006.

The Big Dog would not be what it is today without our readers. Much of the reason for its ever-increasing popularity is that readers have direct input. They tell us where to go. They get to ride along with us. They can win T-shirts in our weekly trivia contest. They get their letters published in our Letter of the Week feature.

In 2001, we started taking readers on our weekly trips. Competition to become a "Muncher" has become fierce; in 2007, we received 400 or so applications. This year? Just take a look at the mountain of paper on my desk!

"Anyone can get into Princeton," Muncher Bob Schwalb said in 2005. "Try getting into Munch U."

Each year's theme is different. For example, in 2003, the theme was Survivor Munch; the same five people rode all summer to complete for valuable prizes and the honor of being named Top Muncher.

The next year saw the Summer of Love; we matched single Munchers: three men, three women on each trip. Two of the Munchers thought it was a great idea — they got married!

In 2008, we went with "The Adventures of Mighty Munch." Our caped superhero — "defending New Jersey eateries since 1998" — bears an uncanny resemblance to the Munchmobile's driver.

One of the more memorable Munch applications came from Emilie Parmalind, a student at East Hanover High School, who made a black-and-white video of herself enduring breakfast, lunch and dinner, with anguished strains of opera music in the background. "Munchmobile, save me from this agony," she said.

Big Dog to the rescue!

Our Munchers come from all ages, occupations and backgrounds. Most are everyday folk, although many became neighborhood celebrities after their names and photos appeared in the paper.

"I walked into one pizza place with my Muncher T-shirt on," Michael Goldberger of Westfield recalled. "They all started coming over to me, 'Can I get you this, can I get you that?' I was treated like royalty."

We never call a restaurant beforehand to let them know we're coming, so the reaction when the Big Dog rolls into the parking lot can range from open-mouth stares ("What is with the giant hot dog on the roof?") to downright shock and awe.

"Oh my goodness!" Judy Church shouted when we showed up at Church's Kitchen in Union in 2001. "Barbara, the Munchmobile is here! I'm having a nervous breakdown!"

It took a while for her to calm down.

For many, being a Muncher is the thrill of a summer, if not a once-in-a-lifetime experience.

"Thanks for taking me along," Dave Brooks said after his Munch ride in 2006. "Now I can die in peace."

There is no dying — or crying, for that matter — on the Munchmobile. Each trip is different: different set of riders, different parts of the state, and different kinds of foods. Some categories we do every year — Down the Shore, Fourth of July picnics, ice cream, healthy food, breakfast — while we try to keep the rest of the trips as diverse as possible.

In 2007, we did everything from chocolate chip cookies, pancakes and delis to soul food Middle Eastern, Caribbean and sushi. In 2008, we did hot dogs, curry, steak sandwiches and pastries — and that was just in the first few weeks!

My favorite trip is probably the Fourth of July excursion, when we crash other people's picnics (with their permission, of course). It's a great trip because you're outside all day, you're always eating something different, and we're treated like family wherever we go.

"I would love to stay in MunchmobileLand for the rest of the summer," Lea O'Shea said during our cookie run last summer.

Yeah, Lea, we know what you mean. Ten years after it began, the Munchmobile has gone beyond being the coolest set of wheels in the state. It's New Jersey's No. 1 roadside food source; by the end of this summer, we will have visited nearly 1,100 places and logged 50,000-plus miles. It's New Jersey, period, celebrating not only the food but culture, diversity and scenic wonder of this lively little state.

"We have Bruce, Bon Jovi, the beach, boys and the Big Dog!" Muncher Donna Helm once said. "What more does a schoolteacher need? Send me out! I'll eat my way through the great state of New Jersey!"

Which is what we've done the past 10 years, and hope to keep doing.

Peter Genovese
Newark, New Jersey

Mangos,
Hackensack

Charlie's
Pool Room,
Alpha

Cliff's
Dairy Maid,
Ledgewood

Santillo's
Pizza,
Elizabeth

DeLorenzo's
Tomato Pies,
Trenton

Ob-Co's
Donuts,
Toms River

The Bait Box,
Greenwich

The Star-Ledger
MUNCHMOBILE

ORIGINS OF THE BIG DOG

James Korpai got a call.

It was an emergency.

"We need a 9-foot hot dog we can bolt to the roof rack of a van," the caller said. "It must be able to survive summer monsoons and lightning strikes. It must be able to travel thousands of miles on rough New Jersey roads and withstand speeds of 65 miles an hour without becoming airborne. It must appetizing — we want a real dog, not a cartoon caricature. And we must have it in 48 hours."

"No problem," Korpai said.

Forty-eight hours later, New Jersey's most famous inedible hot dog was born.

No job is too big for Korpai. He calls his Queens, N.Y., company The Big Idea.

With fellow craftsman Matt Targon, whose Long Island company is called Flying Monkey, Korpai has over the years sculpted a King Kong-sized gorilla, a giant sub sandwich (with three different kinds of meat, Swiss cheese, lettuce and tomato), a 16-foot Nutcracker (as in the ballet) and a whole produce aisle's worth of fruit and vegetables.

"We've done big broccoli, a big tomato, big corn-on-the-cob, a big apple," says Korpai, 26, a graduate of the School of Visual Arts in New York. "They're usually done for farm stands."

The big hot dog is sculpted foam board packed onto a metal frame.

"We used an insulation tube for the basic shape of the hot dog," Korpai says.

A polyurethane foam is then sprayed over the rough shape, then carved and sanded down to the perfect shape.

"Then we coat it with a high-density polyurethane to create a hard shell to make it indestructible," Korpai says. "Then prime it and paint it."

As for the 48-hour deadline, Korpai made it with three or four hours to spare.

"We're used to doing rush jobs," he says. "We did two 18-foot candy canes for a Kmart commercial in less time than that."

(By Mark DiIonno, published Sept. 3, 1998 in The Star-Ledger)

Most pounds lost in one Munch summer: 9½, Pete Genovese, 2000

IT'S ALL ABOUT JERSEY

The Star-Ledger is the voice of New Jersey, so it comes as no surprise that the Munchmobile has become the state's leading roadside food source.

From the beginning, we avoided fancy-schmancy and chain restaurants in favor of independently-owned, mom-and-pop places where you could get good food, cheap. Little-known places and holes-in-the-wall became a Big Dog specialty. We visited and reviewed some nice restaurants over the years, sure.

There was something else about the Munchmobile from the beginning — it was more than just about food and a van with a giant hot dog on top, it was about Jersey. Witness Mark DiIonno's description of Route 22 in the second-ever Munchmobile story in 1998:

The Lido (Diner) sits at the western tip of the shopping center island of the Route 22 we have come to hate: that stretch of death road through Springfield and Union, where megastores and strip malls line not only both sides of the road, but are overgrown in the center median as well. The effect, of course, is bumper car mayhem — people coming in from the right, then shooting across three lanes of traffic to get to, say the Wiz flagship store in the middle isle. Fenders be damned, full speed ahead.

Stories in that first year included quotes from Jerseyans reminiscing about their favorite food hangouts of the past. Anthony DiFumieri mentioned Louie Ting-a-Ling in Newark, who made "the best Italian hot dogs" and "the best homemade lemon ice right in the garage next door."

John Mullarkey fondly recalled Grunning's ice cream stand in South Orange. "They made the best ice cream, especially their mint chip. They used the semi-sweet chocolate, it was more like shavings than chips. I lost a piece of my childhood when the last store closed."

Food memories may be the strongest of all. For proof, you didn't have to look any further than Agostino Fiorarancio's vivid description of the hot dog stands of his childhood:

The Weequahic section of Newark was once home to the all-beef hot dog wars pitting three giants: Sabin's, Mittleman's and Syd's. Sabin grilled and Mittleman boiled. Walking down Lyons one passed Sabin first. Those who liked them boiled were forced to withstand the tirades of Sabin — standing in white apron at his grill, which opened onto the sidewalk — challenging all who opted for his competitor's style. Both have passed into history.

In 1999, my first year behind the wheel, we started expanding the Big Dog's horizons, taking longer trips and introducing all kinds of food to our Munching menu. But the same Jersey pride and spirit, and sense of place, ran through

15

the stories, just as it had during DiIonno's time.

I loved taking the Munchers to parts of the state they had never heard about, much less seen. The Big Dog became an ongoing geography lesson. If there's one line I've heard more than any other in the past 10 years, it's "Where are we?" Or "I can't believe this is New Jersey!"

There's so much North Jerseyans don't know about Central and especially South Jersey. They may know A.C. and the one place down the Shore they visit every summer, but that's about it. I wanted the Big Dog to open readers' eyes not only to the dizzying food choices out there but the state's ethnic and scenic diversity. Often, the scenery was, oh so Jersey.

Tommy's Hot Dogs (Carteret), with its multicolored shingle roof, is located in a former garage. Tables outside offer a scenic view of the tank farms down the street.
— Hot dogs, 1999

And:

The best cheesecakes down the Shore come from a center traffic island, which sounds so Jersey, but one taste of the plain cheesecake at Charlie's Cafe in Normandy Beach may make you swear off supermarket or mail-order cheesecake forever, and think nothing of braving epic Jersey Shore traffic jams to grab a sweet, sinful slice.
— Cheesecakes, 2002

By 2002, the Big Dog had become a trusted roadside food source. No part of the state was off-limits. Since there's only so much time in the Munch day, I started heading out on solo trips to hit towns and restaurants we couldn't reach on our regular weekly trip. This took me down roads less-traveled, to say the least.

Out in the middle of nowhere, past the back of beyond and the end of the road, sits a weatherbeaten, gray-shingled building on stilts overlooking the Maurice River and, beyond it, Delaware Bay.
A furnace-hot breeze blows across the parking lot. The gray building is a restaurant. The waitress brings over good homemade lemonade, served in cylindrical blue plastic cups. The crab cake sandwich — a huge slab of crab with a skin so perfectly fried and flaky you end up peeling it with your fingers and sliding it in your mouth — might be the best you've ever had.
You're in a town called Shellpile. Just down the road is Bivalve. It is about as close to being off the map as you can be in New Jersey.
— Shellfish, 2001

Being a Jersey boy (born in Trenton, spent all but my college years in the Garden State), I wanted to show readers — and Munchers — "my" Jersey. The Jersey not just of crowded highways and strip malls but winding country roads and roadside markets. On our annual Down the Shore trip, I hit the entire Shore, not just popular and over-publicized places like Belmar, Point Pleasant and LBI.

I wanted to take Munchers to places like Leeds Point, home of the unforgettable Oyster Creek Inn, a seafood shack perched at the edge of Barnegat Bay, and, amazingly, just minutes from the Parkway. "That's not the Shore," an editor insisted. Oh, yes it is!

No Jersey Shore summer is complete without a trip to the "other" shore — the Raritan bayfront. The Old Heidelberg, at Keansburg Amusement Park, is bar as carnival funhouse, with its crazily-tilted floor (that's what you get when you're built on sand) and one-item menu. Hot dogs on the open-air grill, and Elvis on the sound system.
— Down the Shore, 2003

Wallington (Bergen County) has the highest percentage of people of Polish ancestry of any incorporated town in the country.

DiIonno riffed memorably on the boardwalk — that quintessential Jersey icon — in a 1998 story:

It is a place of childhood dreams and teenage fantasies, where adults go to recapture both. It is a place inhabited by grifters and immortalized by the Drifters.
It is the boardwalk, down by the sea.
It's a Jersey institution. The Jersey Shore boardwalk — with all its endearing tackiness — was invented in Atlantic City in 1870 and it's been thriving in most places since. It is such an enduring piece of Americana that Disney built a sanitized version of it in Orlando.
But you can't get Kohr's ice cream or Steel's fudge or Joey Tomatoes' pizza or Ann's zeppoles at Disney World. For those, you have to go down the Jersey Shore.
So we did.

We've been to the bottom of Jersey, and the top, and everywhere in between. "Where's Macopin?" one story asked. "North of Newfoundland, the one straddling the Morris/Passaic line." We've done several trips down specific highways where Jersey in all its glorious and maddening variety is on display. Here is an excerpt from our Route 22 field trip in 2002:

Toto Dry Cleaners. See More TV and Appliance Center. Hair in a Pinch. Mr. Lincoln's Highway is a colorful commercial stretch. Strip malls, sure, but strip malls with a sense of humor.

"In Garfield," began another Munch installment, "The Big Dog drove past Whoopee Liquors and Sushi Boy, successfully navigated Confusion Corner — the not-so-well-marked intersection of Locust and Main — and rumbled into Rutherford, the self-titled "borough of trees."

We've visited a golf course restaurant built on the site of a former contaminated industrial tract — and a swanky restaurant right next door to a gentleman's club. How Jersey. We've been to Alpha, Buttzville, Mizpah, Shamong and Zion. We've been down the Parkway more times than I care to remember — and country roads that reveal a Jersey that time forgot.

We've been everywhere, man, we've been everywhere — at least everywhere in this loud, crowded and breathtakingly peaceful state. In 2007, we hit stops in all 21 counties in two whirlwind days. We have could taken the easy way out and done just quick hits like ice cream and hot dogs, but the Big Dog is nothing if not thorough.

Several Munchers on our last road trip of the year are still trying to figure out how they ended up at the Log Cabin Inn in Columbia, which until that moment they thought was a South American country. But the Warren County town is most definitely part of New Jersey, albeit one that most of us never see.
— Readers' choice trip, 2006

The temperature of the freezer at Nasto's Olde World Desserts in Newark is 24 degrees below zero.

OUR MUNCHERS

Munchers are now such an integral part of every mission, it's hard to imagine a road trip, or story, without them.

But in the first five Munch years there were only one or two Guest Munchers per trip. It was not until 2003, and the advent of our Summer Survivor crew, that we started taking groups of readers along.

The results were immediate: the trips became much more fun. There was more laughter and merriment, and more opinions flying around the table.

The most-asked question I get is, "How do I get on the Munchmobile?" The answer is easy. You apply, just like college.

It's funny how many e-mails I receive every year that begin, "Can you send me a Munchmobile application?" There is no "application." Just tell us about yourself and why you want and deserve to be on the Big Dog.

Requests take many forms: letters, poems, videos, collages, sculptures, eating "resumes," short stories and scribbled pleas on everything from napkins to pizza boxes. People have dropped off cake and cookies in a late-minute attempt to win our favor.

Most of the requests are laugh-out-loud funny. Jeri Greenberg of Mountainside wrote she was "very ying/yang personality-wise, but don't worry, I am not Sybil." Kelly Shelsky of Harding said she was "one of those girls people love to hate — skinny and eats like a big fat slob."

A sense of humor, in fact, is probably the most essential quality for any Muncher. Look, you're driving around with a hot dog over your head all day, so if you can't laugh at that you probably don't belong on board. And a sense of humor will help you get through the typically long and exhausting Munch day. Witness this exchange on the 2002 healthy food trip:

Later, the Munchers sat for a spell on Adirondack chairs on the shaded lawn outside the shop.

"I'm doing what I enjoy most," Norine Morando said.

"You sit home all day, watch TV and eat bon-bons," Eileen, her sister, cracked. "Has anyone ever seen her clean her house? And her TV is the size of my rear end."

Readers are always telling us that they have followed the Munchmobile from its beginning and how they clip and save every installment. Elisa Madorsky, a 2007 Muncher, said she had a "special relationship" with the Munchmobile since moving to the Garden Sate from New York City.

"At first the Munchmobile kept me company," she recalled. "All my friends were living in their rented apartments in Manhattan. Every Friday, I eagerly awaited The Star-Ledger to read your reviews and figure out where we would go to eat. I became the Munchmobile's grassroots marketing campaign. If

I read it, then I must go."

Many describe the Munchmobile as a dream come true.

"I've skydived, marched in the Macy's Thanksgiving Day parade, swam with dolphins, bellydanced, and been on a trapeze, but I've never driven around in a van with a giant weiner attached to the roof," Tracy Politowicz of Union wrote in her successful Munch application.

Many see it as a chance to gain instant prestige among family and friends.

"I have a diploma and a law degree, but my wife and kids think being named to the Munchmobile means I've finally accomplished something in my life," Dave Barry of East Brunswick related.

Dedicated? True Munchers are. Herb Raskin of West Orange, who described himself as "the No. 1 Munch fan," said he missed the Munchmobile reports in 2004 because he had fallen into a coma and lost 125 pounds.

"One of the first things that came to mind when I was com-

Total weight gained by the five Summer Survivor Munchers, 2003: 38$^{1/2}$ pounds

ing out of the coma was taking my version of a Munchmobile road trip to favorite places to eat," said Raskin, who would go on a Big Dog ice cream run.

Every Munch trip is memorable for one reason or another, but the 2003 "Summer Survivors" crew will always hold a special place in our hearts. The same five people — Judy Fortunato, Rich Sgrignoli, Dave Brooks, Raymond Goldfield and Jack Sugalski — rode with us all summer, trying to earn points in a competition to be named Top Muncher.

There was Fortunato, of Hillsborough, who readers still ask about and may be the most popular Muncher ever. And the irrepressible Goldfield, of Woodbridge, who was always good for a quote.

"The three most beautiful words in the English language — surf and turf," he once said. And: "I've had my medication for the day: five different kinds of meat."

The random quotes and unguarded moments from our Munchers provide plenty of material for a lively trip — and story.

"My tongue is on the floor," Phil Scharago of Livingston announced during a wing trip in 2006.

"Mussels marinara? I used to wrestle under that name in the '60s," cracked Barry, on our reader's choice trip in 2006.

"I felt surly when I got here; now I feel unsurly," Edith Churchman of Newark said during our day-long doughnut excursion in 2006.

Anything you say or do on the Munchmobile can and will be held against you. Todd Cohen of Edison never heard the end of it from friends when he announced on our seafood trip in 2007, "I'm a happy little girl."

There's always something going on in the van, at the table, or along the way. Twin sisters Stephanie O'Hare, of Morristown, and Sharon Palmer, of Boonton, enlivened a seafood trip in 2007 by "accusing" the male Munchers on board of taking naps and not bringing notetaking essentials like pen and paper. In their Munch application, the twins promised they could "shovel copious amounts of food" down their throats.

"None of this eating like ladies," they wrote.

We love Munchers with attitude.

A day on the Big Dog is a lot of fun — call it a lively road trip with food — but Munchers know they are in for a long day. Many nap in the van during the ride. The trips are 12 hours minimum; the Down the Shore trip lasts 17 hours, or longer. Endurance is tested, perseverance is prized, and cooler heads prevail.

It was blisteringly, mind-numbingly, suffocatingly hot, and while the temptation was to spend the day sipping tall drinks with umbrellas, the Munchers completed their mission. They visited New Jersey's four major boardwalks — Wildwood, Ocean City, Atlantic City and Seaside Heights — staggered several miles, and ate at 12 boardwalk restaurants or stands, no doubt breaking a Jersey Shore record in the process.
— Boardwalk trip, 1999

Sometimes it's better to have a hot head:

The temperature was in the low 40s, and a hurricane-strength wind howled down the beach, so what did Munch photographer Tim Farrell ask us to do? Squat on the sand and eat our pizza! Shaking and shivering, we did our Munch duty. The wind, however, quickly made the pizza inedible. "Can I have a piece without the grass and sand in it?" Rich Sgrignoli asked.
— Down the Shore trip, 2003

How does a typical Munch day go? Well, for one thing, there is no typical day, but this gives you an idea:

Start with sugar-saturated doughnuts and pastry at a bakery in Kearny. Proceed to fat, drippy sandwiches at a little hole-in-the-wall in Newark. Make quick work of a basil, mozzarella and tomato-topped bruschetta at a pizzeria in Caldwell. Savor crispy duck salad, coconut soup, snapper in green curry and other dishes at a Thai restaurant in Stirling. Drive to a steak sandwich joint in Phillipsburg and wolf down a couple with peppers and onions. Back to Elizabeth for refreshing lemon ice and finally to Linden for, uh, dinner.

Yeah, it's like that.

The Munch family is an extended and loyal one, and past Munchers always check in from time to time to let me know of new developments in their lives — or tell Munch-related stories. Cheryl Grant of Neptune reported she was at a trade show in Las Vegas when a woman in the elevator at Mandalay Bay started screaming at her. The reason? Grant, who was on a 2007 ice cream trip, was wearing her Munchmobile T-shirt. "She is screaming, 'I'm from Kearny and I follow the Munch-mobile, it looks like so much fun!' " Grant recalled, laughing.

Our most famous Muncher was probably Federico Castel-luccio, who played Furio on "The Sopranos." He rode along in 2000. Members of the Super Bowl champion New York Giants were on a steak sandwich run in 2008. Other 2008 Munchers included a group of Newark firemen and a half dozen women marathon runners who call themselves Babes to the Waves. Shari Munch — her real name — was on a 2005 trip.

But our typical Muncher is more like Susan Jankolovits of Montclair, who wore a straw hat decorated with plastic pizza, burgers, fries, spaghetti and soda on a 2000 burger trip, where she tossed a hamburger roll aside at one stop.

"Bread doesn't taste like anything," she explained. "Skip the bread, you can eat more food, you can eat more grease."

Munchers are not fussy, finicky eaters. We'll eat everything — and have. And many Munchers are pretty fit. People don't believe me when I say I usually lose weight over the course of a summer.

When all is said and done, the weekly trips and the subse-quent reports wouldn't be quite the same without our Munch-ers, who revel in the instant fame and gustatory glory that goes with riding the Big Dog. "When the story came out, people came up to me on the street and asked for autographs," Eric Williams of Hillside said.

Gil Caminos of Cranford said his 2002 Munch trip "will go into the memory bank for the rest of my life."

Cheryl Gieson of Independence might have said it best.

"Last year, I was a nobody, lonely and isolated in Warren County," Gieson said. "Today, I am a Muncher!"

"Milkshake" first appeared in print in 1889. Early versions contained whiskey.

ROADSIDE FOOD

Food, glorious food. At the end of the Munch day — and the beginning — that's what it all comes down to. In 1998, the Big Dog's first year, the crew paid homage to Jersey standbys like burgers, pizza, ice cream, Italian hot dogs, deli sandwiches and diner food.

The following year, 1999, saw an expansion of the Munch menu. The summer's first report dealt with barbecue; the lead photo showed the manager at Brothers in Newark stirring a huge bubbling pot of barbecue sauce.

Brothers, for those who remember it, looked run-down and low-rent — the plastic sheeting at the front counter made it seem more like a check-cashing service than restaurant —but oh, its barbecue sauce! Peppery and spicy if not incendiary, the sauce was a great find — and a lasting Munchmobile memory. I can still taste it — and it's 10 years later!

Other categories that summer included neighborhood Italian (which included a stop at the late great Emilia's Deli in Newark), drive-ins (you must try the sweet wonderful lemonade at the Circus Drive-in in Wall), all-night diners (don't tell anyone I got lost trying to find the Harris Diner in East Orange in the middle of the night), burgers (the sandwiches at the Rutgers grease trucks are memorable for all the wrong reasons) and a category we called reader's choice, which became the traditional last Munch trip each summer. Reader's choice is a great way to wrap up the summer — everything's on the menu.

By 2000, our horizons had broadened; no longer was the

> The nation's first drive-in was the Dallas Pig Stand, opened by J.G. Kirby in 1921 on the premise that "people with cars are so lazy that they don't want to get out of their cars."

Big Dog just about hot dogs, burgers and pizza. The lineup that summer included Indian food and ballpark food; we even made a special trip to Philadelphia to find the city's best cheese steaks on the eve of the 37th Republican Convention. (Forget Pat's and Geno's; they're for tourists. Head to Tony Luke's or John's Roast Pork instead.)

The Big Dog is not just about grease, fried food, and cholesterol-raising; we've done a healthy food trip every year since 2001. Some of the readers, and Munchers, took this development better than others. "No more rabbit food," hissed one Muncher on one of the first healthy-food excursions.

But the Munch credo never changed: We came, we saw, we

ate. Ate things many of our Munchers had never eaten before. When I saw cow's foot on the menu of a Caribbean restaurant in East Orange, I ordered it for the crew. "Chewy and gluey" was my description of this most acquired of tastes.

We tried cactus enchilada at a Mexican restaurant in Meyersville. Scrapple, at a luncheonette in Chatham. "The Pennsylvania potpourri of pork parts — variously pork livers, pork skins, pork tongue, pork hearts — everything but the oink," read our report.

Oxtail — it's practically become a Big Dog staple. Rodizio — photographer Ed Murray and I did a week straight of rodiz-

Americans consume 13 billion burgers a year.

io, the nonstop meat orgy that is practically a rite of passage in the Ironbound section of Newark. It's a wonder we didn't both become vegetarians on the spot.

Is there anything more deliriously drippy, congealingly cheesy and so wonderfully bad for you than a big, fat plate of nachos? A mountainous pile of crispy tortilla chips, diced tomatoes, black olives, spicy jalapeños and fresh chili, covered with enough cheese to give your cardiologist a heart attack.
— Nachos, August 2003

You can't call someone who rhapsodizes about a pile of nachos a food snob, but the Munchmobile does have standards. As I often tell the Munchers, we're not the Chamber of Commerce — give us your honest opinion of the food. We never call a restaurant beforehand and we always pay for our food, so we don't have to be kind. Just be honest.

Here's my report of a ballpark food trip:

The bread had the consistency of grade-B cardboard. The slice of pizza was lukewarm, overpriced at $3 and on the gummy side. The chicken tenders, bought in the bottom of the eighth, might have been decent six innings earlier.

One Rutgers grease-truck burger was so tough, "it took several yanks to pull it apart." The ribs at one Ironbound legend were "dried out, nearly desiccated." The New England clam chowder at a well-known Shore restaurant "had the consistency of wallpaper paste," Muncher Dave Brooks recalled at the time. The veal saltimbocca at a Italian restaurant in Bloomfield was "swimming — make that drowning — in wine sauce." Here's the verdict on our lunch at one of the state's biggest diners:

The vegetables were mushy and useless. The coconut shrimp could have used more time in the fryer. The yams were candied to the extreme. The Reuben was regrettable and the baked eggplant a mess.

But the food on our trips is uniformly good, sometimes great. The main reason: We visit places recommended by readers. They're regulars of those restaurants, and they can't wait to tell the Munchmobile. Tips come in all forms, and at all hours of the day — one-sentence phone calls from "Laura in Denville" or highly detailed e-mails. When a reader told me about the pizza at DiPaolo Brothers in Newark, I thought, "Pizza? What bakery makes pizza?" But the Sicilian there is great pizza, "with a wonderfully crunchy, you-can-tell-it-was-made-by-a-baker crust."

Opinions? We've got a few. I've insisted for years that the state's best cheesecakes can be found at Mara's Country Desserts in Morristown. I still remember the caramel apple streusel cheesecake there. And the monstrous coffee rolls at Donut Towne in Wharton. The tiny, greasy and altogether irresistible burgers at the White Manna in Hackensack. The sushi pizza at Ocha in Caldwell — sounds like fusion run amok, but the combination of scallion, seaweed, tomato, onion and a spicy barbecue sauce makes it an unqualified hit.

The blueberry pie at the Ritz Diner in Livingston, "dusted with powdered sugar, resting on a not-too-thick crust and filled with a tractor load of berries, it's sweet sensory overload."

The cheese steak at Chick's Deli in Cherry Hill. The butter chicken at Piquant Bread Bar & Grill in New Brunswick. The chocolate brittle-like Chester Crunch at J. Emanuel in Chester. The charcoal-grilled pork chops at After Athens in Rutherford.

The sausage pizza at Tony's Baltimore Grill in Atlantic City. The pepperoni and mozzarella bread at Cheesecake World in Marmora. That's right, Cheesecake World. The perfectly cooked, wonderfully juicy fried chicken at Mangos in Hackensack — these are the things Munchmobile memories, and summers, are made of.

DIVES AND THE BIG DOG

There is nothing like a dive, or a hole-in-the-wall, to stir the Big Dog's soul.

Sure, many of the places we visit on the Munchmobile are modern, spotless restaurants, delis, diners and shops.

But give us a little faded rundown charm any day.

Give us holes-in-the-wall like Boulevard Drinks in Jersey City, with its flickering neon sign, blinding-orange walls and surprisingly good hot dogs. Places like Cooper's Deli in Newark — liquor and lottery counter to the left, deli to the right — where the ladies behind the counter take your order and write cryptic-looking symbols and numbers on a paper bag. "2p WB 1/2 c/s?" That's two pastrami sandwiches on white bread with a half pound of cole slaw.

Those kind of places.

Hangouts with the kind of atmosphere you can't buy, create, or invent. It's just there.

We zigged and zagged our way to Carteret, home of the one and only Tommy's Hot Dogs. Call it a hot dog shack supreme, with shingle roof, screen door and more pots, pans, griddles and grills than a kitchen supply store. Items are written on pieces of construction paper taped to the oven hood. You can get everything from fried clams and crab cakes to nachos and a rib-eye steak. Owner Tommy Lane is a character. "We're looking for the best hot dog in the state," someone said. "You're in the wrong place!" Lane chortled.
— August 2006

India is the world's spice king; the country has a 46 percent share of the global supply of imported spices.

Munchmobile Maxim No. 1: Never judge a place by its looks. Some of our most memorable meals have come at nondescript, rundown, spartan places.

"The subterranean dining spot," began our 2007 report on Caribbean Cafe in New Brunswick, "didn't look promising — dreary-looking front rooms, empty dining room — but once the food started to materialize from the cramped, narrow kitchen, we realized one truth. Better to consume than assume. The whole stewed kingfish swam in a thick, stewy sauce, and would turn out to be one of the day's best dishes. The trip's best plantains, soft and squishy, were here. The red snapper featured a beautifully crispy, crackly skin."

Guernsey Crest in Paterson sure doesn't look like much, inside or out, but they make pretty good ice cream.

A graffiti-splattered, warehouse-like building. One padlocked door; a sign tells you to try the next one. A ceiling that looks like it's about to cave in. Soda machine out of order. In short, a Munchmobile kind of place. That's Guernsey Crest, practically hidden behind the bushes along 19th Avenue.

— Milkshakes, 2006

Mark Koppe's General Store in Bloomsbury is atmospheric, in a different way.

You know you're in the country when you can buy breakfast and bait at the same time.

Mark Koppe's is a hardwood-floored time-warp wonder, stocked with Slim Jims, cookies, candy and self-serve coffee. Grill's out front, frozen bait's out back, and just down the street is a short bridge over the Musky — the Musconetcong River.

— Pancakes/French toast, 2007

The more clutter, kitsch and low-rent charm, the better. The walls at Shut Up and Eat, a luncheonette in Toms River, are jammed with everything from Radio Flyer tricycles, pinball machines and old-time radios to customer snapshots, Gumby figures, and a drawing of a flying saucer with the words, "Abduct Me!"

Signs and messages, the funnier the better, always add atmosphere. Sometimes they can be found in the oddest places. This was a sign in the men's room at a Vietnamese restaurant in Lincroft: "Gentlemen, welcome to the smallest wash bowl in restaurant history. We had originally installed a much nicer one, but ran afoul of building code clearance requirements. We are working with the building department to develop an acceptable design."

We're always on the lookout for this stuff, and for places that dare to be different. The food's got to be good, of course; you can't eat the furnishings. At the White Rose System in Linden, a diner nestled in an industrial area of Linden, specials are written on pieces of blue and red paper, ruffling in the fan-whipped breeze. Definitely a Munchmobile kind of place.

Back Bay in Stone Harbor is a tiny, screen-doored, takeout-only joint with an interesting twist: When you call, you're given the next available pickup time. Select that time or a later one. Show up and your food is ready.

There are hot dog holes-in-the-wall like Tommy's and Jerry's in Elizabeth, both squeezed onto the same side street. There are open-air hangouts like the Smitty's Clam Bar in Somers Point, where you sit around a weather-beaten counter and order first-rate fish sandwiches and platters amidst the bobbing boats in the adjacent marina.

There are great dive bars/restaurants like Crabby's in

Belcoville, outside Mays Landing, and the Old Heidelberg in Keansburg. Roadside holes-in-the-wall like Christine's House of Kingfish in Shamong, which doesn't look promising but serves up some mighty fine barbecue.

The late great Emilia's in Newark oozed atmosphere. You gave your order to one of the ladies behind the counter — the one not stirring the big pot of sauce, anyway — and then sat down at one of the communal tables to enjoy good, cheap Italian food.

Emilia's is the kind of place where the specials are written in Magic Marker on a blackboard, and dollar bills are pinned to pictures of the Blessed Virgin Mary. On the wall are photos of what could be called the Italian Restaurant Bulletin Board Hall of Fame: the Four Seasons, Joe Pesci and the Pope.
— Italian, 1999

The fact that places like Emilia's disappear every year makes finding, and championing, their counterparts that much more important. At one time, dozens of drive-ins were scattered across New Jersey. They were neon-lit American-Graffiti-like hangouts where roller-skating waitresses took your order and every night seemed like Saturday night.

The roller skates are long gone, and there are only a few true drive-ins left: the Circus Drive-in in Wall, with its splendid smiling-clown sign and its incomparable pink lemonade, and Weber's in Pennsauken. Even many Stewart's have abandoned curbside service.

The Harvey Cedars Shellfish Co. Clam Bar — not in Harvey Cedars but Beach Haven — is another Munchmobile kind of place:

From the outside, the white-shingled building looks like any number of other houses on the block. Inside, though, the wraparound counter, fluorescent lighting and happy chatter of diners reveal it as an old-time seafood bar. Give your name to a waitress, drop your beer or wine in the giant iced tub, and wait outside to be called. Cell phones are prohibited inside — thank goodness!
— Readers' choice, 2006

Two of my all-time favorite Munchmobile-visited dives are minutes from each other in Warren County. Toby's Cup in Lopatcong (I can't tell you how people over the years have insisted it's in Phillipsburg) is one of those roadside eateries they just don't make anymore — here or anywhere else. Toby's serves good shakes and dogs, although most people won't go anywhere near the place. It's too, you know, weird.

Jimmy Nicnick stood behind the counter of Toby's Cup on Route 22, a highway landmark that is part fast-food joint, part carnival

funhouse, with its eight-sided structure, grinning clown face painted outside, and what looks like the Sputnik satellite, with tiny flashing lights, atop the roof.

Tall people may have to duck when they walk into the low-ceilinged waiting room, which offers panoramic views of New Jersey's kookiest highway.

— Route 22 trip, 2001

And then there is the one and only Charlie's Pool Room in Alpha, undoubtedly the oddest hot dog joint in America:

In a white-shingled house that once served as the local jail, across squeaky hardwood floors alive with the ghosts of local characters past, beyond the front counter anchored by a 1928 wooden cash register, past the tiny bathroom and fluorescent-lit pool table, through the kitchen where their dad, 91 years young, apologizes for having retired, the brothers Fencz make hot dogs.

These are not ordinary hot dogs, and Charlie's Pool Room is no ordinary pool room, or restaurant. There is just one item on the menu: hot dogs. You can't buy anything else, unless you count Twizzlers and Blow Pops.

In a hurry? Wait. You don't rush through a town like Alpha anyway; it almost demands you slow down, sit a spell, lose yourself.

— Readers' choice trip, 2002

These are the kind of places we love to find. Dives, holes-in-the-wall — call them what you want. One-of-a-kind hangouts in this age of cookie-cutter restaurants. Munchmobile kind of places.

A DECADE OF DOG

Each summer since 1998, Star-Ledger readers have thrilled to the exploits of the Munchmobile and its inquisitive, ever-hungry crew. From burgers, pizza and ice cream to Caribbean, Eastern European and real Chinese, they have covered the culinary map, and all of New Jersey, too. What follows is a complete story from each year, with loads of food and a cast of hundreds, including a guest appearance from a member of "The Sopranos."

ITALIAN HOT DOGS, JUNE 18, 1998

MARK DiIONNO

Philly has its cheese steaks, New Orleans has its po'boys. Every great town makes a great sandwich. Something that's their own. Something you can't get anywhere else — decent, that is.

Newark is no different. Newark is the birthplace of the Italian Hot Dog. Some places pay homage to the birthplace by calling it the Newark-style Hot Dog. Either way, here's what it is: a deep-fried hot dog topped with potatoes, onions, peppers (red and green), all wrapped up in a piece of pizza bread. Ketchup and mustard are optional. A double gets you two dogs.

In most places, a single is under $2.50, a double about $3.25 — cheaper than a Big Mac with large fries. How can you beat that? You can't.

The Italian Hot Dog is a Jersey original. Frank Pacella grew up in Salerno, Italy, but never had one until he came to Newark. He's been making them at his store, Pacella's Italian Super-Deli in Edison, for 25 years now.

Or, as Munchmobile guest food-tester Ira Rubin said, "You haven't eaten Jersey until you've had an Italian hot dog."

Ira's right.

As a tribute to this homegrown concoction, the Munchmobile crew picked the Italian Hot Dog as the first food group we decided to test. (Speaking of food groups, the Italian Hot Dog hits three of the four basic — vegetable, starch and meat, if you classify a hot dog as meat.)

We picked five places based on reader recommendations: Dickie Dee's in Newark's North Ward, Jimmy Buff's in West Orange, Charlie's Famous Italian Hot Dogs in Kenilworth, Frank's Newark Style Dogs in Edison, and Pacella's.

It was a perfect mix. It spread us out over three Ledgerland counties, and it gave us the right balance between big-rep places, like Dickie Dee's and Jimmy Buff's, and hidden gems, like Pacella's.

And in the process of eating five Italian Hot Dogs in one day, the Munchmobile crew discovered the anthropological evolution of this Jersey classic. But unlike other great Jersey inventions — the light bulb and the phonograph (Thomas Edison), the submarine (J.P. Holland) and the steam locomotive (John Stevens) — the Italian Hot Dog does not have a clear-cut originator. Its beginnings are murky.

James Racioppi, the owner of Jimmy Buff's at 60 Washington St. in West Orange, says it was invented by his grandmother, who used to make the sandwiches for his grandfather and his friends during their weekly card games. After a while, the men forgot about the cards and just came for the sandwiches. The Racioppis knew they were on to something and opened up a store at Ninth and 14th Avenue in Newark. That was in 1932. There are three Buff's now: the one owned by James and two owned by his uncle Mike in Irvington and on Route 22 in Scotch Plains.

"The product is the same in all three places," said James. "It's the way we've been doing it for 66 years."

Like Jimmy Buff's, Dickie Dee's is a multigenerational family operation. Dominick D'Innocenzio and Enrico Bruno started the business 40 years ago and have been at their 6th and Bloomfield Avenue for 32 years. Both men have grandchildren who work the store.

"I don't know how it all started," said Rick D'Innocenzio, Dominick's son. "I know we started about the same time as Jimmy Buff's and a place called Ting-A-Ling. They're gone now. But as to who invented them, I don't know."

Pat Martin, the chief cook at Frank's Newark Style, says this: "All I know is I used to eat them all the time back in Newark when I was a little girl."

Rosemarie Pacella said her mother used to make them when she was growing up in the North Ward, and that's where Frank Pacella learned to make them. Frank's first store was on 6th and N. 13th Street in Newark. When he moved to Edison, he dropped the dog.

"We didn't make them here at first, but then all the Newarkers who moved here started asking for them, so Frank started making them again," said Rosemarie Pacella.

One thing is certain: The Italian Hot Dog started somewhere in the North Ward, and all five places we tested can trace their roots back to the old neighborhood. Charlie's founder Charlie Fiorenza even worked at old Jimmy Buff's. Joe Calello, who began working for Charlie at age 12, bought the place after Charlie died. At 32, he's been in the Italian Hot Dog business for two decades already.

Despite the shared genealogy, each place has its own distinctive style. Dickie Dee's deep fries everything in the same oil, but they use peanut oil, which cuts down on the grease load. Jimmy Buff's pan fries the vegetables and deep fries the dog. Charlie's cuts the potatoes not in chunks but in slices and puts them on the side. Pat Martin doesn't deep fry the vegetables. "I don't use a big pan, it makes too much grease," she says. Frank Pacella steams the vegetables and uses steak fries, which end up crispy, not greasy.

Martin and Pacella go light on the vegetables. Charlie's puts on enough to feed a family. The spices at Dickie Dee's and Jimmy Buff's can linger in your mouth for hours.

The atmosphere is different in each place, too. Pat Martin is loud and lovable, making Frank's a laugh a minute. Pacella's is quiet and immaculately clean: a house of worship to Italian food. Charlie's is busy and efficient, with dogs coming out from the back with production line speed. Dickie Dee's and Jimmy Buff's are old-fashioned neighborhood places ... everybody knows the cook and the cook knows everybody.

But there's one thing all the places do the same: make you feel welcome. That's the old neighborhood way.

The results: So who makes the best Italian Hot Dog in New Jersey? Who knows? We don't. The Munchmobile team was split on this one, although Buff's received two of five first place votes.

Guest-taster Ira Rubin: Jimmy Buff's. "I've said it before and I'll say it again, it's the bread that makes the sandwich, and Buff's had the best bread."

New Jersey Online Webpage producer David Hancock: "The bread does make the sandwich, that's why I go with Jimmy Buff's. The bread was nice and firm, you really had to pull it with your teeth."

News 12 New Jersey reporter Melinda Murphy: "I go with Charlie's. Like the onions the best."

News 12 New Jersey cameraman Bill Schlosser: "I like the ratio between meat and vegetable better at Frank's and Pacella's. The hot dog came through more. The other places buried the hot dog in peppers, onions and potatoes."

Star-Ledger editor Mark DiIonno: "Something has to be said for going back to the North Ward for this sandwich. All the places were great, but I go with Dickie Dee's for its Bloomfield Avenue ambiance."

Munch Morsels: Guest food-tester Ira Rubin (alias Pipe Band Manager) is the night manager of the Manischewitz matzoth plant in Jersey City and plays in an Irish bagpipe band ... Ira may know more about New Jersey cheap eats than any man alive, except for Hot Dog John, who has yet to reveal his identity ... Hot Dog John leads the league in reader recommendations. So far he's sent four two-page letters, handwritten ... NJO's David Hancock is the first casualty of the agita patrol. After eating every single bite of all five Italian Hot Dogs on our first trip, Hancock now says he's too busy at work to keep coming out. Yeah, right ... Hancock will be replaced by NJO's Elizabeth Willse. Maybe she can gut it out ... Weight-watch: Mark DiIonno tipped in at 212 before the Munchmobile's maiden voyage, 215 after.

MUNCH BITES 1998:

Eat heavy. Like the traffic on Routes 3, 46, 22, 1 and 9, and all the other old state highways that connect our towns and crisscross New Jersey.

Eat heavy. Like the soles of the shoes of the waitresses who pad the hard linoleum floors in shifts that add up to "Open 24 hours." Like the tired legs of the short-order cooks who stand over sizzling grills for eight hours at a stretch.

Eat heavy. Like the eyelids of the after-hours crowd, downing breakfast after beers, going home some nights lonely, some nights in love. Like the hearts of the single men at the counters. Old men with deceased wives; bachelors for whom home is a bare kitchen and empty bed.

Like the cloud of grease smoke that hangs over the grill. Like the symphonic clinking and clanking of utensils and plates, of hushed and animated conversation, of newspapers rustling, of orders being shout out, of "more coffee, hon," of the jukebox playing.

Eat heavy . . . eat heavy, "hon" . . . eat heavy, my friend . . .

So we did.

If diners are the soul of New Jersey roadside food, then breakfast feeds that soul.

— Diner breakfasts, June 1998

PETER GENOVESE

John Diakakis, undoubtedly the only blind diner waiter/ standup comedian in New Jersey, stood behind the counter of the Bendix Diner in Hasbrouck Heights at 2:30 a.m. trying out material on his customers.

"Can I tell the one about my girlfriend who names her body parts after towns in New Jersey?" the 30-year-old waiter asked the Munchmobile crew.

Uh, no, John.

"How about this one?" he tried. "So I was going out with this blind girl. Know what happened? We stopped seeing each other."

Sitting on a stool was Mike Klimkovsky of Garfield, a Vietnam vet whose tattered cap was festooned with Spice Girls buttons, service patches and peace slogans. "The CIA," he said, to no one in particular, "developed bulletproof underwear. You could get shot in the a— and keep going."

Nearby, Mike Jones of Hasbrouck Heights picked up his bacon-egg-and-cheese on a hard roll and inexplicably dipped it into a cup of mayonnaise.

"What, you think this is weird?" he asked, laughing. "In Holland, this is very common."

Is there anything more wonderfully weird than a diner — and its customers — at 2 or 3 in the morning? You don't even have to be hungry; you can drink in the atmosphere. The open-all-night diner is a sanctuary for dreamers, romantics and lost souls.

"There isn't an all-night place between New Jersey and California that doesn't know me," said Gregory Roberts of Orange, enjoying a 4:20 a.m. bowl of applesauce at the Harris Diner in East Orange. "This one is special. If they ever moved it to Boston, New York or Los Angeles, I probably would follow it."

"This is the most beautiful English muffin I have ever had," Jones said at the Bendix Diner.

Okay, maybe Jones was trying a little too hard to get into the story. But the Munchers found no shortage of diner fanatics — and good food — in the five diners they visited. The all-night tour started at the White Mana on Tonnelle Avenue (Route 1) in Jersey City. "We're the first diner to go worldwide," said owner Mario Costa. If you have a computer and internet access, you can visit the diner from the comfort of your home, thanks to New Jersey Online's 24-Hour DinerCam (go to njo.com/dinercam/).

The flying-saucer-shaped diner, according to Costa, made its debut at the 1939 New York World's Fair — a point disputed by the owners of the White Manna in Hackensack. But Costa says Webster Bridges, original owner of the five White Manas or Mannas in New Jersey, told him the Jersey City Mana came from the World's Fair, and one of Costa's regulars says he visited the Mana at the Queens fair site.

Not long ago, Costa had an agreement to sell the White Mana to businessmen who wanted to turn it into a Dunkin' Donuts. His customers protested. Costa had a change of heart, and eventually reacquired the diner. The Dunkin' Donuts opened a block south on Tonnelle Avenue.

"People said after (Dunkin' Donuts) opened I'd be out of business within six months," said Costa. "But I'd say business has been up 40 percent."

People can really get attached to White Mana burgers. One powerful North Jersey mobster would often send an associate to the Mana to pick up a sack. On his deathbed, the mob guy, stricken with stomach cancer, asked for some burgers — even though he couldn't eat them.

"He just wanted to smell them," Costa said.

Burgers don't get much bigger — or better — than at the Short Stop in Bloomfield, our next destination. Owner Bill Buchanan, wearing a "Property of Alcatraz Penitentiary Swim Team" T-shirt, was at the counter. Buchanan would not make any swim team, not with his sizable girth, but he knows jails. He's a corrections officer at the Essex County Jail annex in Caldwell.

The Short Stop is a greasy spoon par excellence, and regulars wouldn't have it any other way. Spatulas jutted from a wall rack. A big fan above the grill sucked out grease. The fire extinguisher was strategically located nearby.

"I come here all three shifts," said Bil Hughes, a computer programmer. "In the morning, it's a Taylor Ham, egg and cheese sandwich. In the afternoon, it's a He-Man (burger) or a Taylor Ham, egg and cheese. In the evening, it's a cup of coffee and whatever they can cook for me."

The little diner's signature dish: Eggs in a Skillet. Your eggs are cooked and served in a skillet, which is then placed on a wooden board. First-time customers have been known to dump the eggs on the wooden board and then eat them.

The Munchers, naturally, ordered Eggs in the Skillet.

"Go with the bacon," Hughes advised News12 reporter Kate Epstein. "It doesn't go to the hips as much."

As much as what? The Munch crew didn't want to know. It was time to proceed down Route 46, home of the Twilight Zone, Dinette City and Brake-O-Rama, to Hasbrouck Heights. Politicians know the Bendix — Bob Dole was there not long ago — and so does Hollywood. Several movies have been shot at the Bendix, including "Jersey Girl" and "Boys on the Side." "Drew Barrymore comes in and gets sick in our bathroom," John Diakakis said of a scene in "Boys."

His dad, Tony, owns the Bendix. Specials are written on a board — stuffed peppers, spinach pie, broiled salmon. A sign on the wall reads, "I can only please one person a day, and today ain't your day."

Not everyone who eats or works here is funny; it just seems that way. "These are great disco fries," said Mike Jones, attacking the diner's cheese- and gravy-covered fries. He smiled. "I think a little ball drops from the ceiling now."

Spend five minutes with the help here and you will come to one inescapable conclusion: Americans have some very strange eating habits.

"One guy who came here, a trucker, ordered pancakes with mozzarella cheese and gravy," Diakakis recalled. "I said, 'Why?' He said, 'You like pancakes?' 'Yeah.' 'You like mozzarella?' 'Yeah.' 'You like gravy?' 'Yeah.' 'Well, why not all three together?' I told him I like peanut butter and ketchup, but I wouldn't put them together."

The Munchers tried some disco fries, a grilled cheese sandwich, a gyro and a Greek salad.

So how does Diakakis know when to stop filling a coffee cup?

"By the sound," he replied. "The coffee makes a hollow sound when it gets near the top." We left Jones working on his disco fries and Diakakis working on his material, and headed to East Orange.

The Harris Diner is not easy to find — even in the daytime. It's on North Park Street, not to be confused with Park Avenue, East Park Street or Park Place, all nearby. But the L-shaped diner is well worth a visit. The Tums people love the place; they've filmed more than a dozen commercials here. The waitresses at the Harris are friendly and on the sassy side.

"No jelly," waitress Wanda Berry told regular Thomas Jones as she placed his eggs and corned beef hash in front of him.

"I don't want any," Jones, a diabetic, said, smiling.

"You ain't getting none anyway," Berry said sweetly.

"He cheated last week," Berry told another customer. "He sat up here and had some pie."

The diner, opened by Charlie Harris in 1945, is now run by Bill Nicholas and Bill Marmaras. Strange eating habits? Waitress Flecia Blake remembered a customer who ordered liver and pancakes, another who had a grilled cheese sandwich with bacon and bananas.

"Every day customers come in hungry, but they don't know what they want," the waitress observed. "A lot of times you have to pique their curiosity, break the monotony."

The only thing that needed piquing at this moment was the Munchers' energy level. But the team fueled up with coffee and made it to Highland Park, just in time to watch the sun rise over the White Rose System. The System is not as pleasantly seedy as it once was — it's almost too clean inside — but its soul hasn't changed.

"If (employees) stay within the system, a customer can order food and be out of here in 30 seconds," said a cook who goes by the name Joe D. "If they stay within the system."

So what's the system?

"It's how things are done," Joe D. explained. "We have grillmen and a counter person. Each person knows what the next is doing. We know each other, know each other's moves." The system also means knowing what your regulars want, and having it ready.

"Bacon and egg on toast, coffee, three creams, no sugar," Nick Jovani said as a customer opened the door. The customer got his order, paid the bill and left — without saying a word.

"I go to (a fast food restaurant) and say, 'This is fast food?'" Joe D. said cheerfully. "They don't know what fast food is. They should go to the Rose. We are the fastest and quickest. No doubt about it."

There was no doubt about something else — it was 7:15 a.m., and the Munch crew had been up all night. It was time to sleep, perchance to dream of burgers and fries, endless cups of coffee and a jukebox somewhere playing Patsy Cline far into the night.

> Lobster is not as high in cholesterol as many people think. The cholesterol in three and a half ounces of cooked lobster is 72 milligrams, lower than comparable amounts of cooked skinless chicken or turkey breast.

MUNCH BITES 1999:

The Sloppy Joes . . . stuffed with pastrami, corned beef, turkey, pickles, Russian dressing and cole slaw, looked, with all the multicolored toothpicks sticking from the top, like miniature cruise ships.
— Delis, June 1999

Lenny Chill sat at a table in Harold's NewYork Deli rhapsodizing about tongue. "The center cut tongue here is the best tongue I've ever had," said Chill, who teaches at Middlesex County College. "Have you ever seen a tongue before they cut it?"

The Munchmobile team assured Chill that no, they had yet to bear witness to such a beautiful sight.
— Delis, June 1999

Donnie's Dogs is located in front of Fairmount Cemetery in Newark, a source of amusement among customers who figure if you've gotta go, you might as well do it after eating a couple of Pete Caggiano's Bomber hot dogs.
— Hot dogs, July 1999

ITALIAN TRIP WITH 'SOPRANOS' STAR, JULY 28, 2000

PETER GENOVESE

Federico Castelluccio, who plays the baseball bat-wielding enforcer Furio on the HBO series "The Sopranos," sat in the passenger seat of the Munchmobile, his tiny cell phone getting more calls than a pizzeria on a Friday night.

The following day, a casting call for roles on "The Sopranos" would be held in Harrison, and Castelluccio was all of sudden a popular guy. The Italian-born actor, who grew up in Paterson, was besieged with calls from friends seeking advice on how to land a part on the mob show.

Friends like Richie Guido.

"What should I do?" Richie asked Castelluccio.

"Bring a picture, Richie," the actor said.

"A picture of who?" Richie asked.

"A picture of your mother, what do you mean a picture of who?" Castelluccio said, laughing. "A picture of you."

Castelluccio flipped down his cell phone as the Munchmobile cruised down Route 10 on the way to Stretch's Italian Restaurant in Livingston.

"I always knew I wanted to get into acting," recalled Castelluccio, who studied art in college. "But art was more accessible to me. Growing up in Paterson, who becomes an actor, except for Lou Costello?"

And who gets to ride on the Munchmobile, except the lucky few? Castelluccio, the Mystery Muncher in a Star-Ledger contest that drew some 700 entries, accompanied the Munch team to two Italian restaurants, part of a seven-stop restaurant and deli tour that included encounters with one of the original members of the Four Seasons, two guys named Sal Passalacqua, two guys named Francesco Paul Vitamia, and the biggest portions in the Italian restaurant food universe.

But more on all that later.

Fatima's

The journey began at Fatima's market on Bloomfield Avenue in Newark, where the sign on the front door had the Munchers wondering what exactly was going to be on their menu today: We carry quails, rabbits and suckling pigs on order.

Uh, can we order a sausage and peppers sandwich instead?

"I come here every day," said Sgt. Tom Cinque of the Newark police department, walking out with a chicken cutlet sandwich. "It's like Old World here. It doesn't get any more Italian than this."

No, it doesn't. Fresh corn, peppers and other vegetables spilled from boxes just inside the front door. Loaves of bread were stacked at the front counter. The smell of fresh provolone hung in the air. The family business started with Sam Fatima, a produce man whose horse-drawn wagon could be found on Stone Street in Newark. His great-grandson, Joey, now runs the market. Joey's parents, Nick and Theresa, still work at Fatima's, where beefy construction workers with Yankees caps and elderly men in tattered T-shirts sit at long tables enjoying the sausage and peppers and broccoli rabe.

Have Joey make you a fresh mozzarella, tomatoes and roasted red peppers sandwich (the delightfully crunchy bread comes from Nicolo's in Montclair), and you may never go back to your old deli again.

DiMaio's

Next stop: Dimaio Ristorante in Berkeley Heights, where Sal Passalacqua, not to be confused with Sal Passalacqua, greeted the Munch team. The first Sal is the owner and ex-ecutive chef at Dimaio; the second Sal, his cousin, runs the restaurant's takeout side. And don't forget Frank Passalacqua, another cousin, who works in the kitchen.

"I've been making pizza since I was 14," the executive chef said. "We came off the boat and started making pizza." He smiled. "Even though it was a plane."

Passalacqua wears a white cook's outfit embossed with the Food Network logo; he serves as a consultant for Emeril Lagasse's show. The food at Dimaio reflects the owner's Sicilian background.

"Sicilian food is more rustic," Passalacqua explained. "It takes from the abundance of the sea. It has a lot of influence from Morocco. We use a lot of raisins, apricots, pignoli nuts, a lot of sugars and vinegar. In Sicily, for the most part the fish is served whole, head on." He smiled. "People like to look their fish in the eyes."

All the food was first-rate: cheese ravioli, grilled salmon and especially the rigatoni alla serafino, a near-perfect blend of pasta, chicken breast, garlic, sun-dried tomatoes, broccoli, shiitake mushrooms, peas and white wine. The bread is excel-lent; Dimaio makes its own. Then it was time for the most important question of the day.

Sauce or gravy?

"I call it sauce," Passalacqua said, laughing. A good sauce, he added, doesn't need to simmer on the stove all day. "We cook as long as it takes to boil the water and cook the pasta," the cook explained.

Don't dare leave without trying his roasted red peppers. What's special about Dimaio's? "You put them right on the burner," Passalacqua said. "Turn the gas on and char them. Then you peel them, take the black skin off, then lay them in a container to marinate for a few hours."

Portofino's

The crew then headed to Portofino's in Morristown, where hundreds of people ran excitedly towards the Munchmobile as it rolled through town. Were they chasing after News12's Kate Epstein, filling in for Tony Caputo?

Not quite; they were runners participating in the annual Corporate Challenge race. But the dozens of people who waved and screamed "Munchmobile!" convinced us even the physically fit have a soft spot in their hearts, if not stomachs, for the Big Dog.

Portions are big at Portofino's; the seafood marecharia, an avalanche of shrimp, clams, mussels, scungilli and calamari with a pasta of your choice, will give you enough fuel to run several marathons.

"How come you don't have macaroni and cheese?" Epstein kidded owner Bruno Brita.

"We have rigatoni formaggio," Brita replied with a smile.

Sauce or gravy?

"Sauce," Brita replied without hesitation. "I never heard of gravy in Italy. Tomato sauce. Chicken gravy. Beef gravy."

E&V Ristorante

At this point, the last thing we needed was a restaurant known for huge portions. But when the going gets tough, the tough keep eating.

"You're coming to the best place in the world," said Bobbie San Filippo of Montville, at E&V Ristorante in Paterson with her son, Dennis; daughter-in-law, Marcia, and Marcia's sister, Sister Angelina Delvecchio, a member of the Religious Teachers of St. Lucy Filippini in Morristown.

Elio Federico, co-owner of E&V with his brother, Ralph, still works in the kitchen; look for the guy with the raffish white cap decorated with American and Italian flags.

"You've got to be pretty nuts to stay back here," the 53-year-old Federico said, smiling.

"Nobody works like this anymore."

Nobody we know serves portions like he does. The fusilli with sun-dried tomatoes and pesto was split into two dishes, each big enough for two people.

Sauce or gravy?

"Gravy," replied Federico, who was born near Naples. "My mother always told me this was gravy."

The Munchers started with several knockout appetizers: filet mignon bruschetta, thinly sliced steak served over garlic toast topped with diced Jersey tomatoes, fresh basil and extra virgin olive oil; and a dish known as assorted specialty, with its winning combination of mortadella, soppresata, cappicola, prosciutto, imported provolone and roasted peppers. The gnocchi was not only the biggest gnocchi but the biggest dish of pasta this writer has ever seen. One more note: Bring cash; E&V doesn't take credit cards.

Stretch's

The next day, Castelluccio came along for the ride to

Stretch's in Livingston. The restaurant, with its brick exterior, looks unpromising from Mt. Pleasant Avenue, but drive around back, to the restaurant's main entrance. There's you'll find owner Peter Verdicchio, son of Carlo "Stretch" Verdicchio, who ran several restaurants — Lou Carlos on Garside Street in Newark and Stretch's Cellar in the basement of the family house — before opening the Belmont Tavern in Belleville.

The restaurant is known for its Chicken Savoy, and for good reason. The chicken is broiled, then "hit" with red wine vinegar, and that is all Peter Verdicchio will tell you. No one outside the family knows the recipe, and Verdicchio intends to keep it that way. Castelluccio rarely eats pasta and bread — he says they slow him down — favoring chicken and fish. He raved about Stretch's Salad, a mixture of mozzarella, roasted peppers, black olives, red onions, tomatoes, onions and balsamic vinegar.

"This is really good, just the right combination of everything," said the actor, who worked in regional theater and appeared in such daytime soaps as "Guiding Light" and "As the World Turns" before landing the role as Furio on "The Sopranos."

Castelluccio, who lives in North Jersey, is not only an artist — the February 1999 issue of American Artist featured his work — but a collector of art and vintage frames.

"When I read for Furio I said, 'This is me,'" the ponytailed actor said. "The character has to be from Italy, from Naples. I was born in Naples. I came here in 1968, when I was 4."

Tommie DeVito, one of the original Four Seasons and a personal assistant to actor Joe Pesci, stopped by the table. DeVito told the story behind the Four Seasons' hit song "Rag Doll."

He and group member Bob Gaudio were in their car in New York City when a young girl in tattered clothes walked up to the car and offered to clean the windshield. Neither had any change. "Give her $5," DeVito said. "She's just a rag doll." Gaudio went home, according to DeVito, and wrote the song.

Attilio's Kitchen

There was plenty of singing inside Attilio's Kitchen in Denville, our next stop. Pamela Stein DiGesu was singing Italian songs to the accompaniment of accordionist Sal Torino. The Italian restaurant, housed inside the old E.C. Peer Sons General Store, is wonderfully atmospheric. Items from the general store — Prince Albert tins, cookie jars, homemade remedies — line the shelves. Gino Pesci, co-owner with his wife, Lisa, is Joe Pesci's cousin.

"I'll give you the specials, and then get out of your hair," said waiter Dimitri Malki.

"I see we're already out of yours," Castelluccio told the bald waiter.

The braciola — rolled beef and pork stuffed with bread

crumbs, raisins and pignoli nuts and served over penne pasta — was as big as a pound cake, and excellent. Pesci makes his own mozzarella.

"As soon as he gets carpal tunnel, I'm out of here," Lisa Pesci joked. "I'm only in it for the cheese."

Castelluccio finished his tilapia, then eagerly sampled the tiramisu, pear torte and cheesecake for dessert.

"I can't believe I'm off my diet," he moaned good-naturedly. We couldn't believe our evening with him was over.

Vitamia Sons Ravioli Co.

One stop remained for the Mangia-Mobile: Vitamia Sons Ravioli Co. in Lodi, an old-style Italian deli/market if there ever was one.

"We've been associated with cheese making since the 1800s," Francesco Paul Vitamia, the shop's fast-talking owner, said of his family, which hails from Mondello, Sicily. The store's Web site? Pastaboy.com.

Vitamia, which has 100 or so different pastas (including three-color gnocchi and heart-shaped ravioli) at any one time, supplies 200 restaurants throughout the state. "Vietato Fumaro" (no smoking) reads a sign on the wall. The store is known for its sausage bread, mozzarella and other pastas, not to mention the owner's sense of humor.

"You know what they say," he says. "I met you once, I met you twice, and then I foccacia."

Among the regular customers is Lucy Tarabocchia, who is of Croatian ancestry. "I come here all the time, for the ravioli," the Lodi resident said. "They're fresh and the cheese is really good."

"What else are we going to write about?" Vitamia asked. "We make cookies. We make what we call palate teasers. You like that word? Eggplant parmigiana, seafood salad, mostaccioli cake, risotto balls . . . You should come here early in the morning, when the smell — let's call it wafting — the smell of fresh bread is wafting from the oven."

The Munchmobile's driver loaded up his shopping bag with several homemade sauces, plus fresh ravioli, linguine, gnocchi and cavatelli. There were only two words for the pezzetti pomodoro sauce (tomatoes, onions, basil, olive oil and spices) and jumbo ravioli he prepared later for dinner.

Molto bene.

MUNCH BITES 2000:

Gimmee Jimmy's Cookies is located in a low-slung brick building. Founder Jimmy Libman is deaf, and so are five of his 12 employees. When the orange light inside the kitchen goes on, it means a customer has come through the door. White means Jimmy's on his phone. Red: the fire alarm is on. "We're totally high-tech deaf," Libman says.

— Bakeries, June 2000

PETER GENOVESE

Carrot juice and mango smoothies. Tofu parmigiana, tofu scalloppine and pasta with vegan meatballs. Kale juice, veggie enchiladas and the Eden Wrap. Organic chicken curry salad, organic ostrich and organic duck.

Salad bars, juice stations and veggie restaurants.

Wait, is this the Munchmobile?

Yes, Big Dog fans, it is. Man does not live by grease alone, and the Munch Team, in its endless wandering (think David Carradine in "Kung Fu Munchmobile"), will eat anything, even if it's good for you. After a summer spent devouring hot dogs, fried chicken, french fries, milkshakes and the like, the Munchers did the unthinkable — eating healthy, eating right. And enjoying it, with the possible exception of one Muncher who, apparently driven to frenzy by the sight of all the roots and tubers, stopped at Burger King to pick up a burger and bag of fries.

"I need some real food," said the Muncher, who shall remain anonymous.

Real? How much more real can you get than cabbage eggroll, gluten parmigiana and honey BBQ grilled tofu?

Okay, we're having some fun here, but the Munchers were pleasantly surprised by their health food excursion. You can eat well and you can eat right, and you don't have to eat beans and sprouts if you don't want to. If the sight, smell, taste and very essence of tofu bother you, there are plenty of alternatives.

"We're a meat-and-potatoes vegetarian restaurant," said Mark Rasmussen, owner of Veggie Works in Belmar.

A meat-and-potatoes vegetarian restaurant? How can that be? For the healthy answers, read on.

Health Love & Soul, South Orange

You just know, from the name, the place is going to be cool. A wooden bicycle hangs from the wall. Jazz drifts through the air like a faint summer breeze. A sign reads, "You Are What You Eat; What Are You Eating?"

It didn't take Annissa Garrett long to discover Health Love & Soul when she moved to South Orange from Chicago. Her only problem is deciding what to drink every time she stops at the modest, atmospheric, little storefront.

"I like to mix it up," Garrett said. "Mango and pineapple is good. Green apple and pineapple is good. Strawberry is very good. Oatmeal — I can't eat oatmeal but the oatmeal drink is good. Oatmeal and bananas is very good . . ."

Ishiwanda McMillion — just call her Wanda — stood behind the counter, a smile on her face. She has seen this indecision at Health Love & Soul before.

"What's in the grilled chicken wrap?" she said. "Chicken,

cucumber, lettuce, tomatoes, bean sprouts, carrots, wrapped in spinach." McMillion laughed. "You can't go wrong with that."

We didn't. Something labeled "Eden Wrap" would ordinarily have us running for the snack aisle in our local supermarket, but the all-veggie wrap, filled with greens, tomatoes and a honey mustard dressing, was gooey, gushy and good. Buy a wrap, and you get one of HLS' 16-ounce "cocktails" for free, or $1 off any smoothie. The cocktails are made with fresh fruit and contain no preservatives or coloring. A bag of Terra Chips, made from yucca, taro, sweet potato and other vegetables, was the perfect accompaniment to a memorable sidewalk meal.

Sam's Farm, Springfield

Fresh fruit and vegetables, and a bounteous salad bar, within walking distance of Route 22?

The lunchtime crowd at Sam's Farm in Springfield proves that keeping things simple can be the secret to success. Fresh fruits and vegetables, a range of eclectic snacks (nuts, Terra Chips and Veggie Booty, a puffed rice and corn snack), and a salad bar with 30-plus items add up to a country farm stand minutes from Strip Mall Central.

Add dressings like country Italian, sun-dried tomato, and low-fat balsamic vinaigrette, plus pasta, tuna, chicken and fruit salads, and you'll know why getting in and out of Gene DuBeau's parking lot during the lunch hour can be trickier than anything you'll see during a NASCAR race.

"I've lived in Kenilworth 35 years. I've been coming here all that time," said Maryanne Barbella, lugging bags of corn, tomatoes, nectarines and grapes. "He's got the freshest vegetables and best tomatoes. I'm growing tomatoes, and his tomatoes are better."

"Uh-oh, the Munchmobile," moaned one regular, spotting the Big Dog. "That means we won't be able to get in here next week."

Hey, we're just doing our jobs. Busiest day of the week for the salad bar? You'll never guess.

"Monday," Dubeau explained. "Everyone's pigged out over the weekend, so they want to eat healthy."

We'd happily pig out on the salad bar any day. Neat place, a slice of vanishing New Jersey in the unlikeliest of locations.

"People are watching their weight," Dubeau insisted. "They're not just on a diet but eating better, eating healthier."

We had to watch our train schedule. Time to catch a caboose.

Juice Caboose, Summit

Fresh Squeeze is a catchy enough name, but when Stephen Clark bought the Summit business he wanted something jazzy, something juicy. The Juice Caboose is in the station!

"You're in, you're out, you feel good when you leave," said Jason Katz of Long Valley, enjoying one of the Caboose's many drinks.

Juice Caboose gives new definition to the word "tiny." If there are other customers in the store, you don't walk around as much as edge through. The menu's right in front of you; all the juices, smoothies and supplements, and their ingredients, are written in Magic Marker on the wall.

Juices include Good For You (apple, celery and carrot); Green Light (kale, spinach, celery, cucumber and parsley); Eye Opener (apple, carrot, orange, lemon and ginger) and the Universal Health Kale (kale, parsley, carrot). Smoothies range from Arctic Java (coffee, maple syrup, cinnamon, milk and fresh yogurt) and Surfside (mango, papaya, pineapple) to Elvis (banana, strawberry and peanut butter) and Passion Switch (papaya, strawberry and banana). There are also wraps and daily soups.

The mango berry smoothie was not quite as fruity as the name promised, but the Tropical Wave won the Munchmobile Seal of Approval with its cool, creamy blend of pineapple, coconut milk, banana and orange juice. Catch this Wave; you'll love it.

Health Shoppe, Morristown

Talk about choices. In the center of Morristown is a Burger King. Next to it, the Health Shoppe, a health food supermarket offering everything from Boca burgers and turkey franks to Uncle Sam cereal and organic gelato.

"All the produce is organic," said Brant Shapiro, co-owner of the Health Shoppe. "The chicken in the chicken salad is organic." He laughed. "Those chickens have lived a happy life. They're fed natural grains. They're free to roam about."

The store, which his dad, Steve, and uncle, Herb, opened in 1970, is a great place to roam around. Our destination was the deli at the back of the store.

"The juice bar is huge, huge, huge," Shapiro said. "The guys who are hungover come in Monday for their wheat grass (said to detoxify and cleanse the system). It's like 'Cheers.'" The deli offers nearly 20 different kinds of hot food daily, plus an array of salads.

The Thai tofu, lightly baked and accompanied by a fresh peanut sauce, is a "huge hit," according to Shapiro.

We spread our plates and containers in the back seat and on the floor of the Munchmobile, and chowed down. The chicken curry salad is a subtle, satisfying curry, dotted with raisins. Good spinach salad, with tomatoes, black olives and feta. The blackberry cheesecake, with walnuts and oats, maple syrup, cream cheese, sour cream, Florida crystals, butter, salt, vanilla, lemon juice and peel, plum jam and fresh blackberries (whew!), is a tasty alternative to your standard diner pie.

The standouts, though, were two sandwiches — the New Yorker, succulent roast beef with horseradish and Russian dressing on rye, and the Mastermind, with Genoa salami, provolone, balsamic vinegar and tomato on a Tuscan hero roll.

Super sandwiches.

Veggie Works, Belmar

"PEACE" reads the message outside Veggie Works in Belmar. "Love animals — don't eat them," says a note inside. Hendrix, Marley and Sinatra provide the background music.

"We look loosey-goosey back here, but we're all pretty well-trained," said Mark Rasmussen, owner of Veggie Works.

Veggie Works is a popular place; you may have to wait for a table. Rasmussen chalks it up to an increasing interest not just in vegetarianism but in healthy, nutritious food in general.

"We've had a 15-20 percent increase in customer base every year," he said. "And at least half of our regular customers are not vegetarians."

He calls Veggie Works a "meat and potatoes" vegetarian restaurant because it offers high-protein vegetable meat "analogs" and concentrated vegetable flavorings.

"We have a salad bar, but we're not about low-calorie raw food," Rasmussen explained. "We're about getting a power-packed meal with all your proteins."

Even "the most reluctant cynic," he says in his "Veggie Works Vegan Cookbook" (available at the restaurant) "will easily succumb to the satisfying meals that you prepare."

Okay, okay, we succumbed!

We started with hummus and baba ghanoush, both good. The nachos, with baked cheese and diced veggies, did not rise much above the movie-theater variety.

But our entrees were uniformly good. Got something against tofu? The grilled tofu sandwich, with tomatoes and greens, may forever change your mind. The Paul Bunyan, a 12-ounce soy "chuck" steak with diced garlic and veggies, pan-seared and sauted with mushrooms and gravy, was a big hit with News 12 cameraman Anthony Cocco.

And the Munchmobile's driver, the world's No. 1 meatloaf hater as a kid, loved his vegan meatloaf, made with a TVP (textured vegetable protein) burger blend, tomato paste, black pepper, thyme leaf, diced onion and bread crumbs.

"Meat is Dead," reads another sign inside Veggie Works. That could have been the motto on this Munchmobile trip, which was eye-opening and consciousness-raising. The Muncher who needed the Burger King fix? He has been given a good talking-to.

MUNCH BITES 2001:

Teddy Miller works out of a battered old white camper marooned in the parking lot of an abandoned Bradlee's on Central Avenue in Clark. The camper, Teddy's third in his 30 years as a hot dog vendor, has a right rear flat tire Teddy has no intentions of fixing any time soon. Why bother? The truck is not going anywhere. And neither is Teddy.

— Hot dogs, July 2001

PETER GENOVESE

Right from the start, we knew we were in trouble. The Big Dog had pulled up, innocently enough, in front of Essex Grand Buffet in West Orange. Led by Guest Muncher Harvey "You'll Never Starve with Harv" Tekel, also of West Orange, the Munch Team waltzed inside.

How hard could this be, everyone thought — a day of all-you-can-eat buffets? Eat as much or as little as you want. No menus to fuss with, no daily specials to worry about.

As soon as we stepped inside, we shuddered. Rows of stainless-steel buffet tables stretched as far as the eye could see. For all we knew, they went straight through the back wall and into the parking lot.

About 200 different dishes beckoned, everything from sushi, salads and soup to spare ribs, shrimp and salmon (and that's just a smattering of the selections starting with "s").

"This," said an awestruck Star-Ledger photographer Ed Murray, "is frightening."

The kind of frightened you get when confronted with a staggering amount of food and the realization you cannot begin to do it justice. Like showing up at your mother-in-law's for Thanksgiving dinner with a full stomach.

"My natural inclination," Tekel said after returning with his fourth dish from the buffet, "would be to go back and back and back. But that would be suicide."

It was the first stop on a five-restaurant, four-county search for the state's best all-you-can-eat buffets. Would the Munchers have to be wheeled out by the end of the day? What is the difference between General Tso's chicken and the General's chicken? How much can you eat of all-you-can eat, anyway? For a smorgasbord of answers, read on.

Essex Grand Buffet, West Orange

It is not known who put on the first buffet, and of what foods it consisted. Smorgasbord is Swedish for "bread and butter table," although the smorgasbord has come to mean a variety of dishes. The breakfast buffet is a staple of hotels worldwide, and American truck stops, for one, have raised, or debased, the genre, depending on how you feel about truck stops and buffets.

Around 1900, a French poet penned these lines:

Aussitot que la lumiere
Vient eclairer mon chevet
Je commence ma carrier
Par visiter mon buffet

Which means, roughly, if you're going to pay any of these buffets a visit, don't eat for a week beforehand.

There are nearly 200 different items at Essex Grand Buffet. Mountains of crawfish. Mussels and clams, white rice and fried rice, veggie low mein and veggie low mein fun. Sweet paste buns and steamed roast pork buns. Ten kinds of chicken. Pizza. Noodle bar, soup bar, sushi bar, salad bar. Salt and pepper squid. Even pigs in a blanket!

Where does one begin? How can one end?

The broccoli is fresh and crunchy. Good, viscous egg drop soup. Juicy fried chicken, although it could have been crisper. Excellent salmon — thick, moist slices. The sushi won't win any Jersey-fresh awards, but decent selection. The pepperoni pizza? A slice above the super market frozen variety. The salt and pepper squid sounded tempting, but was rubbery. Chicken teriyaki: greasy. Try the chicken with mushrooms instead. One tip: If you order tea, ask for it unsweetened; the sweetened variety here is way too sugary. We loved the "dim sum dessert"— flaky, nut-topped tiny pastries.

"We come here every time we have a doctor's appointment," said Stacy Kosmides of Glen Ridge, enjoying the buffet with her husband, Bill.

"The variety is unbelievable." Among her favorites: spring rolls and steamed buns.

We checked the messages in our fortune cookies, as we would the rest of the day. "May you have a good appetite," read Ed Murray's message.

Not a problem with the Munch Team. Buffeted by a hot summer breeze, we headed to Wayne.

Oriental Buffet, Wayne

"Super buffet. All You Can Eat. Great Food. Great Prices," announces the menu at Oriental Buffet, formerly King Chef Buffet. The menus at our all-you-eat buffets — produced by such companies as Sino Printing and Oriental Art Printing — make for great kitchen kitsch, decorated with glistening Peking duck, saucy spareribs and other dishes.

Buffets have been around for years, but all-you-can-eat Chinese-themed buffets have mushroomed in New Jersey in the last few years. All showcase a variety of "American" food — fried chicken, buffalo wings, roast beef, prime rib and so on. You'll find sushi and shrimp chow mein — and, at Oriental Buffet, pollock with white wine and butter, roast beef, and self-serve soft ice cream. Popular? At 1:30 on this Tuesday afternoon, the restaurant is packed.

All the buffets we visited preach sensible eating. "Please help us maintain our reasonable prices by taking only what you (can) eat," reads a sign at Oriental Buffet. The lunch buffet here is $6.25 Monday through Friday, $7.80 on Saturday and Sunday; dinner buffet is $9.95 Monday through Thursday, and $11.95 Friday to Sunday. All five buffets we visited are in that price range. Beverages are included in the buffets, and you can even do takeout; you're charged by the pound. No doggie bags, though, if you eat in.

It's chicken galore at Oriental Buffet — roast chicken,

honey chicken, black pepper chicken, chicken with shrimp, chicken and shrimp, chicken with broccoli, General Tso's chicken. Good — and hot — egg drop soup, better than the Essex Grand Buffet's. But the egg roll is inferior. Fried chicken: plump and crisp. BBQ chicken-on-a-stick: greasy, but nicely charred on top. Roast beef: thin-sliced and juicy. Pollock with white wine and butter: you can barely taste the butter, even less the white wine. And the "chicken balls" tasted more like pork than chicken. One recommended dish: the mussels with black bean sauce. "The pepper steak is good but a lot of the other meat is bland," Murray said.

Tekel, who weighs 250 pounds, said that "on paper" he's healthy. On paper, the Munchmobile driver's future looked promising: "You will advance socially without any special effort."

We advanced, with little special effort, to our next Munch stop.

King Chef, Union

Our all-you-can eat buffets all seemed to be designed by the same person: same green color scheme, same high-backed chairs, same light fixtures, same neon tiara sign in the window. One difference at King Chef: the carve-your-own meat stations, including ham and roast beef. The selections are slightly more adventurous: steak au poivre, lobster roll, cod with white wine and butter sauce, stuffed shells. The King Chef does what buffets do most, if not best: chicken. Peking chicken, chicken chow mein fun, chicken with cashew nuts, among others.

Porfirio's in Trenton makes about 4,000 pounds of pasta every week. The top-seller: gnocchi.

Good salad bar; we liked the tomato/green-and-black-olive salad mix. The sushi could have been fresher, but Tekel liked the variety. Fair fried chicken, on the undercooked side. We couldn't pick out the lobster in the lobster roll. Our Guest Muncher liked the "seafood delight," a combination of scallops, shrimp and lobster in a light butter sauce. General's Chicken turned out to be the ubiquitous General Tso's chicken. The egg drop soup is not as rich as the Oriental Buffet's but it's hotter. Stuffed shells: not bad, considering. Rare roast beef, but it showed the effects — picked apart, dried out — of sitting out there for buffet line forever, which can be a long time.

Buffets lend themselves to curious eating patterns. Murray brought back one dish laden with boneless ribs, stuffed mushrooms, cantaloupe and coconut macaroons. "I'm impressed with the variety here, especially the meats," Tekel said. "There's more red stuff here."

Murray's fortune cookie read: "You may attend a party where strange customs prevail."

Empire Buffet, Pompton Lakes

"This is like watching the same movie," Tekel said as the waitress at Empire Buffet took our drink orders and said the magic words: "Help yourself to the buffet."

David Cheng and his father, Tom, own this Empire Buffet; David's brother, Michael, owns an Empire Buffet in Stanhope. "Proud to be American" balloons fly inside, and there's that same neon tiara in the window again.

Huge, tasty clams and crunchy spring rolls. Tekel, searching for a standout hot and sour soup, again came away disappointed. "I've had hot and sour soup at each place; none of them were that good," he observed.

Stuffed shells, hold the stuffing; there's nothing inside the three shells on our plate. The fried chicken would have been the best of the day if it had not been sitting out so long. A buffet is, more than anything else, a waiting game: Wait for those fresh pans to come out of the kitchen, then attack.

Tough pork ribs, okay shrimp rolls. The chicken and mushrooms came in a too-syrupy sauce. Much of the buffet food we sampled all day tasted like it was cooked in the same central commissary: same BBQ glaze on the ribs, same taste to the teriyaki. Best thing about the Empire: the hard ice cream. And it had the best buffet soundtrack — a folk/pop mix.

The message inside one of our fortune cookies (from the Ha-Ha Fortune Cookie Co. of Brooklyn): "The best of profit is the past."

"What does that mean?" asked a befuddled Tekel.

No idea, Harv. We left, hoping to find enlightenment at our next and final stop.

Lodi Buffet, Lodi

We rumbled past Castle of Gourmet Nuts and Elegant 99 Cents or Less in Clifton on our way to Lodi, where Howard and Vicki Rubenstein sang the praises of their favorite thin-crust pizza as they sat in their classy convertible outside Lodi Buffet.

"Naples, on Broadway in Bayonne," Howard Rubenstein said. "Thin crust so thin you can put it up to the Star-Ledger and read the paper through it."

The two are big fans of Lodi Buffet. "It's consistently good, it's clean, and they're constantly replacing; very rarely do you ever come to a tray that is empty," Howard Rubenstein said.

True on all counts. We liked the twinkling lights around the buffet table and the friendly waitresses. This is the most far-ranging buffet of the bunch: veal with mushrooms, pasta vodka, sausage and peppers, lentil soup, Singapore chicken and corn on the cob.

The Munchmobile's driver, sampling the egg drop soup at each location, found the best here, a rich, golden-hued brew. Crispy fried chicken, but it could have been hotter. Freshest sushi of the day. Passable chicken parm. Great to see prime rib, but it was dried out from sitting under those bright buffet lights. Easily the day's best egg roll here, bursting with flavor. Not-so-fresh honeydew melon. Good, thin-sliced cheesecake, but the same generic chocolate pudding. Good rice pudding, though. Nice touch: You pay as you enter, so there's no waiting at the register later.

We made multiple trips to the buffet line, then sat back, sated and a little silly. Tekel, the Guest Muncher, drew the best fortune cookie message of the day.

"I'm full," it read. We were stuck in Lodi again, and enjoying every minute of it.

Neatest T-shirt seen: "My mother was a travel agent for guilt trips" (Wildwood boardwalk)

MUNCH BITES 2002:

Five straight nights, 12 to 15 different meats each night (everything from filet mignon and top sirloin to alligator and ostrich), and somehow, with all that, finding room for appetizers and dessert at each restaurant.

Who said Munchmobile duty isn't fun?

"I prefer this chicken heart over the one from yesterday," Guest Muncher Mickey Horne said at Solar do Minho in Belleville. "That one tasted like chicken. This one tastes like a delicacy."

"The thing that impresses me here," Star-Ledger photographer Ed Murray said at one point, "is that I haven't been attacked by the salt."

— Rodizio, June 2002

Around 1900 a French poet penned these lines:
Aussitot que la lumiere
Vient eclairer mon chevet
Je commence ma carrier
Par visiter mon buffet
Which means, roughly, if you're going to pay any of these buffets a visit, don't eat for a week beforehand.

— Buffets, August 2002

FOURTH OF JULY TRIP, JULY 18, 2003

PETER GENOVESE

You didn't need to be a pig at Grace and Travis Fryzow-icz' Fourth of July weekend picnic in Spotswood, but it sure would have helped to appreciate the 25th annual event. The guest of honor each year is a 100-pound-or-so roasted suckling pig named after a different letter of the alphabet. Previous guests of honor: Lucinda (after former Gov. Jim Florio's wife), Madonna, Quincy and Tootsie. This year's prize piggie: Yo-Yao, after a TV commercial featuring Yogi Berra and Yao Ming.

The names of all 25 pigs were written on pieces of paper flapping in the breeze above a table laden with food. Mussels marinara. Chicken wings. Oriental salad. Noodle pudding. Fruit salad in the shape of a majestic peacock. Dozens of other dishes, all made by friends and neighbors.

When it was time for dessert, the entire table was cleared and filled with cakes, pies, cookies and brownies.

> About 1,500 clams and oysters each are shucked on a typical summer weekend at Martell's Raw Bar, Point Pleasant Beach.

No, you didn't need to be a pig at Grace and Travis' annual shindig, but it didn't hurt.

"We have followed your tasty jaunts from east to west and north to south in our great state of New Jersey," Grace Fryzow-icz wrote when we asked readers to invite the Munchmobile to their holiday cookouts and barbecues. "Now come and enjoy one of the most scrumptious July 4th barbecues ever. We usually have between 80 and 100 people here in our backyard, which is only 100-by-100 feet. But we do have fun, and it is truly a neighbor and friend barbecue as everyone chips in with salads, desserts. . ... all-American chili dogs, chicken and corn on the cob."

Another reader, Hilary Bragar of Millington, promised the Munchers potato salad ("I have been told by more than one it is the best in the land!") and a "crystal clear" swimming pool. Jodi Howard of Montclair, inviting the Munch Bunch to her Long Beach Island home, said her friend Eric "prepares a mean whole chicken — with a beer can up its behind — as well as many other goodies."

Marge and Gary Drozd, also of Spotswood, were celebrating not only the Fourth of July but their middle son's high school graduation and their youngest son's eighth-grade graduation. "Best food this side of the Mississippi," Marge said.

We crashed readers' bashes between Kearny and Long

Beach Island, sampling everything from suckling pig to sinful desserts. Oh, the picnics we did not attend, the sights we did not see! Kathy Mongello invited us to the picnic/pool party at Grand Centurion Pool in Clark.

"Ask for the tree people," she said cryptically.

Jackie Sullivan of Readington teased us with offers of spinach salad with cherries, "Granddad's spare ribs," "classic cole slaw" and "the best burgers you could ever eat." Jackie Schatell invited us not to one but two cookouts at the retirement communities where she works — Seabrook, in Tinton Falls (barbeque baby back spare ribs, shrimp and scallop stir fry, honey cornbread) and Cedar Crest in Pompton Plains (grilled chicken kabobs, burgers, grilled Italian sausage, waffle fries).

And we weren't sure whether to be tempted or terrified by Christine Cocca's invite: "If you haven't been to Bear Country, N.J. yet — then come on up," the Jefferson resident wrote. "We have such a big population of black bears around here. We had one in our yard after last year's barbeque. We had one on our front walk last week around 7 p.m."

Aside from that minor distraction, the food sounded good — her husband Michael's "delicious sausage and peppers," his "equally delicious" venison chili and his "famous" macaroni salad.

Some of the invites were Proustian in nature, others Hemingwayesque.

"We are having a barbecue at 4 p.m.," one reader announced. "We will be at Calandra's at 8 a.m. to pick up hot bread."

It was our second straight Munchmobile 4th of July weekend excursion, and the Munch crew hopes it becomes an annual feature. Flag-draped and jam-packed, the Big Dog did its patriotic duty, pigging out from north to south. The full report, we rib you not:

Trinity Episcopal Church, Kearny

A sweat-soaked Nick Giaquinto stood in front of a grill outside Trinity Episcopal Church in Kearny. The smell of burgers, chicken and ribs — the smell of summer — drifted through the air.

"These ribs are marinated for about two hours, then cooked in the oven, then we put them on the grill to touch them up," Giaquinto explained.

His chicken and ribs are flavored with honey, molasses — and coffee.

"It enhances the flavor," added Giaquinto, opening a Sears Craftsman-like toolbox filled with every conceivable barbecue implement.

"Exceptional" is how Dave Brooks described the ribs. "The coffee gives the barbecue a smoky flavor," he added. "My objection to most barbecue is that it's too sweet."

Good eggplant, made by Nick's mom, and potato salad, by

Carol Stec.

"Everything is so good," Judy Fortunato marveled.

"You have made my year," gushed Giaquinto, as the Big Dog pulled away.

Hey, Nick, you made our summer! On to Millington.

Hilary and Jeff Bragar, Millington

Biggest mistake the Munchers made on their pool-packed Fourth of July excursion last summer? Not bringing their bathing suits! Duh! The Summer Survivor Munchers were not about to let that happen; almost all immediately headed straight for the pool behind Hilary and Jeff Bragar's house in Millington.

"My daughter is bringing her mouth-watering tomato tart, and I will be serving my legendary zucchini pie," Hilary Bragar had written.

When it comes to barbecues and cookouts, of course, everyone's a four-star cook. The barbeque ribs, made by Rich Raymond, Hilary's son, were another attraction. Ingredients for the sauce?

"Two tablespoons of sugar and a can and a half of Foster's (beer)," according to one highly-placed party source.

"Combine Nick's ribs with this sauce," said Rich Sgrignoli, rolling his eyes.

"I'm pushing the baked beans," said Raymond Goldfield, who, to no one's surprise, was the first to grab a plate. "They're not sickeningly sweet like many baked beans."

Loved the zucchini pie, and the potato salad. Fortunato added an apple pie from Delicious Orchards to the dessert pile. We noshed on snap-crackly edamame, the Japanese green soybeans. The Dixie Chicks sang "Landslide."

We wished it were Stevie Nicks instead, but we couldn't have wished for better company. We bid the Bragars, and their pool, good-bye.

Grace and Travis Frzyowicz, Spotswood

"You just missed the pig," Travis Fryzowicz said as we strolled into his backyard.

Story of our life.

Actually, we didn't miss the pig, just the pig on the spit. We couldn't possibly have passed up this invite. Big crowd, roasted pig, "special family secret recipes" and enough desserts to stock a bakery. The couple even printed up 500 T-shirts reading "I Smell Bacon Bacon Bacon."

We smelled good food, mostly. Tomato, mozzarella and cucumber salad. Chicken wings. Homemade pepperoni bread. Sausage and peppers. Great baked beans, a mixture of variet-ies. Most inventive dish: noodle pudding, a Frosted Flakes-topped concoction of creamed cheese, sour cream, noodles and eggs.

"Basically a coronary on a plate," family friend Donna Savarese said, laughing.

Delicious, too!

The first pig's name was Alice, who was followed by Bertha. Two years ago, it was Wilbur, last year, Xenia.

"Twenty five years, a pig every year," said Travis Fryzowicz, a former Marine. "We've had lots of fun."

The picnic's most poignant moment would come later, when a brief memorial service would be held in honor of the 20 or so people — all regulars of the Fryzowicz picnic — who had passed away over the years.

We dug the desserts — strawberry rhubarb pie; red, white and blue-frosted layer cake; cream puffs; cupcakes; cherry-topped Black Forest brownies; and Carole Ott's fabulous chocolate chip cookies.

"Wow, wow, wow," Fortunato said of the astounding array.

"I am so stuffed," Kathryn Little sighed.

We've heard that from you before, Deputy Muncher!

The Big Dog's driver summoned the troops together. Next stop? Oh, about six blocks away.

Marge and Gary Drozd, Spotswood

"There're drinks and food," Marge Drozd announced.

"Don't have to tell me twice," said Goldfield, the self-described "buff hunk on the Munchmobile."

We dove immediately into, not the pool, but the stuffed cabbage made by Drozd's 82-year-old mother-in-law, Rose.

"This is a Polish-Hungarian crowd," Gary Drozd said. "They know how to eat."

He longingly described a Hungarian dish called solona, which essentially consists of melted fatback dripped on cucumber and onion-topped rye bread. Yumm!

Like the Fryzowiczs, the Drozds were celebrating their 25th anniversary picnic.

"Food means a lot of things," said Marge Drozd. "It's family and friends and friendship and a whole lot of love. We are blessed in America to have all this bounty."

"I feel too blessed," said Dave Brooks, patting his stomach.

Once again, it was hit (the food table) and run. Next —and final — stop: Long Beach Island.

Jodi and Doug Howard, Beach Haven

We couldn't turn down an invite to LBI on a hot day like this. Or a chance to see a "mean whole chicken with a beer can up its behind," as Jodi Howard had so succinctly put it. The beer adds flavor, and who was going to argue with chicken this good anyway? We poured out big glasses of Jodi's lime juice-sweetened watermelon juice, and enjoyed a luscious fruit-salad-like mix of watermelon, mint, serrano peppers, cucumbers and lime juice.

"I've never made it before," the Montclair resident confessed.

What does she call it?

She thought a moment, and said, "Watermelon blast!"

Flank steak on toast points, clams with garlic and oregano, bean salad, delicious pulled pork sandwiches, wings smoked on apple wood: What a cookout!

"This pork is growing on me," Sgrignoli said.

Yikes!

"Does anyone want a piece of ice cream cake?" Howard asked later. "It's moving."

Double yikes!

We sat on the back deck, caressed by the softest of breezes. It would be a long ride home, and we wouldn't pull into the parking lot until 2:30 — in the morning! — but it was all worth it.

"Best day of the summer," the one Muncher who was awake at the time marveled. Couldn't agree more.

> The first ice cream ad appeared on May 12, 1777, when confectioner Philip Lenzi announced ice cream was available "almost every day."

MUNCH BITES 2003:

It was perfect bread-eating, coffee-drinking weather: dreary, miserable. Dawn-to-dusk bread? It was the yeast we could do.

— Breads, June 2003

All the way to Bound Brook, we puzzled over the provenance of the oddest-sounding name of Munch 2003 — Stan's Chitch's Cafe.

"Chitch was the first owner; Stan is the current owner," explained Myra, the bartender.

But of course! Stan's Chitch's is a funky little place: football and hockey banners in the tiny front bar, spacious dining room off to the side.

— Pizza, August 2003

When a nun tells you to make a run to her favorite ice cream stand, you listen.

"I never tasted such good (ice cream) in my life," Sister Joan Marie Maliszewski said of Custard's Last Stand in Ventnor. She is a member of the Felician Sisters who works at St. Cecilia's in Iselin. "The hot fudge was absolutely delicious."

Sister Joan Marie, who recently vacationed in Ventnor, is a big Munchmobile fan. "I just eat those stories up!" she said.

— Ice cream, August 2003

PETER GENOVESE

Crabs are low-lifes, no way around it. They spend their beady-eyed existences scuttling along the ocean floor, scavenging for crabapples, crabgrass or whatever it is they eat. Ugly, unathletic, apathetic, they look as if they're born to have a bad day.

No wonder "crabby" has become synonymous for grouchy, cranky and ill-tempered. But put a steamed, boiled or sautéed decapod on your dinner table, tie a bib around your neck, and the lowly crab suddenly transforms into a sublime, albeit messy, delight. When they're right, that is.

To every season, turn, turn, turn; you'll run into one crab or another. Soft shells are available from May to September. Dungeness, one of the larger species, are best in winter and early spring. Timing is everything in beautiful downtown Crabville.

"We had some great crabs last night; I wish you were here," Brian Sexton, chef/manager of Crabby's Suds and Seafood in Belcoville, told the Munch-mobile crew. "Blue claws. We sold out."

Crabby's, in the Pine Barrens, is proof you don't have to be near the water to find good crabs. Blue Claw Seafood & Crab Eatery, meanwhile, is located on Route 130 in Burlington Township, which does not usually come to mind as prime crab territory.

"Blue crabs can swim rapidly forward, backwards or sideways," according to one of the many crab-educational signs on the walls at Blue Claw Seafood & Crab Eatery.

Yeah, but they're still ugly. And cranky.

Our Munchmobile mission took us to five crab joints around the state. Four Love Munchers were along for the ride — three women, one guy, and he, not surprisingly, didn't act crabby at all.

"The garlic pieces at the bottom of the bowl make me excited," Muncher Melyssa Quintana said at one point.

It's been that kind of summer.

Does eating crabs all day improve your disposition? Would our lone male Muncher bear up under the terrible strain of accompanying three beautiful women? And who is Jean LeFeet, anyway? For the swimmingly sweet report, read on. And stop being so crabby.

Blue Claw Seafood & Crab Eatery, Burlington Township

"Make as much mess as you want" is the motto at Blue Claw Seafood & Crab Eatery, open since 1961. Plush, plastic and wooden crabs dangle from the ceiling. Fresh crabs, flounder, catfish, scallops and shrimp rest atop ice in a display case. Posters and charts provide an instant education to menippe mercenaria (stone crab) and friends. "Forget the stress, relax and enjoy," counsels the menu. The tables are covered in brown construction paper, and crayons are provided. Rolls of hand towels are positioned at the end of each table, so you don't need to use your shirt to wipe your hands.

"Snows are longer and skinner," explained waitress Jessica Rein. "More of an orange look to them. King are even longer, and have spikes on them. Dungeness are short and fat." Have your crabs your way here; get them steamed, or with garlic, Old Bay, or a cayenne-enlivened hot sauce. The garlic snow crabs? "Amazing," according to Quintana, not loosening her grip on the bowl.

The hot-sauced blue crabs were not far behind. The crab cake wouldn't win any awards, but the Old Bay-seasoned fries get our vote for the summer's best fries. Simply irresistible.

The spicy crab soup and clam chowder are good and rich, although the former was lukewarm. Cool touch — drinks served in Mason jars. The menu is expansive — fried and broiled fish, shellfish, pasta, ribs — and we'll be back again. Maybe take a shot at Blue Claw's all-you-can-eat crab dinners, see just how messy we get.

Crabby's, Belcoville

Belcoville? You've never heard of it, but it's easy enough to find, south of the Black Horse Pike and west of Atlantic City. Crabby's is off the beaten path, but don't let that deter you. Or the signs on the walls.

Rules of the Inn: no thieves, fakirs, rogues or tinkers. No skulking, loafers or flea-bitten tramps.

Guess we'd better leave! Crabby's is a lively back-roads hangout, and Sexton, the chef, knows his stuff, and crabs. Dollar bills are taped to the ceiling — at the end of the year, they are taken down and donated to charity. Sign above the kitchen door: "This stairway off-limits to patients." No crabby people here, apparently.

Got off to a great start here, with the soups. The seafood gumbo is spicy, rice-y and recommended, but we loved the sherry-flavored he-crab soup. It's terrific, stopping just short of too rich and too sweet. "A really nice blend of comforting flavors," Amanda Brown observed.

Order your crabs "dirty" — uncleaned — or have the staff clean them for you, no extra charge.

Crabby's house spice contains "less salt, more spice" than Old Bay, but some of us found it saltier.

The king crab legs here are first-rate; Star-Ledger photographer Tim Farrell would put them on his favorites list. The garlic crabs didn't seem quite as successful, or sea-worthy, as the blue crabs. The crab cake could have been better. The crab and linguine marinara, though, was a pleasant surprise.

Good homemade desserts in a bar? What's this world coming to? Crabby's strawberry delight, fresh strawberries meant to be dipped in granulated brown sugar and sour cream, more than lives up to the name. "Simple and effective," Jessica Russell said succinctly.

We bid the Pine Barrens goodbye, and went looking for Bum.

Bum Rogers, South Seaside Park

We arrived at this venerable Seaside restaurant, right outside the entrance to Island Beach State Park, just in time. The line was already out the door soon after we were seated.

If you want your crab tasting to be a tranquil, meditative experience, go elsewhere; Bum's can get noisy, especially on the weekend. This place rocks — almost literally. "A communal, spirit-lifting watering hole," according to the menu. That's one way to put it.

But if you want great garlic crabs, look no further. Pull up a seat and order Jean LeFeet, Bum's name for its "oven-blasted" zesty-spiced garlic crabs. They're nice and garlicky, tender and slightly sweet.

Crabs arrabiatta — garlic crabs baked in a marinara-like "Cajun spicy" sauce — was a muddled mess; the dish didn't know whether it wanted to be Cajun, Italian, or something else. The hot-n-spicy crabs are not particularly hot, but the spiced crumbly topping makes them a tangy, tasty treat. The deep fried soft shells: okay, at least on this night.

Nice, meaty mussels, in a garlic and white wine sauce. The jumbalaya, sautéed in a Cajun scampi-style sauce, didn't have much going for it; right ingredients, wrong result. Corn on the cob is an overcooked afterthought in many seafood joints, but Bum's mushy version is even worse; why did the kitchen bother?

Afterwards, the paper-plate-strewn table and floor looked like the aftermath of a crab hurricane. Think "The Wizard of Oz," with Jean LeFeet and Toto being tossed about.

Crab's Claw Inn, Lavallette

Permit the Big Dog's driver to be, well, crabby for a moment. What is with colder-than-a meat-freezer restaurants when it's 65-70 outside? It doesn't make for pleasurable dining, and didn't the night we stopped at Crab's Claw. We shivered through dinner, even if much of it was memorable.

Old-time photos of Lavallette decorate the walls; the bar is a lively late-night gathering spot. And the kitchen stays open late. The spicy crab chowder was little more than a Manhattan. But the homemade crab cake is recommended — fine, fried texture and a soft but not mealy filling. "Best crab cake we've had all day; good balance to it," R.J. Charles said.

The Dungeness crab, steamed in beer and Old Bay, does this crustacean proud — tender, oh-so-sweet meat. The verdict on the soft shells, in a garlic/butter sauce: so-so crab, nice sauce. The flounder stuffed with crabmeat is excellent. The seafood lasagna seemed overly cheesy, but Jessica Russell listed it among her favorites. One word for the double fudge chocolate ice cream cake: delicious.

The Big Dog's driver, properly chilled, hit the beach one more time several days later.

Rooney's Ocean Crab House, Long Branch

It won't be long before Long Branch is back on the tourist map again; condos and townhouses are popping up quicker than fast-rising biscuits on the waterfront. Rooney's, with its oceanfront wrap-around bar, dining room and outdoor cafe, is in a perfect position to take advantage.

Looking for good, fresh oysters? Try a dozen Emerald Cove oysters, from Canada; they're fresh and near-fabulous. And they come with three dipping sauces: your standard cocktail, plus a ginger lime and chipotle pepper, both standouts.

The blue claws, available either in a beer/Old Bay mix or in a garlic herb scampi oil, didn't distinguish themselves. Couldn't find much evidence of the beer, or Old Bay. But the 1 1/2 pound steamed snow crab clusters and the 2-pound steamed Dungeness, in a garlic herb broth, will please the most finicky crab eater. The Dungeness, in fact, was the best of its kind sampled on our two-day jaunt.

Rooney's Key West crab salad is super — loads of crab; fresh, crisp Romaine; grape tomatoes, hearts of palm, mandarin oranges and roasted pistachios, all in a prickly pear vinaigrette.

> Sushi is not raw fish; that's sashimi. Sushi is the sweetened rice the raw fish is wrapped in.

MUNCH BITES 2004:

Ahh, the Jersey Shore. Early-morning walks on the boardwalk, picture-perfect sunsets. Banner pilots — two for one drinks early bird dinner specials six bands tonight free camera phone with activation — chugging back and forth across a bright blue sky. Lazy, languorous days on the beach; weeks you wish would last forever.

That your Jersey Shore?

It's not the Big Dog's!

Glaze-y, gluey cinnamon buns; drippy sausage and pepper sandwiches. Custard, cookies and cotton candy; fudge, funnel cakes and curly fries. Two chili dogs with the works, washed down with a giant cup of fresh-squeezed lemonade.

That more like it?

— Down the Shore, June 2004

ICE CREAM, JULY 22, 2005

PETER GENOVESE

The identity of the first person to scream for ice cream is shrouded in mystery. How many people had murmured, whispered or spoken in a normal conversational tone up to that point is not known either.

But this much is indisputable — nothing beats the heat like a creamy smooth cone or sundae. The first ice cream ad, according to the International Ice Cream Association, appeared in the New York Gazette on May 12, 1777, when confectioner Philip Lenzi announced ice cream was available "almost every day." Thomas Jefferson had an 18-step recipe for his favorite ice cream dish.

Here is a time-honored two-step recipe:

Pick up cone.

Start licking.

"For my 21st birthday coming up in August, I'm going to get loaded," announced Nicole Georgio of Clark.

Mom and Dad, don't worry.

"Loaded on a 21-scoop sundae at Emack & Bolio's," added the Kean University student. Georgio was one of six Munchmobile University students on a statewide search for first-rate ice cream.

Vanilla and chocolate account for 52 percent of supermarket sales of ice cream, but we were looking for unusual, offbeat ice cream. Funky flavors, if you will. We wanted edible, delectable ice cream; there would be no fettucine-flavored or other designer ice cream for this crew. We would take many lickings and keep on ticking, sampling 100-plus flavors at eight stops. What we hope will be a smooth, sweet story, delivered during National Ice Cream Month, follows.

Uncle Mike's, Kenilworth

Vanilla is No. 1 around the world, but funky vanilla sells, too. The most popular ice cream at Uncle Mike's since April 2004 has been vanilla cake batter. Owner Mike Philipone makes about 150 gallons of ice cream a week.

"Looking for a flavor we don't have?" reads a sign. "Suggest it."

Hmm. How about Munch Madness?

"What do they use, antifreeze?" Herb Raskin marveled at the brightly colored blue raspberry. "It's good!"

"Grab some of this," Flanders resident and Newark fireman Kamal Brown said of the pistachio almond. "It's outstanding."

Meltingly-soft metaphors abounded. "Like a kid's party in a cup," Sue Marinello of Montville said of the vanilla cake batter.

We also loved the chocolate cake crunch. One flavor we weren't crazy about: the almond joy. Raskin described the mango ice as "unbelievable, refreshing."

Gabriel's Fountain, Martinsville

"This is a beautiful thing!" Brown exulted as he happily dug into cotton candy ice cream at Gabriel's Fountain, both walk-up ice cream stand and sit-down restaurant. "I'm going to be Santa Claus when I take my kids to see this!"

SpongeBob the ice cream, like SpongeBob the TV character, evoked varying reactions. Raskin called it "creative," but Jack Parker dismissed the peanut-butter-flavored ice cream. "Bob tastes more like Patrick," he cracked.

Star-Ledger photographer Tim Farrell admired the peach's "subtle" flavor. The chocolate hash, smooth and nutty, was terrific. "Dazzling" was Dwayne Florenzie's description of the black raspberry.

The clear, cool winner here was the peanut butter and jelly, amazingly authentic. "Not the Holy Grail, but close to it," Parker said.

"Almost better than a sandwich," Georgio gushed. "Thank you for finding this!"

Emack & Bolio's, North Brunswick

Georgio quickly acquired a nickname among her fellow Munchers — Dairy Queen. "Am I embarrassed that at 20 years old ice cream is my life? No way!" she said.

She seemed about to blast off into dessert orbit after sampling a dozen flavors at Emack & Bolio's.

"Mud pie," she said of the java ice cream, Oreo and chocolate-flake-flavored ice cream, "is beyond belief . . . the ultimate frozen tasty delight."

Funky flavors fill the display case. Deep purple cow (black raspberry ice cream with white and dark chocolate chips and blueberries). Grasshopper pie (creme de menthe, Oreos and chocolate flakes). Vanilla Bean Speck (Madagascar vanilla with marinated vanilla beans and an egg custard base).

"Ka-ching!" Parker exclaimed after one lick of the eminently lickable and likable espresso chip.

"The flavors just burst, explode in your mouth," Raskin said.

Other flavors we liked: chocolate sol, rich and creamy; almond joy; deep purple cow. Heaven — vanilla ice cream, marshmallow swirl and white chocolate chips — was a letdown.

Confectionally Yours, Franklin Park

There's an outside deck and a water cooler inside to quench that inevitable post-cone thirst at Confectionally Yours, open 24 years.

"Wait until next year," promises co-owner Stacey Gondek. "We're going to have a kick-butt party."

Sweet-toothers will like her Candy Catastrophe, laden with peanut butter, malted milk balls, Snickers, M&Ms and other treats. Overall, the flavors here did not pack quite the same punch as those at other stops, but there were several we liked. Marinello said the key lime exemplified "summer fun," while Raskin found the cantaloupe "fun and refreshing." Dwayne Florenzie was a big fan of the chocolate malt.

One important question needed to be asked: sprinkles or jimmies?

"Sprinkles," Gondek replied, laughing. "It depends on one's age. Then again, I have one customer who calls them bugs."

The Bent Spoon, Princeton

Talk about using local ingredients. Gabrielle Carbone and Matthew Errico used nearby pear and grape trees and shrubs to make Concord grape ice cream and Princeton pear sorbet at their year-old bakery/ice cream shop.

"We use hormone-free dairy," Carbone explained. "Eventually we hope to move to all-organic everything."

The Bent Spoon, named after an object in "The Matrix," offers a dozen kinds of ice cream and sorbet. The day's boldest flavors were found here. The dark chocolate habanero — heady and intense — had several Munchers straining for superlatives.

"Awesome," Parker said.

"A chocolate with a killer bite," according to Brown.

The organic coconut streak "had just the right amount of chocolate and coconut," one Muncher observed. And the organic blueberry tasted like it was scooped right out of the fields. Carbone and Errico have made 200-plus flavors to date, using an ever-changing ice cream palette.

"These are very adult flavors," said an admiring Parker. "There's nothing called SpongeBob in here."

Jersey Freeze, Freehold

"Let me wax nostalgic about Jersey Freeze," wrote Christina Leslie, who reminisced about driving down Route 9 in her 1970 Catalina.

"I still navigate the now-truncated (traffic) circle when my inner Dairy Demon rears its head to visit this ice cream mecca," she added.

It's all soft-serve here, and don't expect the ice cream to have the complexity of artisanal makers like The Bent Spoon. The nonfat gourmet chocolate tasted "flat," according to Georgio, and the mint did not exactly taste minty fresh.

But two kinds of ice cream here rocked our world. The juicy strawberry burst with fruity flavor. The grape — soda in a cone, only better — was the biggest hit.

"Oh my God, it's really good!" Marinello exclaimed.

"A religious experience," Raskin added.

Chocolate Carousel, Wall

"This is her baby," John Porada said of his wife, Lisa, and Chocolate Carousel. "I just got sucked into it."

There are worse places to get sucked into. During her first summer of operation, Lisa Porada sold Hershey's ice cream. Now they make her own.

The fudge chunk-filled chocolate carousel was one of the day's best chocolates. Marinello described the key lime as "zesty." Georgio was not enamored of the cappuccino explosion, but Marinello liked its creamy subtlety. The creamsicle did not wow anyone, but Raskin loved the banana — "very realistic, a true banana." Marinello said the cotton candy didn't "twang," this apparently being one flavor she didn't have a song in her heart about. Parker's verdict on the hazelnut chip? "Real nice."

"This being a sweet shop gives it some character," Brown said.

Our six Munchers, characters all, jumped in the Big Dog for one last stop.

Ice Cream at Days, Ocean Grove

Ice cream with a generous scoop of history — that's Days. The building has housed a restaurant or ice cream shop since the late 1800s, according to David Fernicola, co-owner with Arnold Teixiera of both Days and the Starving Artist. About 70 percent of the ice cream is supplied by Double Rainbow in San Francisco. Fernicola doesn't hesitate to replace unpopular flavors, which has not exactly endeared him to suppliers.

"They yell at me," he said, laughing. "I play around, pull flavors. I get yelled at a lot." One big seller: It's a Goody, with vanilla, peanut butter swirl and chocolate chips. The Dairy Queen herself approved.

"It's a chocolate-peanut butter chunk sensation," Georgio said.

The last of our eight stops produced some of the day's most memorable flavors. The peppermint stick, hazelnut truffle latte, black raspberry chip and dulce de leche all were excellent. The ultra chocolate, while dark and luscious, was not quite in their class.

Days closes for the season in October, and from the sound of it, Fernicola is not entertaining any thoughts of staying open year-round.

"In the winter I think about it, but when the summer comes, I think, 'What am I, crazy?'"

MUNCH BITES 2005:

Generations of students would concur: Campus eats rank at the very bottom of the food chain.

You know what we're talking about. Suspicious-looking beef stroganoff and dubiously-dated pudding, cardboard-like pizza and funky fries. The kind of food more endured than eaten, survived more than savored.

— Campus eats, August 2005

PETER GENOVESE

Forget Mom and Chevrolet for a moment. A piece of apple pie — or cherry, blueberry, peach, raspberry, or any flavor you like — is the perfect summertime dessert. Light, fruity, flaky, sugary — what's not to like? Serve with a scoop of ice cream, or a cold glass of milk, and you're on the stairway to comfort food heaven.

"It's not overly lemony," Ben Cozin of Bernardsville said during a long and winding Munchmobile road trip for good pies. "It's not that lemony goo you get on those 99-cent pies."

We didn't want goo, we wanted pie Mom would be proud of. Good, homemade pie. Baked on the premises.

Make that baked on someone's premises. Not one of the five farm markets we visited actually made their own pies. Baked them, yes. But didn't make them from scratch; the pies are made by outside vendors and shipped frozen. In terms of significant world events, this isn't exactly stop-the-press-news. But it came as a surprise nevertheless.

Which is not to say the farm market pies were middling. In fact, many were first-rate. In several cases, we couldn't tell the baked-on-premises pies from the made-from-scratch pies. Throw in the sugar/sweet factor, and you have the recipe for an eye-opening, head-spinning day. How many pies can you eat in one day? (35, if you have six people helping you). Where would we find true pie happiness? For the answers, read on.

Terhune Orchards, Lawrence

For a while there, you could pick up your apple pie and talk to the mayor at the same place; Pam Mount, co-owner with her husband, Gary, of Terhune Orchards, served as mayor of Lawrence Township in 2005.

The Mounts bought Terhune Orchards in 1975; the original 55 acres of farm is now 200 acres, spread across four farms, and the Mounts grow 36 crops.

Most popular pie: apple. They'll turn out 10,000 pies during the Thanksgiving holiday. "Every person in America eats pie at 2 p.m. (on Thanksgiving day)," Pam Mount said with a smile.

You don't have to wait until Thanksgiving to sample their apple cider slush; it's summer brain freeze in a cup — cold, sludgy, sweet and sensational.

We loved the red raspberry pie. "Nice fruitiness and balance of tart and sweet," said Karen Ann Kurlander of Morristown. Mike Dalzell dug the blueberry. "You cut it, it oozes fruit," the Lambertville resident said.

The apple pie was average; one Muncher found the crust "hard." But Terhune's coconut custard pie, smooth and creamy, would make it on two Munchers' favorites list.

Battleview Orchards, Freehold Township

This farm market is a roadside cornucopia, with neatly arranged shelves and bins of fruit, produce, jams and jellies, and baked goods.

We selected a half dozen pies and with paper plates, and our official set of Munchmobile knives in hand, made our way to a picnic table on the sloping front lawn. Several pies stood out, and several should have stayed in the shadows. Kurlander admired the "liveliness" of the lemon krunch pie. "Not too tart, very creamy consistency," she said. At the end of the day, she would name it the best of the "off-premises pies."

The very berry pie was bursting with berries, but strangely lacked much of a berry flavor. Battleview's peach pie was nowhere as good as Terhune's. Loren Mochari of Jamesburg called the apple pie "too sweet." Kurlander found the peach praline "far superior" to the peach, but it was a bit overcooked.

Two markets down, and we had sampled some worthy-of-homemade pies. We would find pie paradise at our next stop.

Mr. Tod's Pie Factory, Somerset

First off, it's Mr. Tod, not Sweeney Todd, so you won't be getting any surprises in your pie.

Tod Wilson opened a wholesale pie business in 2002, selling his sweet potato pies to fast food restaurants and other clients.

"One day, my landlord said, 'Tod, you've got to do better than selling that sweet potato pie,'" Wilson recalled.

He now offers an array of 10-inch and 4-inch pies, plus choose-your-own-crust cheesecake. This pie man with the simple storefront is getting noticed; he will open a Mr. Tod's Pie Factory kiosk in Terminal C at Newark Liberty International Airport in October. One look at the pies told you they were made with care and craft.

"They're more sincere-looking," Kurlander said. "They don't mind being draped over the edge. They're not perfect-looking."

But several tasted nearly perfect. The banana cream was a fluffy, puffy, dense delight. "Real whipped cream, not out of a can or tub," Mochari noted.

Dalzell found the Key lime pie "pretty close to heaven," its "very limey" flavor "blending perfectly with the graham cracker crust."

The cherry pie was another winner. "What I like is that the cherries don't dominate," Cozin said.

The blueberry was a decided improvement over Battleview Orchards' version, but it was not on the same lofty level as the cherry.

Strip mall pie 1, farm market 0.

Wightman's Farms, Harding

The Wightman family has been growing and selling fruit

and vegetables at its farm since 1922; Albert Wightman would drive through neighboring Morristown and sell his produce. The pies are perched invitingly in display cases.

The apple and blueberry pies are average. The coconut custard is nicely constructed — Kurlander admired its crusty edge — but the filling is inferior. "It's very nice — tastes more like flan — but it's not coconut," Tina Papetti-Noll said.

Kent Stein would put the lemon crunch on his best-of-day list, and Kurlander, our resident rhubarb expert, liked the rhubarb pie for its tartness.

Keeping score? She was.

"We're up to 23 pies," she said. "Now we're showing a little backbone."

Country Pie Factory, Long Valley

"I'm a member of the Pie Council," Sally Vilardi announced as we walked into her pie store. "For $100, you can be a member, too."

We like pie makers with a sense of humor. Vilardi, former owner of the Schooleys Mountain General Store, opened the Country Pie Factory last October.

"We tripled our commute — now it's 6 miles," she said, laughing.

Vilardi and her daughter, Kate, make pies in the kitchen. Cute place — black and white tile floors, sunshiny-yellow walls.

Her blueberry Diane, named after a deceased friend, was a big hit in a small package, a tart-like confection with fresh and cooked berries. "It took all day to find a great blueberry pie," Mochari sighed.

The powdered-sugar and crumble-topped peach pie was the day's best pie, as far as the Munchmobile driver was concerned. The only disappointment: the Key lime. "Not very limey," Dalzell pronounced. "It's not Mr. Tod's."

It was shaping up as a two pie-maker race for Top Dog honors. Or would an unknown rise out of the sugary shadows?

Peaceful Valley Orchards, Union Township

"Meet our sheep, Elijah and Joey," reads a sign at this farm market. "Our goat, Red, and our cows, George and Gladys."

Presiding over this farm family are Meredith and Jeremy Compton. They took over Peaceful Valley Orchards in 2001. He's from Flemington, she's from Neshanic, and they met at a Rutgers University research farm.

The open-air market stocks fruit, vegetables, dressings, even fresh and frozen pork from a local supplier. And pies.

The best of the bunch was the red raspberry. "It tastes like red raspberry; I can feel the seeds crunching," Dalzell said happily.

Kurlander pronounced the strawberry-rhubarb the day's

best rhubarb. Several Munchers admired the apple and its cinnamony flavor.

"It's your basic all-American apple pie," Papetti-Noll said. The same could be said for the cherry pie, straightforward and honest.

The Munchers' day was done. The Big Dog's driver, whose favorite childhood meal was a slice of cherry pie and a glass of milk, would make one more stop.

Melick's Town Farm, Oldwick

This is one farm family that goes way back. The Melicks trace their origins to Johan Peter Moelich, who arrived in this country with his two brothers between 1725 and 1735 and settled in Hunterdon County.

The Oldwick farm stand, minutes from Route 78, offered the best pies of the roadside markets. The apple was a sweet success, with its sugary latticed crust and cinnamon-laced fruit. The red raspberry was not quite as tart as Terhune's, but it was a worthy contender.

The peach seemed to have lost some of its fruitiness on the way to market, but the crust was first-rate. The cherry was simple and straightforward, nothing special.

But the very berry was lovely and luscious, a near-perfect blend of tart and sweet. The pies were quickly dispatched back at the office. "Are you bringing more tomorrow?" someone asked.

"You're on your own," was the reply.

MUNCH BITES 2006:

Seven sub shops, dozens of sandwiches: The Munchers immersed themselves in the substantial mission, promising to be subjective while not resorting to any subterfuge. Okay, enough already with the substandard jokes. Time to chow down. We promise this story will not contain any subplots or subliminal messages. Remember, no substitutions!

— Subs, June 2006

PETER GENOVESE

Beware of redheads with knives.

There was Meredith Neubeck in the kitchen at Fat Cat's Cafe in Harvey Cedars, deftly slicing sandwiches with a rather wicked-looking blade.

"We don't have Wonder Bread, we don't have American cheese," the waitress/sandwich maker extraordinaire proclaimed.

"You have something against Wonder Bread?" the Munchmobile driver teased.

Her withering look said it all, and there was the matter of that knife, and besides, we had work to do. It was our annual Shore run, when the Big Dog cruises the coast in search of good breakfast, lunch and dinner from Sandy Hook to Cape May.

"The trip," said Muncher Chris Kossup of Belleville, "was out of this world."

If we had driven any farther, we would have been out of the state. We started at 7 a.m., returned home at midnight, and ate doughnuts, crumb buns, wraps, grilled cheese sandwiches, burritos, clams, oysters, bread pudding, pizza, Key lime tacos, and scampi, to name just a few.

Videographer Ed Ruggieri got everything down on tape, and the Munchers turned out to be a fun — and well-prepared — bunch.

"I brought Gas-X," announced Elisa Madorsky of Livingston. Not to mention Mylanta, dental floss and a tube of Colgate, packed in what amounted to her Munch Survival Kit.

It all sounded like fun, but this was serious business; not once did the Munchers' feet touch water. Ocean's Thirteen? Call this Ocean's Six, with the Munchmobile in the role of Best Supporting Dog.

Colonial Bakery, Lavallette

So we drive all the way from Newark to a doughnut shop in Lavallette and the amiable Kossup orders. . . a buttered roll?

"Highly recommended," the Belleville resident said, laughing.

The jelly doughnuts here are worth the sugary trip from anywhere.

"Juicy, meaty, a doughnut diner's delight," Madorsky marveled.

The owner of Colonial's two Lavallette locations is Brian O'Neill, who also owns Mueller's in Bay Head. He playfully chided us for giving Mueller's legendary crumb buns a tepid review during Munchmobile 2006, then said Colonial's crumb buns are better anyway. O'Neill turns out 150 18 x 26 pans of crumb buns a week at Colonial Bakery.

Colonial offers good sugar twists and other doughnuts, decent cinnamon and raisin bread, and excellent coffee, considering most bakery java is weak, watery and woeful. Suitably sugared up, we moved on.

Fat Cat's Cafe, Harvey Cedars

Fat Cat's is the former Joe's Market Cafe, and there really is a fat cat, and his name is Andy. One look at the menu board tells you these people mean business — but want to have some fun doing it. Sandwiches include Grilled Cheese For Grownups, Almost Croque Monsieur, and Good 'Ol BLT — all fresh-tasting, expertly made, and served with a side of chutzpah.

"Tomatoes or bacon on the grilled cheese?" Neubeck asked.

"Okay," the Munchmobile's driver replied.

" 'Okay' is not an acceptable answer!" she chided.

If you can get past the self-serve baskets of scones, muffins, cinnamon buns, croissants, cheese pockets, crumb cake and cookies, order sandwiches, as we did, and take them outside to the deck.

The salads are way outside the box — lentil seaweed, carrots and orzo, and juniper chicken were among those on display, along with more commonplace garden and Greek salads.

The Fat Cat Breakfast Sandwich — two scrambled eggs with Vermont cheddar and choice of bacon, sausage or pork roll on multigrain ciabatta — is a morning, or afternoon, delight.

The yellowfin tuna salad sandwich, on kalamata olive bread, is superb. The Beef and Blue sandwich got mixed reviews. Some loved the combination of steak, bleu cheese and caramelized onions; others thought it jarring. But everyone liked the roasted breast of turkey, and Parma prosciutto, sandwiches.

"We are not a full-service breakfast place with pancakes and waffles," manager Donna Schmid said.

With sandwiches this good, who cares?

Gecko's, Cape May

Then it was a long, lazy ride past Milepost 0 on the Parkway to ever-charming Cape May. There are inside tables at Gecko's; you'll want to grab a table at the umbrella-shaded, red chile-pepper-lit outdoor patio. Nice breeze, a little Doors and Joe Cocker on the sound system, and gecko figurines everywhere.

"Easy on the beans, guys," Madorsky said.

Uh, thanks for the advice, or warning. We liked the crab enchilada and chorizo-filled quesadilla and loved the pork posole, stuffed with stewed pork, lime-cured blue corn kernels, and green chile.

Muncher Gerard Drappi of West Orange said the Prince Edward Island mussels, a special, "tasted very fresh, as if they were plucked from the ocean earlier in the day."

But the BBQ chicken sandwich deserved a better roll than the pasty one here. One surprise: the irresistible corn mini-muffins. Bigger surprise: the delicious desserts, made by Susi Bithell, wife of owner Randy Bithell.

"That's a big yum," Madorsky said one bite into the bread pudding.

"Whoa," she added, sampling the chocolate decadence cake.

Another dessert slam dunk: the Key lime taco, sprinkled with toasted coconut.

"The desserts overwhelmed the entrees," Drappi observed.

Would the Munchers be overwhelmed with all this food and distance driven? Time, and their tummies, would tell.

Oyster Creek Inn, Leeds Point

There is no place in New Jersey quite like the Oyster Creek Inn, a rambling, weather-beaten seafood shack in Leeds Point, down the road from Smithville.

Grab a cold one, head out to the deck and drink in a whole lot of marsh-filled peace and quiet, minutes from the Parkway. "Beware of attack waitress," cautions a sign. "'An old crab lives here," reads another.

The head crab is Bill Kuppel; the building, a former hotel, has been in his family since 1946. Looks like it will stay there for a while; his sons, Scott and Jason, run the restaurant while

> The first malted milk appeared in 1897; it was designed as a restorative for invalids and children.

his daughter, Erin, is a waitress.

"The only thing they let me do now is dock boats," Kuppel grumbled good-naturedly.

There may have been meals more quickly dispatched in the Big Dog's 10 years, but the Munchmobile driver can't remember them. Lemon and pepper scallops, crab claws, steamed clams, garlic steamers, garlic shrimp, tuna wrap and a dozen oysters — judging by the aftermath, we wondered if the Munchers had eaten all day.

Kurt Koerner called the garlic clams the best he's had anywhere. Marilyn Francis admired the jumbo lump crab cocktail's "unadorned simplicity" and said all the items sampled were "ultra-fresh and prepared perfectly."

Great stop, even if none of the Munchers knew exactly where they were or how they had gotten here.

"Are you sure we're still in New Jersey?" Drappi wondered.

Sawmill Cafe, Seaside Park

Lights, cameras, plenty of action, and a barrage of bells, whistles, screaming and shouting: It can only be Seaside on a Saturday night. Most of the hubbub is in the Heights, but let's not forget the Park, home to Maruca's, best pizza on any Jersey boardwalk, and the legendary Sawmill Cafe, which bears as much resemblance to a cafe as Ocean Grove does to a swinging seaside resort.

There's the sprawling, open-air boardwalk bar; the Green Room, a venue for top bands, and the World's Largest Slice of Pizza, available at the bar or a walk-up counter. How big is it? Even owner Steve D'Onofrio doesn't know.

"I've never measured it," he said, laughing. "But the pizza (from which the slices are taken) is 28 inches in diameter."

The humongous slice is actually better than you might expect: not very tomatoey or cheesy, but a dependable, doughy crust. Toppings? Go with the sausage over the less-than-worthy mushrooms.

"The perfect end to a perfect day," Ruggieri sighed.

Hey, Ed, snap out of it; we're not done yet!

The Inlet Cafe, Highlands

A waterfront table, with views of Sandy Hook and, in the distance, the New York skyline. Small boats silently gliding across the inky water. An American flag snapping in the nighttime breeze.

Was there any better way to end this Munch day?

"Why is there a hot dog on your truck?" a patron asked as the Big Dog rolled up in front of the Inlet Cafe.

"Because we couldn't get a hamburger?" some wag responded.

Forget the "cafe" moniker; this is a full-service restaurant, and an excellent one. Start, as we did, with a dozen bluepoint oysters, slightly fresher-tasting than those at the Oyster Creek Inn. Or the lobster escargot — chunks of Maine lobster sautéed with garlic in a cream sauce. Proceed to the sesame-crusted ahi tuna, rare and wonderful, with its side of delicious seaweed salad. Or the Inlet Scallops.

"Cooked perfectly, and literally melted in your mouth," according to Koerner.

One disappointment: the heavily battered fried soft shell crabs.

"I am at the coma stage right now," Madorsky sighed, speaking for the stuffed crew.

But wait — a miraculous recovery! Four desserts materialized, including a show-stopping Chocolate Volcano, and suddenly everyone was hungry again!

"The food here," Drappi observed, "was just a cut above the rest."

You could say the same about the trip, always one of the favorites of any Munch summer. We walked — waddled? — back to the Big Dog. One ocean; several bays, rivers and creeks; and nearly 400 miles later, our Shore run was done.

"I am the Candy," proclaimed the friendly, smiling woman behind the counter of the gingham-curtained luncheonette on Route 57 in New Village, Warren County.

Really, she was. Candy Bratkovics is the proprietor of Candy's Country Cafe, filled with chicken and rooster kitsch in every form imaginable — figurines, drawings, lampshades, menus.

We didn't hear, or see, any real chickens or roosters, but maybe they were hiding, awestruck by the rather large food object parked out front.

"There's a big hot dog on that van!" said an excited Cindy Corcoran, a waitress at Candy's.

— Pancakes/French toast, May 2007

When someone told us about great cookies in a liquor store by a train station, we were dubious. When you step into Towne Liquors & Delicatessen, ignore the packaged snacks and the bottles of wine, red or otherwise, and check out the cookies in the display case.

They're square, they're huge, and they're pretty close to great.

We wondered, though, if Lea O'Shea was noticing any of this.

"This is cute guy heaven," said O'Shea, making note of the all-male counter crew.

— Cookies, June 2007

No fish goes anywhere without a porpoise, and eating fish every day won't give you a haddock. Enough already with the bad jokes; it's time to stop floundering around and eat.

— Seafood, August 2007

ROUTE 46, MAY 30, 2008

PETER GENOVESE

Route 46 dips and weaves its way across North Jersey, essentially running from river (Hudson) to river (Delaware) and from one of the country's most magnificent bridges (the George Washington) to one of its more modest (the Portland-Columbia Toll Bridge), showing off New Jersey in all its marvelous, maddening diversity.

It manages to be both cluttered, chaotic highway and winding country road. At one end, strip malls, used car lots and 99-cent stores; at the other, roadside markets, country churches and one-traffic-light towns.

Near the eastern end is Totowa, which Dutch scholars translated as "where you begin," "suggesting that it was once the frontier to the wild west," according to "The WPA Guide to 1930s New Jersey."

The guidebook, a good read to this day, describes Route 46 as "the most direct route between the George Washington Bridge and New Jersey's inland lake country."

Not to mention the most direct, though not quickest, way to Budd Lake, Buttzville, and Belvidere. Or is that Belvedere? The sign marking the beginning of Route 46 in the Warren County seat spells it, incorrectly, with an "e" in the middle.

The road passes through Dover, Great Meadows, Vienna, Hackettstown (named after landowner Samuel Hackett, who became instantly popular by offering free drinks at the grand opening of a hotel).

And don't forget Manunka Chunk, once the location of Manunka Chunk Junction, "one of the most euphoniously named railroad (stops) in America," according to the WPA guide.

The food choices on 46, not surprisingly, are all over the map, and our crew of Munchers intended to try them all. We started with bagels; segued to pizza; jumped to Jamaican; chowed down on chili, quesadillas and mac and cheese at a picturesquely-placed roadhouse; then really got down to business at a rib/barbecue joint in Independence.

Fitting choice — the Munchmobile is all about declaring independence from chain and cookie-cutter restaurants.

After six stops, it was time to call it a day. Not so fast! What would a journey on Route 46 be without a stop at its best-known ice cream stand? And arguably its most celebrated pizzeria? Where slices of pizza were first introduced in New Jersey, or so they say.

"Our Big Munch Leader asks: one last pizza stop, Munchers?" Lorrie McGough recalled. "It's 9:30 p.m. and we are ready to bust; but we are not quitters! We say YES!"

After the last greasy slice was greedily devoured, after the last zeppole disappeared from the powdered-sugar-doused bag, the Munchers were finally ready to head home. Route 46: Mission accomplished.

Pizza 46, Little Falls

According to owner Larry Coppa, Pizza 46 was the first pizzeria in the area to introduce five-cheese pizza, back in the 1960s. Known for its fleet of pizza-delivering Jeep Wranglers.

"Quintessential Jersey pie," noted Muncher Ryan Peene. "Greasy where it should be on top, not on the bottom." Nice, chewy crust. Garlic knots boasted "the perfect amount of garlic and oil," according to Ashley Antoniello, but she found the pepperoni sausage pinwheels inferior. "Great" dipping sauce, according to Liz Driscoll.

Smokehouse Barbecue & Tavern, Independence

We call for an immediate ban on the use of "world famous" on restaurant storefronts and menus! The ribs here are fall-off-the-bone tender — and practically tasteless. The monstrous beef ribs, charred and oh-so-chewy, easily the best entree.

"Crazy good," Nina Wilson raved. Helen Leba described the barbecue chicken as "extremely tender" and the onion rings as "crunchy and delicious." Good French fries. Best side: the Southern mashed sweet potatoes.

M&S Pizzeria II, Rockaway

Not to be confused with M&S Pizzeria, just down the hill in Dover. Several readers raved about M&S II, but it was average, at best. Garlic knots had me wondering: Where's the garlic? Dipping sauce "tasted right out of a jar," according to one taster.

Pizza consensus: Decent crust, so-so sauce. Danny Benz gave the sausage sandwich an "A," but the meatball sandwich an "F." The most disappointing stop of the day.

Sam I am Bagels, Totowa

Highway-based bagel store claims "the most exotic specialty bagels in the state."

Who's Sam? Owner Sam Abdullah. The 40-plus kinds of bagels range from plain, egg and cinnamon raisin to banana, strawberry cheesecake, and French toast, the most popular. Fat, chewy bagels, and fresh, funky spreads.

Muncher Lorrie McGough described the strawberry cream cheese as "oh so yummy," and Helen Leba loved the walnut raisin cream cheese. One disappointment: the chocolate muffin, mushy, nearly tasteless.

Jamaican James Jerk Pit Restaurant, Ledgewood

Asked what he did before opening his restaurant five months ago, James Woolery replied, "Pressure washing and detailing."

Colorful storefront with bright green and yellow walls. Munchers not wowed by the soups, but I liked the conch chowder, tangy and muscular.

The jerk chicken was neither savory nor spicy, but we loved the oxtails (slow-cooked 2-3 hours) and the curry chicken.

I couldn't get enough of the curry goat. "I've never seen you eat so much of one dish," Munchmobile photographer Tim Farrell said.

Gunnar's Landing, White Township

The food (sports bar-worthy, nothing more) takes a back seat to the lovely location, on the banks of the Pequest River.

"The chili is good for Willie," Will McGough cracked.

Our favorite item: the crackly-good chicken quesadillas, left. Not sure what's Cajun about the J.D. Cajun chicken wings. Pulled pork sandwich is huge, but not otherwise memorable. "Baked to perfection" mac and cheese anything but. "Good roadhouse food," Farrell concluded.

Cliff's Dairy Maid, Ledgewood

We've been to Cliff's twice in two weeks and loved it both times. Antoniello quickly polished off a banana split, much to the awe of her fellow Munchers (see the video on nj.com). "Insanely delicious," she said.

Driscoll reported "no problem" with "scraping clean" her double peanut butter sundae. I loved my single-scoop double-dark chocolate fudge crunch in a sugar cone. The regular chocolate is just as creamy-good.

Pizza Town USA, Elmwood Park

Circus-tent-like, flag-decorated pizzeria celebrating its 50th anniversary. Claims to have served the first pizza slices in New Jersey, back in the 1950s; until then, so the Pizza Town story goes, you could get only whole pies.

It's a decent, straightforward pie: no superlatives, no surprises. We liked the powdered-sugar-dusted zeppoles more. "I think they used an entire container of powdered sugar in our bag," Driscoll mused.

MUNCH BITES 2008:

The most peculiar thing about our epic-length Down the Shore Munchmobile trip?

The relative lack of traffic on the Parkway on a picture-perfect beach day?

No.

The claim by one waitress that she was once voted "the best waitress in the state of Philadelphia?"

Nope.

The entire female staff of a Toms River luncheonette dressed in their pajamas?

Yeah, that's it.

— Down the Shore, June 2008

ROAD TRIPS

So you want to hop in your car and do your own Munchmobile-type road trip? You can, with the help of our handy-dandy Official Munchmobile Road Trip Guide. I've put together 20 different trips, listing must-stops in food categories ranging from baked goods, breakfast, diners, hot dogs and healthy food to delis, brew pubs, barbecue, Spanish/ Portuguese and more.

ASIAN

In the past five years, Asian restaurants have spread across the Jersey culinary map. And we don't mean just Chinese; Indian, Japanese; Thai, Korean, Malaysian and other Asian cuisines are readily available.

Dim sum is a weekend treat and spectacle; one of the better ones can be found at the stone lion-fronted **Dynasty** (100 Route 22 West, Green Brook; 732-752-6363). For sheer food quantity, it's impossible to beat a Chinese buffet. One of the biggest is at **China Gourmet** (468 Eagle Rock Ave., West Orange; 973-731-6411).

For authentic if not adventurous Chinese, **Hunan Cottage** (14 Rt. 46 east, Fairfield; 973-808-8328); **Noodle Chu** (770 Route 46 west, Parsippany; 973-299-6518) and **Chef 81** (81 N. Beverwyck Road, Lake Hiawatha; 973-335-9988) will expand your culinary horizons.

Interested in Indian? The easy answer is to drive down Oak Tree Road in Iselin, where Indian restaurants and food markets are more common than gas stations. Elsewhere, try **Saffron** (249 Route 10 East, East Hanover; 973-599-0700), where the lamb jardalo is a must. **Star of India** (496 Boulevard, Kenilworth; 908-272-6633) offers some of the more fragrant, overpowering curries anywhere. In Central Jersey, try **Passage to India** (2495 Business Route 1 South, Lawrence Shopping Center, Lawrenceville; 609-637-0800).

For Thai, try **House of Thai Cuisine** (319 Route 22 East, Sansone Plaza, Green Brook; 732-968-0085). It's a bit of a drive, but **Khun Thun** (179 Cahill Cross Road, West Milford; 973-506-4942) is well worth it. The golden curry puffs and Singapore noodles are great! One of the more beautiful, and tranquil, dining rooms anywhere can be found at **Sukhothai** (186 Orlando Drive, Raritan Borough; 908-707-4747).

Good Japanese food, and creative presentation, meet at **Ocha** (403 Bloomfield Ave., Caldwell; 973-228-8856). The sushi pizza is super! Tomonori Tanaka is a character, and a good cook, besides, making a visit to **Tomo's Cuisine** (113 Route 23, Little Falls; 973-837-1117) a must. One more Japanese recommendation: **Zen** (277 Eisenhower Parkway, Livingston; 973-533-6828).

BAKED GOODS

If I could take one type of food to my desert island, it would be baked goods: cookies, cakes, pies, muffins, and last but not least, doughnuts.

Best doughnuts in Jersey? My vote would go to **Ob-Co's Donuts** (547 Fischer Blvd., Toms River; 732-270-3882).

Best pies? Roadside markets are fine, but be advised: Their

"homemade" pies are usually made elsewhere, baked off the market's premises. For delicious, really-homemade pies, visit **Country Pie Factory** (67 E. Mill Road, Long Valley; 908-876-8500) or **Mr. Tod's Pie Factory** (1760 Easton Ave., Somerset; 732-356-8900). In North Jersey, **Best's Fruit Farm** (11 Route 46, Independence; 908-852-3777). In South Jersey, **Emery's Berry Patch** (346 Long Swamp Road, New Egypt; 609-758-8514).

There's no place quite like **Delicious Orchards** (36 Route 34 South, Colts Neck; 732-462-1989), a sprawling market filled with fruit, produce and baked goods. I can't get enough of their trolley buns!

In Central Jersey, try **Baker's Treat** (14 Turntable Junction, Flemington; 908-782-3458) and **The Dessert Plate** (34 E. Main St., Somerville; 908-722-9881). Sussex County stand-outs include **Cafe Pierrot** (19 Sparta Ave., Sparta; 973-729-0988) and the windmill-shaped **Holland American Bakery** (246 Route 23, Sussex; 973-875-5258).

Down the Shore: **Flaky Tart** (145 First Ave., Atlantic Highlands; 732-291-2555) makes small batches of high-quality items. One must: the almond danish.

In Sussex County, **Everything Homemade** (68 Olde Lafayette Village, Lafayette; 973-300-3336), offers excellent pastries and strudel in a country setting.

For an old-fashioned Italian bakery, it's **Carlo's City Hall Bake Shop** (95 Washington St., Hoboken; 201-659-3671).

The rugelach at the **Swiss Pastry Shoppe** (1711 E. Second St., Scotch Plains; 908-322-4751) are other-wordly; make sure you get them warm, out of the oven.

Next time you're down Wildwood or Cape May, stop in at **Cheesecake World** (228 Route 9 South, Marmora; 609-390-2468). Good cheesecakes and amazing stuffed breads. Probably the best high-end bakery in South Jersey is **Miel Patisserie** (1990 Route 70 East, Cherry Hill; 609-424-6435).

Good cookies in an unlikely location? **Feed Your Soul** (520 Jersey Ave., Jersey City; 201- 204-0720) is a spare-looking storefront in downtown Jersey City. The chocolate fudge brownie cookie is one of my favorite cookies, ever.

An even more unlikely cookie paradise is **Towne Liquors & Delicatessen** (810 Old Springfield Ave., New Providence; 908-464-5400). They make big, chewy, delicious cookies; try to get them right out of the oven.

Best cheesecakes in Jersey? That's easy: **Mara's Country Desserts** (281 Speedwell Ave., Morristown; 973-682-9200).

One of the more unusual cookie operations is **Gimmee Jimmy's Cookies** (23-25 Church St., Montclair; 800-454-6697). The owner is deaf, as are many of the employees.

BARBECUE

Great barbecue is harder to find than $3 gas in New Jersey. North Jersey? Forget about it; it's just not there. One of the better ones is **Hot Rod's** (19 N. Main St., Wharton; 973-361-5050).

Here's a quartet of good barbecue joints in Central Jersey: **C.T.'s Bar-B-Que** (920 Hamilton St., Somerset; 732-418-8889), **Dunellen BBQ** (626 Bound Brook Road, Dunellen; 732-968-3200), **Grub Hut** (307 N. Main St., Manville; 908-203-8003) and **Hog Hollow Bar-B-Que** (400 Route 57, Lopatcong; 908-454-4294).

For the real deal, set your compass, or GPS, south, and head to **Christine's House of Kingfish Barbecue** (926 Route 206, Shamong; 609-268-3600). It's nothing more than a roadside shack, but the sturdy outdoor smokers tell you these people mean business.

Uncle Dewey's BBQ Pavilion (Mile Marker 40, Route 40, Mizpah; 609-476-4040) is just that: a huge outdoor tent with tables.

Next time you're in Atlantic City, make a stop in neighboring Pleasantville for **Kelsey & Kim's Soul Food and Bar-B-Que** (52 Main St., 609-484-8448).

BREAKFAST

It's the most important meal of the day, and I'm not talking about a bag of chips and a soda at 10 a.m.! I never ever miss breakfast, even if it means just a bagel or muffin. It's disappointing how many diners serve mediocre breakfasts. The **Americana Diner** (Route 130 North, East Windsor; 609-448-4477) and its sister diner, the **Skylark Fine Diner & Lounge** (Route 1 and Wooding Aveue, Edison; 732-777-7878) serve consistently good breakfasts.

The next time you're on LBI, hit **Mustache Bill's** (Eighth and Broadway, Barnegat Light; 609-494-3553) for first-rate omelets and a '50s diner atmosphere.

For country atmosphere and cooking, visit **Mark Koppe's General Store** (39 Church St., Bloomsbury; 908-479-6100), a former general store, and **Candy's Country Cafe** (2423 Route 57, New Village, Franklin Township, Warren County; 908-213-1889), with its delicious French toast.

In Hunterdon County, the **Cafe at Rosemont** (Routes 519 and 604, Rosemont, Hunterdon County; 609-397-4097) exudes country charm.

Down the Shore? **Allenwood General Store** (Allenwood-Lakewood Road, Allenwood; 732-223-4747) is a colorful combination of general store, second-hand shop and breakfast spot.

The Shore's liveliest breakfast hangout is **Shut Up and Eat!**

(213 Route 37 East, Toms River; 732-349-4544). The wait-resses wear pajamas, and everything short of the kitchen sink — tricycles, record albums, license plates — is on the walls. The food, particularly the stuffed French toast, is pretty good.

Gronsky's Milk House (125 W. Main St., High Bridge; 908-638-6030) is known for ice cream, but its breakfasts are better.

Pondering pancakes? In North Jersey, head to the **Stack Pancake and Steak House** (205 River Road, North Arlington; 201-991-1023). Down the Shore, we'd recommend **Uncle Will's Pancake House** (3 South Bay Ave., Beach Haven; 609-492-2514). For memorable brunches, **The Mad Batter** (Carroll Villa Hotel, 19 Jackson St., Cape May; 609-884-5970).

BREW PUBS/BARS

There are 20-plus brew pubs and breweries in New Jersey; the best brew pub, food-wise, is **Trap Rock Restaurant/ Brewery** (279 Springfield Ave., Berkeley Heights; 908-665-1755). Not far behind is **Basil T's** (183 Riverside Ave., Red Bank; 732-842-5990). For a homey Irish pub atmosphere, and good food besides, visit **St. James Gate Publick House** (167 Maplewood Ave., Maplewood; 973-378-2222).

Others: **Krogh's Restaurant and Brew Pub** (23 White Deer Plaza, Sparta; 973-729-8428), **Triumph Brewing Co**. (138 Nassau St., Princeton; 609-924-7855), **Long Valley Pub and Brewery** (1 Fairmount Road, Long Valley; 908-876-1122) and **Ship Inn** (61 Bridge St., Milford; 908-995-0188), which in 1995 became the first business in the state to legally brew beer on premises since Prohibition.

CHOCOLATE

As far as I'm concerned, there is not enough chocolate in the world.

My two favorite shops in North Jersey are **Donna & Company** (19 Eastman St., Cranford; 908-272-4380) and **J. Emanuel** (57 Main St., Chester; 908-879-0500), where the brittle-like Chester Crunch is a must.

If you want anything made of chocolate, the folks at **Enjou** (8 DeHart St., Morristown; 973-993-9090) would be more than willing to oblige.

Other recommended shops: **Birnn Chocolates** (314 Cleveland St., Highland Park; 732-545-4400), **Brummer's** (125 E. Broad St., Westfield; 908- 232-1904), **Krause's Homemade Candy** (203 McLean Blvd., Route 20, Paterson; 973-345-4606), **Lee Sims** (743 Bergen Ave., Jersey City; 201-433-

1308) and **Sweet Cravings** (165 Ridge Road, North Arlington; 201-998-3641).

CUBAN/CARIBBEAN

Most of the Caribbean and Cuban restaurants in New Jersey are unpretentious places. **The Caribbean Cafe** (85 Bayard St., New Brunswick; 732-846-2620) looks uninviting, but once the food starts coming out of the kitchen you won't care what the place looks like.

For Cuban food, try **El Sol de Cuba** (161 Passaic St., Passaic; 973-472-4400) and **Havana Sandwich Cafe** (17 Franklin St., Bloomfield; 973-429-3303), the latter for the Cuban sandwich especially.

For a good and cheap Cuban steak sandwich, visit **Dos Amigos**, 5300 Bergenline Ave., West New York; (201) 348-2255. Great shakes there, too,

For spicy if not downright fiery jerk and other Caribbean standards, sail away to **Caribbean Cuisine** (5 Winans St., East Orange; 973-674-2992). **De Island Breeze** (676 Franklin Blvd., Somerset; 732-214-8611) is one of the state's more colorful restaurants. **Island Life Cafe** (307 Irvington Ave., South Orange; 973-763-7900) is one of its more spartan. Let owner Carol Allen whip you up one of her fruit drinks, especially the watermelon-ginger.

One more suggestion: **Jamaican James Jerk Pit Restaurant** (1034 Route 46 East, Ledgewood; 973-252-4339). You'll love the curry chicken and the curry goat.

DELIS

Delis, surpassed only by pizzerias in number, are a Jersey staple. They come in all shapes and sizes. For great old-school Italian delis, look no further than **A&S Pork Store** (281 Browertown Road, West Paterson; 973-256-0115), **Benanti's Italian Delicatessen** (16 W. 22nd St., Bayonne; 201-437-5525) and **Ciccone's Italian Deli** (658 Bloomfield Ave., West Caldwell; 973-228-4070).

For a quintessential Jewish deli, you can't go wrong with the legendary **Eppes Essen** (105 E. Mt. Pleasant Ave., Livingston; 973-994-1120), **Livingston Bagel & Deli** (37 E. Northfield Road, Livingston; 973-994-1915) and **Noah's Ark** (493 Cedar Lane, Teaneck, 201-692-1200).

The food could be better at **Harold's New York Deli Restaurant** (Ramada Inn, 3050 Woodbridge Ave., Edison; 732-661-9100) but the outrageously-sized sandwiches and baked goods are worth a look, if not taste.

Three excellent in-town delis: **Millburn Deli** (328 Millburn Ave., Millburn; 973-379-5800), **Watchung Delicatessen** (117 Watchung Ave., Montclair; 973-744-1452) and **Town Hall Deli** (60 Valley St., South Orange; 973-762-4900), which claims to have invented the Sloppy Joe.

DINERS

If you love diners, I have one suggestion: Don't move. Jersey is Diner Central; there are nearly 600 here, more than in any other state.

The stainless steel **Harris Diner** (21 N. Park St., East Orange; 973-675-9703) is one of my all-time favorites. So are the **White Mana** (470 Tonnele Ave., Jersey City; 201-963-1441), which looks like a brick-walled flying saucer, and the **White Manna** (358 River St., Hackensack; 201-342-0914), the state's cutest — and smallest — diner. At the latter, the burgers are tiny — and addictive.

Generations of Rutgers students know the **White Rose System**, (154 Woodbridge Ave., Highland Park; 732-777-1881). The **White Rose System** (1301 E. Elizabeth Ave., Linden; 908-486-9651) is more atmospheric and better overall. The **Summit Diner** (Summit Avenue and Union Place, Summit; 908-277-3256) is a barrel-roofed, wooden-walled wonder, and probably the state's oldest diner.

Morris County's best diner? I'd choose the **Alexis Diner** (3130 Route 10 West, Denville; 973-361-8000). Two of my favorites in Middlesex County: **Menlo Park Diner** (Route 1 South, Edison; 732-494-1760) and **Skylark Fine Diner & Lounge** (Route 1 North, Edison; 732-777-7878).

HEALTHY

Munchers do not live on grease and cholesterol alone. We make one healthy-food-only trip every summer. And no, that doesn't mean reduced-salt French fries!

One of my all-time favorite health food stops was the **Greenmarket Cafe** (195 E. Franklin Turnpike, Ho-Ho-Kus; 201-652-7733). In Morris County, choose between **Jeremiah's** (84 N. Beverwyck Road, Lake Hiawatha; 973-334-2004), for first-rate sandwiches and salads, and **Mrs. Erb's Good Food** (20 First Ave., Denville; 973-627-5440) for overall selection.

It's a Wrap (9 Village Plaza, South Orange; 973-762-7474) offers fine wraps and smoothies. **Basil Bandwagon Natural Market** (276 Routes 202/31, Raritan Township, Hunterdon County; 908-788-5737) is one of the state's biggest health food emporiums; the cafe is in the back. **Sussex County Food Co-op** (30 Moran St., Newton; 973-579-1882) is one of the smallest, but no less enjoyable.

Veggie Heaven (1119 Route 46, Parsippany-Troy Hills; 973-335-9876) is one of the state's best-known vegetarian restaurants. **Twisted Tree Cafe** (609 Cookman Ave., Asbury Park; 732-775-2633) offers good food and a laid-back vibe.

I have two words for you when it comes to **Piquant Bread Bar & Grill** (349A George St., New Brunswick; 732-246-2468): butter chicken. Two more words: Order it.

HOT DOGS

One could argue New Jersey is Hot Dog Heaven: The Italian Hot Dog and the Texas weiner (chili dog) were born here.

Two classic Italian hot dog joints are **Dickie Dee's** (380 Bloomfield Ave., Newark; 973-483-9396) and **Jimmy Buff's** (60 Washington St., West Orange; 973-325-9897).

Dizzy for dirty-water dogs? You won't do better than **Tony's Specialized Hot Dogs** (Lake Street and Park Avenue, Newark) and **Donnie's Dogs** (South 15th Street and Central Avenue, Newark).

Hiram's (1345 Palisade Ave., Fort Lee; 201-592-9602) was named the state's best chili by our S.W.A.T. Dog Patrol in 2006, but the chili at the **Dover Grill** (Route 46 East, Dover; 973-989-4007) is equally memorable.

Two hot dog roadhouses: **Galloping Hill Inn** (325 Chestnut St., Union; 908-686-2683) and **Hot Dog Johnny's** (Route 46, Buttzville; 908-453-2882).

Two doggie joints with plenty of history: **Libby's Lunch** (98 McBride Ave., Paterson; 973-278-8718) and **Lou's/The World's First Italian Hot Dogs** (202 14th Ave., Newark; 973-621-9468), where Jimmy Buff's started.

There is only one **Rutt's Hut** (417 River Road, Clifton; 973-779-8615), a shrine to cholesterol excess.

Best dogs down the Shore? It's a tossup between **Max's** (Ocean Boulevard and Matilda Terrace, Long Branch; 732-571-0248) and **The WindMill** (200 Ocean Ave., Long Branch; 732-229-9863). If you're in Cape May, swing by **Hot Dog Tommy's** (Jackson Street, just off the beach, Cape May; 609-884-8388).

What's with all the Tommys? Go to **Tommy's** (900 Second Ave., Elizabeth; 908-351-9831) for Italian hot dogs and top-notch potatoes, and **Tommy's Hot Dogs** (114 Grant Ave., Carteret; 732-541-8409) for the charmingly low-rent atmosphere and lovably nutty owner.

Two hot dog destinations in Bergen County: **Hot Dog House** (510 Route 17 South, Carlstadt; 201-935-5803), perched on the edge of the highway, and **Karl Ehmer's** (120 Broadway, Hillsdale; 201-664-1477), where a hot dog stand is set up outside the meat store.

If you like it hot, try **Big Daddy's** (62A Main St., Little Falls; 973-785-0206) with its staggering collection of hot sauces.

ICE CREAM

You don't have to scream too loud for ice cream in New Jersey, because you never have to drive far to find it. The trick, of course, is getting the good stuff. In Essex or Morris County, you can't go wrong at **Applegate Farm** (397 Centre St., Nutley, 973-661-1166; 17 Church St., Montclair; 616 Grove St., Upper Montclair, 973-744-5900; 134 Ridgedale Ave., East Hanover; 973-884-0222;). "The Sopranos" fans know **Holsten's Ice Cream Parlor** (1063 Broad St., Bloomfield; 973-338-7091) as the setting for the show's very last scene.

Ice cream and Newark's Ironbound can mean only one thing: **Nasto's Olde World Desserts** (236-40 Jefferson St., Newark; 973-589-3333).

Classic roadside ice cream stands? The most noteworthy include **Cliff's Dairy Maid** (Route 46 West, Ledgewood; 973-584-9721), **Polar Cub** (Route 22 West, Whitehouse; 908-534-4401), and, in South Jersey, **Hudock's Custard Stand** (Route 49, Quinton; 856-935-5224).

In Bergen County, the two best-known ice cream names are **Bischoff's** (468 Cedar Lane, Teaneck; 201-836-0333) and **Van Dyk's** (145 Ackerman Ave., Ridgewood; 201-444-1429). **Ice Cream Charlie's** (200 Park Ave., Rutherford; 201-939-8133) offers creative, quality ice cream.

For the state's best artisan ice cream, visit **The Bent Spoon** (35 Palmer Square West, Princeton; 609-924-BENT).

In Middlesex County, the cream of the crop includes **Country Cow Creamery** (523 Inman Ave., Woodbridge; 732-882-1234).

In Morris, must-stops include **Denville Dairy** (34A Broadway, Denville; 973-627-4214), **Jefferson Dairy** (Route 15, Jefferson; 973-663-1750), and **Taylor's Ice Cream Parlor** (18 E. Main St., Chester; 908-879-5363).

The best ice cream in Jersey City can be found at **Torico Homemade Ice Cream Parlor** (20 Erie St., Jersey City; 201-432-9458).

It looks ramshackle from the outside, but **Guernsey Crest Ice Cream Co**. (134 19th Ave., Paterson; 973-742-4620) makes good ice cream and shakes.

For Italian ice, there's only one place to go: **DiCosmo's Homemade Italian Ice** (714 Fourth Ave., Elizabeth).

The Shore and ice cream go together. **Kohr's** (Boardwalk and Dupont Avenue, Seaside Heights; 732-830-1833) is a boardwalk soft-serve legend. Another cool spot: the **Margate Dairy Bar** (9519 Ventnor Ave., Margate; 609-822-9559).

It's a ride, but **Vanilla Bean Creamery** (958 Route 109, Lower Township) may well be the best ice cream down the Shore. The chocolate fudge chip is a chocoholic's vision, or taste, of paradise.

MIDDLE EASTERN AND GREEK

In recent years, Middle Eastern restaurants have spread throughout New Jersey, away from traditional strongholds like Paterson and Clifton.

Ibby's Falafel (303 Grove St., Jersey City; 201-432-2400) advertises world's famous falafel; grab a table outside in nice weather. **After Athens** (19 Park Ave., Rutherford; 201-729-0005) has one of the state's more unusual dining rooms, a subterranean, cavelike space.

For Turkish, try **Bosphorus Restaurant** (32 N. Beverwyck Road, Lake Hiawatha; 973- 335-9690), **Toros** (489 Hazel St., Clifton; 973-772-8032) and **Sultan Gyro** (307 Ridge Road, Lyndhurst; 201-728-9542).

For Lebanese, **Headquarters** (647 Georges Road, North Brunswick; 732-247-5454) and **Tabboule** (90 N. Maple Ave., Ridgewood; 201-444-7044).

And there's always **King of Shish Kabob** (932 McBride Ave., West Paterson; 973-812-9888), whose owner is Syrian.

Want to sample food spanning the Middle East and Mediterranean? The best introduction can be found at **Sahara Restaurant** (165 Easton Ave., New Brunswick; 732-246-3020).

ONE-OF-A-KIND EXPERIENCES

In a special category all their own are those singular, dare-to-be-different places that are as much about atmosphere as food.

Boulevard Drinks (48 Journal Square, Jersey City; 201-656-1855) is a neon-lit hot dog hole-in-a-wall across from the PATH station. Speaking of hot dogs, there isn't a more wonderfully odd hot dog joint than **Charlie's Pool Room** (1122 East Blvd., Alpha; 908-454-1364).

Also in Warren County are the **Log Cabin Inn** (47 Route 46, Columbia; 908-496-4291), with its rustic charm and view of the Delaware, **Red Wolfe Inn** (130 Route 519, White Township; 908-475-4772), and **Toby's Cup** (857 Memorial Parkway, Route 22, Lopatcong), a fast food stand as carnival funhouse, with its grinning clown face, low ceiling and other oddities.

Drive-ins — both the movie and food variety — have practically disappeared from New Jersey. The most splendid example of the latter is the **Circus Drive-In** (Route 35, Wall; 732-449-2650), where the pink lemonade is a must. The best-preserved drive-in in South Jersey is **Weber's** (Route 38, Pennsauken; 856-662-6632).

Shocking news! The **Old Heidelberg** (20 Boardwalk, Keansburg; 732-787-3131) recently underwent a renovation, but its low-rent charm remains. It's one of the great Shore hangouts, as is the **Oyster Creek Inn** (41 N. Oyster Creek Road, Leeds Point; 609-652-8565), a seafood shack that manages to be in the middle of nowhere and minutes from the Parkway.

A unique happy hour spot down the Shore is **Schooner American** (Lobster House, Fisherman's Wharf, Lower Township; 609-884-8296), a docked ship where you can enjoy drinks and a light menu.

The **Rutgers University Grease Trucks** (College Avenue and Hamilton Street, New Brunswick) are the stuff of legend, some of it digestible. It's the kind of scene, and food, best appreciated after a night on the town.

At **Steve's Sizzling Steaks** (620 Route 17, Carlstadt; 201-438-9677), jackalopes and other oddball ephemera adorn the walls of this steak roadhouse.

Ever want to eat in church? Now you can, at **Trinity Restaurant** (84 Broad St., Keyport; 732-888-1998), a church-turned-upscale restaurant. Best item: the soft-shell crab.

There's only one **White House Sub Shop** (Mississippi and Arctic avenues, Atlantic City; 609-345-1564). Excellent subs and steak sandwiches, charmingly gruff staff, celebrity photos on the walls.

PIZZA

My Jersey Hall of Fame pizzeria list would begin with **DeLorenzo's Tomato Pies** (530 Hudson St., Trenton; 609-695-9534), with its wooden booths, straight-out-of-Grandma's-attic plastic glasses and near-perfect pie, and **Santillo's Brick Oven Pizza** (639 S. Broad St., Elizabeth; 908-354-1887), a tiny, takeout-only joint with great, saucy pies.

Any discussion of thin-crust pie must include **Star Tavern** (400 High St., Orange; 973- 675-3336), **Mario's** (710 Van Houten Ave., Clifton; 973-777-1559), **Pete & Elda's** (Route 35, Neptune City; 732-774-6010), **Miller's** (Beaver Avenue, Annandale; 908-735-9915), and **Nancy's Towne House** (1453 Main St., Rahway; 732-388-8100).

Dig sausage pizza? Two of the best ones can be found at **Lombardi's** (597-F Pompton Ave., Route 23, Cedar Grove; 973-239-6600) and the neighborhood bar-like **Tony's Baltimore Grill** (2800 Atlantic Ave., Atlantic City; 609-345-5766).

Great Sicilian? Try **Mr. Nino's** (442 Bergen St., Harrison; 973-484-5770). A Morris County legend is **Reservoir Tavern**

(Intervale Road and Parsippany Boulevard, Parsippany; 973-334-0421).

The best boardwalk pie is **Maruca's Tomato Pies** (Boardwalk and Porter Avenue, Seaside Park; 732-793-0707). Not far behind is **Mack and Manco's** (12th and Boardwalk, Ocean City; 609-398-0720).

Good pizza in a bakery? Yes, when it's **DiPaolo Brothers Bakery** (399 Bloomfield Ave., Newark; 973-485-6737).

SEAFOOD

You don't have to be near the water to find top-notch seafood. **Caldwell Seafood Market & Cafe** (390 Bloomfield Ave., Caldwell; 973-226-2031) is a recommended fish market and restaurant.

Blue Claw Seafood & Crab Eatery (4494 Route 130, Burlington Township; 609-387-3700) is much closer to the Delaware River than the ocean, but you may not find better, fresher crabs anywhere. A good crab joint in the Pine Barrens? **Crabby's Suds & Seafood** (1413 Route 50, Belcoville; 609-625-2722).

Crockett's Fish Fry (162 Bloomfield Ave., Montclair; 973-746-2114) is fried food heaven; the catfish sandwich is the bomb. **Dick's Dock** (452 Main St., Metuchen; 732-744-1274) offers good, creative seafood in the Brainy Borough. Don't be put off by the strip mall location of **Hillsborough Lobster Dock** (424 Route 206, Hillsborough; 908-874-3337). The food's excellent.

It's a long way from most anywhere, but **The Bait Box** (30 Hancock Harbor Road, Greenwich; 856-455-2610) is a scenic spot minutes from Delaware Bay.

Down the Shore, from north to south:

Pirate's Cove (901 Port Monmouth Road, Belford; 732-787-6600) is nestled amidst the boats at the Belford Seafood Co-op.

Located within walking distance of each other are **Red's Lobster Pot Restaurant** (57 Inlet Dr., Point Pleasant Beach; 732-295-6622) and **Spike's Fish Market Restaurant** (415 Broadway, Point Pleasant Beach; 732-295-9400).

Martell's Shrimp Bar (Boardwalk, Point Pleasant Beach; 732-295-CLAM) is not to be confused with the raw bar outside the renowned Shore tiki bar; the Shrimp Bar is located just inside the boardwalk entrance to Martell's).

On LBI are the open-air **M & M Steam Bar** (13301 Long Beach Blvd., Beach Heaven Terrace; 609-492-9106); **Beach Haven Fishery** (2115 Long Beach Blvd., Spray Beach; 609-492-4388); the takeout-only **Off the Hook** (20th and Bayview, Barnegat Light; 609-361-8900); the seafood shack-like **Pinky Shrimp's** (Long Beach Boulevard and 83rd Street, Beach Haven Crest; 609-492-0706); and the wonderfully atmospheric **Harvey Cedars Shellfish Co. Smitty's Clam Bar** (506 Centre St., Beach Haven; 609-492-2459).

On the way to LBI is the excellent, but often crowded, **Mud City Crab House** (1185 E. Bay Ave., Manahawkin; 609-978-3660).

In Ocean City for the weekend? Stop at the **Clam Bar** (910 Bay Ave., Somers Point; 609-927-8783), just off the Somers Point Circle, for first-rate sandwiches and platters, and great views.

SOUL/SOUTHERN FOOD

Attending an event at the Prudential Center or NJPAC? Within walking distance is **Je's** (260 Halsey St., Newark; 973-623-8848), which may be the center of the Jersey soul food universe. Nearly as well-known is **Freshwater's** (1442 South Ave., Plainfield; 908-561-9099).

Church's Kitchen (2117 Springfield Ave., Union; 908-810-1686), in the old Vaux Hall post office, does fried chicken, and other Southern standards, well. For great smothered pork chops, visit **MaDear's** (39 Glenridge Ave., Montclair; 973-746-5600). Also in Montclair is **Sweet Potato and Pecan** (103 Forest St., Montclair; 973-746-3444).

Best fried chicken in the state? It can be found at **Mangos** (136 Main St., Hackensack; 201-343-8533); the co-owner is Queen Latifah's mother .

Call **Nubian Flavor** (410 Springfield Ave., Newark; 973-242-2238) a soul food diner, and a good one.

Shack's (1160 E. Grand St., Elizabeth; 908-436-0005) is no-frills, but you'll love the ribs, mac and cheese, and tuna pasta salad.

Another spare-looking, but surprisingly good, stop is **Sisters of Soul Southern Cuisine** (1314 St. Georges Ave., Route 27, Linden; 908-587-0100).

SPANISH/PORTUGUESE/BRAZILIAN

Sprawling restaurants, huge portions and pitchers of sangria: sounds like Newark's Ironbound. But some of the better Spanish/Portuguese restaurants are the smaller ones, and not located in the Ironbound at all.

Portuguese Manor (310 Elm St., Perth Amboy; 732-826-2233) is one. The rodizio at **Solar do Minho** (15 Cleveland St., Belleville; 973-844-0500) is better than any of those in the Ironbound.

Casa Vasca (141 Elm St., Newark; 973-465-1350) is one of the smaller, and better, Ironbound restaurants. **Spanish**

Sangria (157 Magazine St., Newark; 973-344-9286) is well off the Ironbound track, which means parking is easier.

You haven't had a burger until you've tried a Brazilian burger at **Hamburgao** (288 Lafayette St., Newark; 973-465-1776).

Sangria and steak lovers will find much to love at **Fernandes Steak House** (152-170 Fleming Ave., Newark; 973-465-4533).

Across the river is the long-established and ever-reliable **Spanish Pavilion** (31 Harrison Ave., Harrison; 973-485-7750).

SPECIALTY STORES/MARKETS

When it comes to food, you can find just about anything you want in New Jersey. When we went looking for Ghanian food and beer, for example, we didn't have to go any further than downtown Newark.

The state's best ravioli is made at **Casa di Trevi** (534 Westfield Ave., Route 28, Roselle Park; 908-259-9000).

The sprawling **Pulaski Meat Products** (123 N. Wood Ave., Linden; 908-925-5380) provides one-stop Polish food shopping. Smaller but no less noteworthy is **European Provisions** (301 Old Bridge Turnpike, East Brunswick; 732-254-7156). Pierogis? The tiny, un-palace-like **Pierogi Palace** (713 W. Grand Ave., Rahway; 732-499-8411) is a must.

For lovely liverwurst and other German deli standards, try the **Forked River Butcher Shop** (109 Lacey Road, Forked River; 609-693-7100).

At the top of New Jersey, **Clove Brook Market** (800 Route 23, Wantage; 973-875-5600) makes excellent pies, pastries and cookies.

Olive-lovers will swoon at the selection in **The Greek Store** (612 Boulevard, Kenilworth; 908-272-2550), which also offers everything from Greek olive oil, wine and cookies to moussaka, octopus and squid.

Shopping at the Flemington outlets? Minutes away is **Verducci's Food Market** (176 Route 202 North, Raritan Township; 908-788-7750) with its staggering selection of sandwiches, salads, baked goods and foodstuffs.

WINGS

Most sports bar and restaurant wings are of the Buffalo-wing variety, which means they're instantly forgettable. A handful of places — they refuse to be Buffalo-ed — stand out.

Broadway Bar & Grill (106 Randall Ave., Point Pleasant Beach; 732-899-3272) makes the best wings I've had in Jersey;

they're deep-fried, then grilled.

Close behind are the jerk-flavored wings at the simple, spare **Callaloo Cafe** (1401 Maple Ave., Hillside; 973-391-1550).

Hottest wings in the state? Probably the "ludicrous" wings at **The Chicken or the Egg** (207 N. Bay Ave., Beach Haven; 609-492-FOWL), where the prize for surviving them is getting to wear a dunce-like cap.

If you're in the Brick/Point Pleasant area, sample the barbecue wings at **Chicken Town** (2791 Hooper Ave., Brick; 732-920-3870).

For spicy, extra-crunchy wings, hit **Chuck's Spring Street Cafe** (16 Spring St., Princeton; 609-921-0027), a campus hangout. At the **Iron Horse** (20 Washington Ave., Westwood; 201-666-9682), you can dine to the accompaniment of passing trains.

The "super famous" wings at **Jimmy Geez** (436 Belmont Ave., Haledon; 973-790-9729) are pretty good; order them "wimpy," with no sauce of any kind.

The **Old Mill Tavern** (55 Route 24, Chester Township; 908-879-9815) makes its own barbecue sauce and blue cheese dressing, and the "suicidal" wings may have you breathing flames.

THE MUNCH PHOTO ALBUM

The Big Dog would be nothing without the talented photographers who have made the Munch-mobile experience come alive with their beautiful pictures. Every trip, they'll take up to a thousand photos, which are narrowed down to the select few you see in the paper and online every week. Here is a gallery of some of the past decade's most memorable Munch moments, captured on camera.

ABOUT THE MUNCH PHOTOGRAPHER

Star-Ledger staff photographer Tim Farrell has been a photojournalist for over 30 years. He's worked for newspapers in Westchester County, N.Y. and Morris County, N.J., before joining the Ledger in 1995. There he's covered the gamut of news, sports and feature assignments. He has covered the World Series, the NBA Finals, the Stanley Cup finals and two Super Bowls. Since 2003 he has been the staff photographer of the Star-Ledger's Munchmobile. A native of Nyack, N.Y., Tim lives with his wife Susan and their dogs. He enjoys working in their garden, cooking, playing golf and billiards and listening to classical music.

TIM FARRELL'S 10 THINGS YOU SHOULD KNOW ABOUT THE MUNCHMOBILE

1. Surprisingly, most of the people who ride the Big Dog are relatively "normal"! (Driver and photographer not included.)

2. Go ahead. Fill up on the bread. You'll be sorry later.

3. Pace yourself at the first stop.

4. Think forkfuls, not platefuls.

5. Eating chocolate all day sounds like a dream come true, but it's a lot harder to do than you would think. A LOT harder.

6. Pete Genovese can't resist good olives.

7. It's hard to exaggerate the reaction of people, in their cars or on the street, when they see the Big Dog.

8. A decent burger is a much sought-after, yet elusive prize (the same can be said of French fries).

9. Spending an entire day eating in Newark's Ironbound was my single favorite Munchmobile trip. That was the true test of a Muncher.

10. What happens on the Munchmobile stays on the Munchmobile!

School lunches, 2006

Fourth of July picnics, 2008

Burgers, 2005

Diners, 2007

Doughnuts, 2006

Mexican, 2005

Fourth of July picnics, 2005

Wings, 2006

Kickoff festivities, 2002

Route 206, 2008

New Jersey Devils tailgates, 2003

Around the world, 2005

Fourth of July picnics, 2005

Fourth of July picnics, 2008

Healthy food, 2004

Hot dog trucks, 2001

Japanese, 2001

Kickoff festivities, 2002

Reader's choice, 2005

Reader's choice, 2001

Down the Shore, 2005

Fried chicken, 2001

Golf course restaurants, 2005

4th of July picnics, 2007

Pastries, 2008

Milkshakes, 2006

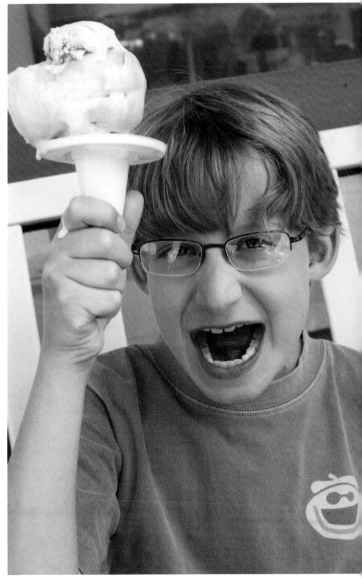

Ice cream, 2007

Chocolate chip cookies, 2006

Down the Shore, 2008

Route 206, 2008

Down the Shore, 2006

4th of July picnics, 2008

Fried chicken, 2008

4th of July picnics, 2007

Route 46, 2008

Real Chinese, 2008

Pizza bloggers, 2007

1998-2000

2001-2003

2004

2005

2006

2007

2008

PETER GENOVESE'S BEST-OF LISTS

Peter Genovese's
Best-Of Lists

You've been following the Munchmobile year after year, but there's one thing you really want to know: Which places are the all-time best? How about most memorable dishes, coolest hangouts, best views and year-by-year Munchmobile stats? It's all in the following pages. Did your favorite place make one of Pete's lists?

A&S Pork Store, West Paterson (2000)

Beach Haven Fishery, Spray Beach (2000)

Benanti's Italian Delicatessen, Bayonne (2007)

The Bent Spoon, Princeton (2005)

Casa Vasca, Newark (2004)

Charlie's Pool Room, Alpha (2002)

Country Pie Factory, Long Valley (2006)

Crockett's Fish Fry, Montclair (2003)

DeLorenzo's Tomato Pies, Trenton (2007)

The Dessert Plate, Somerville (2005)

DiCosmo's, Elizabeth (2003)

Emery's Berry Patch, New Egypt (2001)

Feed Your Soul, Jersey City (2007)

Freshwater's, Plainfield (1999)

The Greek Store, Kenilworth (2002)

Hillsborough Lobster Dock, Hillsborough (2005)

Hog Hollow Bar-B-Que, Lopatcong (2007)

Mara's Country Desserts, Morristown (2002)

Martell's Shrimp Bar, Point Pleasant Beach (2007)

Mud City Crab House, Manahawkin (2003)

Nubian Flavor, Newark (2005)

Ob-Co's Donuts, Toms River (2006)

Santillo's Brick Oven Pizza, Elizabeth (2006)

Solar do Minho, Belleville (2002)

Sweet Potato & Pecan, Montclair (2004)

25 BEST DISHES OR ITEMS

Blueberry Diane, Country Pie Factory, Long Valley

Bubbie sandwich, Eppes Essen, Livingston

Butter chicken, Piquant Bread Bar & Grill, New Brunswick

Caramel apple streusel cheesecake, Mara's Country Desserts, Morristown

Catfish sandwich, My Two Sons, Englishtown Auction, Manalapan

Charcoal-grilled pork chops, After Athens, Rutherford

Chester crunch, J. Emanuel, Chester

Chicken cheesesteak, Chick's Deli, Cherry Hill

Cilantro garlic fries, Tabboule, Ridgewood

Fried chicken, Mangos, Hackensack

Jerk wings, Callaloo Cafe, Hillside

Maryland crab cake sandwich, Mad Batter, Cape May

Omelets, Mustache Bill's, Barnegat Light

Peach berry pie, Emery's Berry Patch, New Egypt

Pepperoni and mozzarella bread, Cheesecake World, Marmora

Prosciutto de parma sandwich, Ciccone's Italian Deli, West Caldwell

Raspberry white chocolate tofu cheesecake, Greenmarket Cafe, Ho-Ho-Kus

Sausage pizza, Tony's Baltimore Grill, Atlantic City

Scallops, Off the Hook, Barnegat Light

Seafood salad, Cosimo's, Bloomfield

Sicilian pizza, Mr. Nino's, Harrison

Sushi pizza, Ocha, Caldwell

Vietnamese spicy and sour prawn soup, Saigon II, Lincroft

Wings, Broadway Bar & Grill, Point Pleasant Beach

Yams, Sisters of Soul Southern Cuisine, Linden

BEST VIEWS (20)

Bahrs, Highlands

The Bait Box, Greenwich

Barnacle Bill's, Rumson

Blue Rock Cafe, Cliffwood Beach

The Chart House, Weehawkin

Gronsky's Milk House, High Bridge

Gunnar's Landing, White Township

The Inlet Cafe, Highlands

Log Cabin Inn, Columbia

Kelly's Old Barney Restaurant, Barnegat Light

Klein's Waterside Cafe, Belmar

Off the Hook, Highlands

Owen's Pub, Ballyowen Golf Club, Hardyston

Oyster Creek Inn, Leeds Point

Pirate's Cove, Belford

Red's Lobster Pot Restaurant, Point Pleasant Beach

Rooney's Ocean Crab House, Long Branch

Seabra's Armory, Perth Amboy

Smitty's Clam Bar, Somers Point

The Windmill, Long Branch

GUILTIEST PLEASURES (20)

Apple cider slush, Terhune Orchards, Lawrence

Baklava, Toros, Clifton

Blackberry doughnuts, Abma's Farm Market & Nursery, Wyckoff

Blue sangria, Fernandes Steak House, Newark

Caramel apple streusel cheesecake, Mara's Country Desserts, Morristown

Cheesesteak-stuffed pizza, Slice of Heaven, Beach Haven

Chocolate brownie chunk cookies, Feed Your Soul, Jersey City

Chocolate horn, Natale's Summit Bakery, Summit

Chocolate lava cake, The Mad Batter, Cape May

Croissant doughnut, Ob-Co's Donuts, Toms River

Fried ravioli, Mario's Italian Market, Surf City

German chocolate cake icing, The Baker Boys, Ocean Grove

Jelly doughnuts, Colonial Bakery, Lavallette

Outrageous oatmeal cookie shake, McCool's, Madison

Pork roll, egg and cheese sandwich, Summit Diner, Summit

Publick House chips, St. James Gate Publick House, Maplewood

Roasted pork skins, Havana Sandwich Cafe, Bloomfield

Salty balls, Maui's Dog House, North Wildwood

Sticky buns, JR's Bakery, Raritan Township

Warm upside-down chocolate soufflé, Zoe's by the Lake, Sparta

LATE AND LAMENTED (GREAT PLACES THAT HAVE SINCE CLOSED)

Abin's, Newark

All Things Cranberry, Monmouth Beach

Cafe Cafe, Butler

Callahan's, Fort Lee

Cozy Drive-In, Netcong

Fat Cat's Cafe, Harvey Cedars

Karen's at Brookside, Hopewell

Hofbrauhaus, Atlantic Highlands

Michele Lorie Cheesecakes, Trenton

Palmyra Tea Room, Bound Brook

Rockingham Coffee Lounge, Boonton

Screamin' Nelli's, Whitehouse Station

Sebastian's, Rahway

Shellpile Restaurant, Shellpile

Short Stop, Bloomfield

White Crystal Diner, Atlantic Highlands

ALL-TIME COOLEST HANGOUTS (20)

Allenwood General Store, Wall

Boulevard Drinks, Jersey City

The Cafe at Rosemont, Rosemont

Charlie's Pool Room, Alpha

Christine's House of Kingfish, Shamong

Circus Drive-in, Wall

Crabby's, Belcoville

Gronsky's Milk House, High Bridge

Log Cabin Inn, Columbia

Miller's, Annandale

Old Heidelberg, Keansburg

Red Wolfe Inn, White Township

Rutt's Hut, Clifton

Schooner American, Lobster House, Lower Township

Smitty's Clam Bar, Somers Point

St. James Gate Publick House, Maplewood

Toby's Cup, Lopatcong

Uncle Dewey's BBQ Pavilion, Mizpah

White House Sub Shop, Atlantic City

White Mana, Jersey City

YEAR BY YEAR STATS

1998: 60 stops

1999: 74 stops; 4,024 miles

2000: 111 stops, 5,100 miles

2001: 97 stops, 4,700 miles

2002: 84 stops, 3,452 miles

2003: 105 stops, 4,365 miles

2004: 92 stops, 4,394 miles

2005: 84 stops, 3,561 miles

2006: 177 stops (Munchmobile and SWAT Dog), 6,335 miles

2007: 102 stops, 4,500 miles

THE MUNCH DIRECTORY

Looking for the most comprehensive, up-to-date directory of casual eateries in New Jersey, complete with incisive reviews? Look no further. In the next 80 pages, you'll find summaries of every Munchmobile stop since the beginning, listed by county. You can also look up a particular restaurant or type of cuisine in the indexes at the back of the book.

Atlantic

Costello's, 615 E. Moss Mill Road, Smithville; (609) 652-0378. Offerings include Fuhgeddaboutit pizza and a bruschetta chicken sandwich. Novel item: warm antipasti (sauteed Italian sausage, broccoli rabe, roasted red peppers and white cannellini beans tossed in garlic and olive oil). "Buffalo tails" — chicken tenders in tangy sauce — are excellent.

The Crab Trap, 2 Broadway, Somers Point; (609) 927-7377. Longtime Shore favorite — you may have to wait several hours on a summer evening — delivered the day's best soup, a Maryland crab. Manhattan clam chowder almost as good. The deviled crab fared better than the more expensive crispy crabcakes.

Crabby's Suds and Seafood, 1413 Route 50, Belcoville; (609) 625-2722. Good crabs in a Pine Barrens bar? Sure. Seafood gumbo spicy and ricey, but we loved the sherry-flavored he-crab soup. First-rate king crab legs; garlic crabs didn't seem as successful or sea-worthy. Crab and linguine marinara a nice surprise.

Custard's Last Stand, 107 N. Dorset, Ventnor; (609) 823-4033. Plenty of inventive toppings — chocolate pretzels, dark chocolate drops, Nerds, Kit Kats and more. Chocolate, while smooth and creamy, not as memorable as its counterpart at Margate Dairy Bar. One Muncher said the soft ice cream "was a little loose," but another liked it just fine that way.

East Bay Crab and Grille, 6701 Black Horse Pike, Egg Harbor Twp.; (609) 272-7721. Came highly recommended, but this was the least memorable meal of the summer. New England clam chowder had the "consistency of paste," according to one Muncher. The mahi wasabi a good enough piece of fish, but the accompanying cream sauce the wimpiest wasabi you'll ever experience.

Kelsey and Kim's Soul Food and Barbecue, 52 N. Main St., Pleasantville; (609) 484-8448. Good barbecue is hard to find in New Jersey. This may be the best. Simple, spare storefront. You'll wait a while, but it'll be worth it. The ribs are highly recommended. Good barbecue chicken. The pulled pork sandwich tasted almost as good the morning after, straight out of the fridge.

Lo Presti's Pizza and Grill, 2601 Boardwalk, Atlantic City; (609) 345-6339. Okay food, but at least you're serenaded by Italian popular and operatic music.

Margate Dairy Bar, 9210 Ventnor Ave., Margate; (609) 822-9559. A real roadside throwback — green-awninged, pink-lettered, fluorescent-lit stand that screams for a starring role in a Hollywood production. Maybe the richest chocolate of the day, and both the vanilla and chocolate the creamiest of all those sampled.

Oyster Creek Inn, 41 N. Oyster Creek Road, Leeds Point; (609) 652-8565. About as far from New Jersey as you can get without leaving the state, this rambling seafood shack offers scenic vistas and fine fare. Garlic clams, jumbo lump crab cocktail and the lemon and pepper scallops among the better dishes.

Smithville Bakery, 615 Moss Mill Road, Smithville; (609) 652-6471. Smithville, with its shops and pond, makes for a great excursion the next time you're in AC or on LBI. The bakery offers good doughnuts and cakes, but if you have time, sit down and enjoy their country breakfasts.

Smitty's Clam Bar, (formerly The Clam Bar), 910 Bay Ave., Somers Point; (609) 927-8783. "You can't lick our clams," announces a sign at this indoor/outdoor snack bar with great waterfront views. Excellent fried shrimp. New England clam chowder a big hit. Check the daily "fishburger." The grouper burger — strips of lightly fried grouper on roll — is terrific fish fast food.

Tony's Baltimore Grill, 2800 Atlantic Ave., Atlantic City; (609) 345-5766. Local landmark, colorful change-of-pace from the antiseptic casino scene. Crab cake, fried shrimp, linguine in white sauce did not rise above the bar-food norm; you come to the Baltimore Grill for one thing — the sausage pizza, with some of the best sausage you'll find anywhere. Great pie.

Uncle Dewey's BBQ Pavilion, Mile Marker 40, Route 40, Mizpah; (609) 476-4040. Roadside barbecue tent, where workers tend grills in a tin-roofed cooking shed. Excellent brisket, spilling from a Kaiser roll. Decent ribs, and dry chicken. But good cole slaw and potato salad, and the homemade lemonade is marvelous.

White House Sub Shop, 2301 Arctic Ave., Atlantic City; (609) 345-1564. Everyone from the Beatles to Joe DiMaggio has visited this legendary sub shop. The help is charmingly gruff, the atmosphere borderline chaotic. The first-rate subs are marked by great bread, from Formica's.

Bergen

Abma's Farm Market and Nursery, 700 Lawlins Road, Wyckoff; (201) 891-0278. Petting zoo and farm market make for a great day out with the kids. The summer smash pie a smash hit and the blackberry turnovers — when was the last one you saw a blackberry turnover? — are great. Don't forget to bring home a bag of the sugar doughnuts.

After Athens, 17 Park Ave., Rutherford; (201) 729-0005. Co-owner Dimitri Valavanis turned the basement of a former hardware store into a cave, with faux columns and miniature friezes. The portabello After Athens, a stunning construction of crabmeat-stuffed flaky filo dough, drew raves. Lamb in the souvlaki: dried out. Pastichio the day's best. Charcoal-grilled pork chops meaty and monstrous, perfectly cooked and wonderfully juicy.

Arlington Diner, 1 River Road, North Arlington; (201) 998-6262. "Creamiest cheesecake around" is how one reader describes the cheesecake here. The plain cheesecake is not up to the level of the Westfield Diner's; the strawberry cheesecake — fluffier, cheesier — is markedly better. And a terrific chocolate topping distinguishes the chocolate cheesecake.

Bendix Diner, 464 Route 17, Hasbrouck Heights; (201) 288-0143. Only blind diner waiter/standup comedian in New Jersey. You gotta try the disco fries. Nothing special about the rest of the food; it's the ambiance that counts.

Bischoff's, 468 Cedar Lane, Teaneck; (201) 836-0333. If you're looking for thick, lumpy shakes, this is not the place; shakes here are frothy on top, almost milk-like. The chocolate shake, pistachio shake and chocolate fudge brownie shake were the group favorites.

Callahan's, 146 Route 46, Little Ferry; (201) 440-8516. Hot dog legend, but our panel was not kind to the hot dog. "Should be put down," one groused. Cold sauerkraut.

Candlewyck Diner, 179 Paterson Ave., East Rutherford; (201) 933-4446. Any diner offering 18 kinds of cheesecake is worth visiting in our book. Mediocre soups, but first-rate New York strip: thick, juicy, perfectly cooked. Fine French toast. Start with the plain cheesecake, smooth and creamy; you can try the rest another time.

Country Pancake House, 140 E. Ridgewood Ave., Ridgewood; (201) 444-8395. For sheer pancake excess, no restaurant can match it. Offers a staggering 112 kinds of pancakes with nutty names (Peter Rabbit, Heavenly Celestial Body, etc.). Monstrous pancakes — 12 inches in diameter. The Maine Delicacy (whole grain and blueberries) is good and chewy without being rubbery. The Banana Nut tastes fresh and nutty.

Cubby's Q, 249 S. River St., Hackensack; (201) 488-9389. The Cubby's Special Texas Weiner is a train wreck of a sandwich — chili, cheese, onions, bacon and mustard all smooshed together on crunchy French roll.

Danny's Dogs, 100 River Road, Garfield; (973) 249-8700. Decent dog, but thick, meaty, spicy chili. Worth a try: The Texas Flame Thrower, with chili, raw onions, hot sauce and chopped hot peppers.

Dayi'nin Yeri, 333 Palisade Ave., Cliffside Park; (201) 840-1770. The shepherd salad a fresh, feisty mix of tomatoes, cucumbers, onions, green peppers and parsley in vinegar and virgin olive oil. Creamy-smooth hummus. Chicken kebab tender and delicious. Kunefe — unsalted mozzarella and walnuts inside shredded wheat-topped filo — a cheesy, sugary success.

Fireplace Restaurant, 718 Route 17 North, Paramus; (201) 444-2362. How many fast food joints have been around since 1956? The

Fireplace, opened by former FBI agent Frank Reilly, has. Best known for their burgers, fries and milkshakes, but you can also get salads, steak sandwiches, cheesesteaks, chicken sandwiches and pizza.

Greenmarket Cafe, 195 E. Franklin Turnpike, Ho-Ho-Kus; (201) 652-7733. Terrified of tofu? Give the Thai vegetables and tofu over organic rice a try. The veggie burger, unlike others we've sampled, actually packs taste and flavor. It sounds a little on the weird side, but the raspberry white chocolate tofu cheesecake is amazing.

Hiram's, 1345 Palisades Ave., Fort Lee; (201) 592-9602. Hot dog roadhouse, with beer on tap. Chili named the state's best by our S.W.A.T. Dog team. But so-so kraut.

Hot Dog Heaven, 176 Kinderkamack Ave., Emerson; (201) 261-0073. Sabrett dog and house mustard a winning combination.

The Hot Dog House, 510 Route 17 South, Carlstadt; (201) 935-5803. Sit outside, with dump trucks roaring mere yards from your feet, and enjoy hot dogs with barbecue sauce, German white potato and other unusual toppings. Good fries and sweet relish, too.

Ice Cream Charlie's, 200 Park Ave., Rutherford; (201) 939-8133. There's a DQ down the street, but we doubt they have Rice Krispie and ginger lemon chiffon ice cream there. Some of the day's best, most consistent flavors found here.

Indian Chef, 370A Essex St., Lodi; (201) 587-1087. "Sopranos" fans should have no trouble finding the International Food Warehouse, where Indian Chef is located. The food emporium is across Route 17 from Satin Dolls, known as the Bada-Bing on HBO's mob show. The tandoori chicken — there's a tandoor oven behind the counter — is near perfect. The coriander chutney and naan bread make for an unbeatable combination. We also liked the ginger chicken.

Iron Horse, 20 Washington Ave., Westwood; (201) 666-9682. Bar and dining rooms decorated with train memorabilia. Orders come with pickles and terrific — creamy and extra crunchy — cole slaw. The Buffalo wings the day's plumpest, but not otherwise distinguished. Highly recommended: the Iron Horse cheeseburger, with juicy fresh meat and the cheese melted inside the burger.

It's Greek to Me, 21 E. Ridgewood Ave., Ridgewood; (201) 612-2600. Indoor courtyard-look, with blue-shuttered windows and blue mosaic-tiled windows. Portions healthy if not humongous. Lamb kokkinisto — cinnamon-scented lamb chunks in tomato sauce over orzo — had several Munchers straining for superlatives. Baked feta nicely charred on top and soft and squishy inside. Baklava the day's best.

Jim Dandy's, 448 Ridge Road, North Arlington; (201) 998- 8006. Order shakes and ice cream at the walk-up window. Homemade ice cream. Chocolate shake thick and frosty but not particularly distinctive; cookie dough shake is better. Burgers, ribs, homemade chili also available.

Johnny and Hanges, 20-30 Maple Ave., Fair Lawn; (201) 791-9060. All-beef Thumann's overcooked, and served on bland roll besides. The Texas weiner fared better.

Karl Ehmer's, 120 Broadway, Hillsdale; (201) 664-1477. Butcher shop with sidewalk hot dog cart. Top-of-the-line German-style beef and pork dog.

Lodi Buffet, 1 S. Main St., Lodi; (973) 777-2277. Most far-ranging buffet visited; includes veal with mushrooms, pasta vodka, lentil soup, Singapore chicken. Egg drop soup best of those sampled. Crispy fried chicken, but it could have been hotter. Freshest sushi of the day. Passable chicken parm. Easily the day's best egg roll. Not-so-fresh honeydew melon. Good rice pudding.

Mangos, 136 Main St., Hackensack; (201) 343-8533. You may not find better fried chicken anywhere — it's crisp, crunchy and wonderfully juicy inside. Near-perfect cornbread and pretty good sides, particularly the collards.

Market Basket, 813 Franklin Lakes Road, Franklin Lakes; (201) 891-2000. What a bakery — doughnuts, cakes, pies, cookies, fruit tarts, bread, in a display case that seems to stretch forever. The frosting-topped brownies received thumbs-up, the teardrop cake an emphatic thumbs down. Juicy, plump chocolate-covered strawberries.

Mazur's Bakery, 323 Ridge Road, Lyndhurst; (201) 438-8500. Cherry turnovers, mini-fruit boats, cream puffs, chocolate truffle cheesecake and scores of other items: The display case is a sugar lover's wildest fantasy.

Natalie's Cafe, 17 S. Broad St., Ridgewood; (201) 444-7887. Cute, cheery place. Recommended salads: the house special with baby greens, apples, walnuts, Gorgonzola and a light balsamic dressing, and the sliced marinated steak, with the fattest, juiciest strips of steak you may ever see in a salad.

Naturally Good, 152 Main St., Hackensack; (201) 487-0651. Good salads in this spare storefront. Tabouleh salad features perfectly cooked bulgur wheat dotted with tomatoes and parsley. Artichoke and tomato salad a straightforward, Fourth-of-July cookout kind of salad. Best of the bunch: the cabbage, apple and walnut salad, in a creamy but light dressing.

Noah's Ark, 493 Cedar Lane, Teaneck; (201) 692-1200. Their corned beef sandwich once voted best in nation. Matzo ball soup to write home about, onion rings the size of dinner plates.

Seafood Gourmet, 103 W. Pleasant Ave., Maywood; (201) 843-8558. One of summer's best soups: the Maryland crab. Rich, creamy New England clam chowder. Also recommended: the steamers, oysters and stuffed sole.

Ski's Weenie Bus, Midland Avenue, Garfield. Undoubtedly the wildest-looking hot dog stand in the state, a converted school bus decorated with purple flames and cartoon characters. Owner Linda Leschynski offers unusual toppings — potatoes, mushrooms, plain and German sauerkraut, baked beans. Try her "kick-butt" onions and peppers.

The Stack Pancake and Steak House, 205 River Road, North Arlington; (201) 991-1023. Pancakes with a view; tables look out on the Passaic River. Wooden beams, country decor, real syrup. Buttermilk pancakes fluffy and fat without being leaden. "Best buttermilk pancakes in the state," according to one reader.

Steve's Sizzling Steaks, 620 Route 17, Carlstadt; (201) 438-9677. Bar/steakhouse/roadhouse with oddball ephemera (showshoes, a jackalope hunting license) on the walls. The steaks indeed come sizzling to the table, spitting and sputtering grease and fat.

Sultan Gyro, 307 Ridge Road, Lyndhurst; (201) 728-9542. We love holes-in-the-wall, and Sultan Gyro, owned by Turkish-born Ahmet Tekin, qualifies. The doner kebap — a gyro-like stuffed pita — is outstanding. The lamb and chicken kabobs, with chunky, savory pieces of meat, are every bit as good.

Super Deli, 125 Wallington Ave., Wallington; (973) 773-7277. The Bergen County town has the highest percentage of people of Polish ancestry of any incorporated town in the U.S. The Super Deli provides one-stop Polish food shopping. Great kielbasa.

Sweet Cravings, 165 Ridge Road, North Arlington; (201) 998-3641. Everyone from Ludacris to Christie Todd Whitman has ordered chocolates from Patty Sickinger's cheery candy shop. Excellent chocolate-covered pretzels, with their great sweet-salty taste. A finger-licking favorite: the dark chocolate coconut custard candies. Fresh, juicy, chocolate-covered strawberries.

Tabboule, 90 N. Maple Ave., Ridgewood; (201) 444-7044. Friendly, likable owners, from Lebanon, run this casual restaurant. We found the tabboule too lemony, but the hummus and baba ghanoush are first-rate. The bright-purple pickled turnips look like something out of a cartoon, but they're amazing.

Van Dyk's, 145 Ackerman Ave., Ridgewood; (201) 444-1429. Peach-colored ice cream parlor in residential neighborhood. Peanut butter shake "like drinking straight peanut butter," marveled one Muncher. But the rest of the shakes seemed average, and the peach shake had us wondering: Where's the peach?

Vitamia Sons Ravioli Co., 206 Harrison Ave., Lodi; (973) 546-1140. About 100 different pastas (including three-color gnocchi and heart-shaped ravioli), plus homemade sauces, fresh mozzarella, sausage bread and a funny, fast-talking owner.

White Manna, 358 River St., Hackensack; (201) 342-0914. The state's most photogenic diner, this glass-blocked jewel is right across the street from a McDonald's. Talk about choices. White Manna's minuscule burgers are marvelous. All the basic ingredients — meat, cheese, bun, ketchup — blend together in burger bliss.

Burlington

Blue Claw Seafood and Crab Eatery, 4494 Route 130, Burlington Twp.; (609) 387-3700. You'll make a mess at this roadside crab joint and love every minute. Tables covered in brown construction paper; crayons are provided. Terrific garlic snow crabs; hot-sauced blue crabs not far behind. Summer's best side — the Old Bay-seasoned fries here.

Christine's House of Kingfish Barbecue, 926 Route 206, Shamong; (609) 268-3600. Before you squawk about driving all the way to the Pine Barrens for good ribs, know this: There's no top-notch barbecue anywhere in North Jersey. You want the real deal, stop at this roadside shack. The ribs are lip-smackingly tender. Try the juicy pulled chicken sandwich and a side of coleslaw.

Gaetano's, 498 Beverly Rancocas Road, Willingboro; (609) 871-5588. Super steaks, jammed with tender, juicy meats. There's a Jersey cheesesteak, with potatoes, green peppers, fried onions and A1.

Mastoris, 144 Route 130, Bordentown; (609) 298-4650. One of the state's biggest diners, Mastoris seems to have slipped some-what, judging by our visit. Overcooked prime rib; mushy and useless vegetables, and yams candied to the extreme. Excellent salads and better-than-average onion rings.

Palermo's, 674 Route 206 South, Bordentown; (609) 298-6771. The Old-Fashioned Pie here is simple, straightforward and good. The Giulio pizza — prosciutto, roasted peppers, sun-dried tomatoes and olives — alone is worth the ride down the Turnpike.

Camden

Big John's, 1800 Route 70 East, Cherry Hill; (856) 424-1186. One of the top two or three South Jersey cheesesteak names, but we found better at several other places. Go with the provolone; it comes off better than the American cheese. Service could have been friendlier.

Chick's Deli, 906 Township Lane, Cherry Hill; (856) 429-2022. Not easy to find — it's wedged into an alleyway off Route 70 West — but Chick's delivers the best cheesesteak you'll find in New Jersey, maybe even in Philly. The plain cheesesteak is a molten marvel, the meat, cheese and bread blending beautifully together. Chicken cheesesteaks may be even better.

Miel Patisserie, 1990 Route 70 East, Cherry Hill; (856) 424-6435. This shop is almost a fine arts museum of sweets — everything looks so delicately constructed and exquisitely shaped. Good sticky bun, but we've had better. Forget your diner Danish and try one of the cherry Danish here. Chocolate eclair coated with a terrific chocolate glaze. Okay cheesecake, but the fruit tart is near-perfect.

Weber's, Route 38, Pennsauken; (856) 662-6632. One of New Jersey's classic drive-ins; roll down your window and let one of the girls attach a tray and take your order. Snappy hot dogs, nestled in toasted rolls and slathered in spicy brown mustard.

Cape May

Back Bay Seafood, 8305 Third Ave., Stone Harbor; (609) 368-2022. Tiny, screen-doored, takeout-only joint; when you call up, you're given the next available pickup time. Day's best crabcake. "Famous" lobster bisque nearly lived up to its billing, but the she-crab soup received a quick thumbs-down.

The Blue Pig Tavern, Congress Hall, 251 Beach Ave., Cape May; (609) 884-8422. Excellent crab sandwich, despite the overpowering bernaise topping. Good grilled sirloin burger. Filet mignon tender and terrific, but we could have done without all the trappings — a crown of greens, bacon and roasted red peppers and a bed of middling mashed potatoes.

Cheesecake World, 228 Route 9 South, Marmora; (609) 390-2468. The father-daughter owners turn out 15,000 cheesecakes a year. Our favorites: the chocolate chip and the Bodacious, a peanut butter cheesecake. The pepperoni and mozzarella stuffed bread is amazing.

Crab House at Two Mile Landing, Ocean Drive, Wildwood Crest; (609) 522-1341. Peaceful setting; perched at edge of marsh. Subtly sweet Dungeness crabs, terrific conch fritters — crispy outside and sensationally smooshy inside.

Curley's Fries, 3501 Boardwalk, Wildwood. Opened at Morey's Piers in 1978, and as popular as ever. "Curley's fries chased by a Lemon Shakeup can't be beat," went our Munch report.

Del's Oceanside Grill, 934 Boardwalk, Ocean City; (609) 399-3931. Open-air diner/luncheonette on boardwalk. The Big Misteak — a cheesesteak smothered with fried onions, sweet peppers and mush-rooms — is excellent.

The Fish Factory, 8606 New Jersey Ave., Wildwood Crest; (609) 522-9582. Clam chowder rich and creamy, maybe too creamy. Manhattan clam chowder thick with clams, potatoes and celery. Nicely-seasoned colossal shrimp seemed adrift in an oily sea. Good crab cake.

Gecko's, 31 Perry St., Cape May; (609) 898-7750. Outdoor patio is a pleasant, shaded spot, but the food seems hit-or-miss. Liked the crab enchilada and pork posole, didn't like the barbecue chicken sandwich. Outstanding desserts, especially the Key lime taco.

Hot Dog Tommy's, 319 Beach Ave., Cape May; (609) 884-8388. If you're not smiling by the time you leave here, you'd better check your sense of humor. Floppy hot dog hat perched on his head, Tommy Snyder dishes out the jokes while wife Mary makes the dogs. They're plump and juicy, from Berks. Plenty of toppings available. Mary makes good chili and a homemade cranberry cole slaw. Open summer only.

Ike's Famous Crab Cakes, 1344 Boardwalk, Ocean City; (609) 814-1700. Very good crabcake sandwiches. Try the lemon, orange and lime-flavored Iced Fruit Tea.

Mack and Manco Pizza, 12th and Boardwalk, Ocean City; (609) 398-0720. You haven't truly sampled boardwalk food until you've had a slice of Mack and Manco's pizza. A good thin-crust pie, with none of that warmed-over taste you get at some places.

The Mad Batter, Carroll Villa, 19 Jackson St., Cape May; (609) 884-5970. Breakfast/brunch here is a Cape May tradition. Maryland crabcake sandwich the best sandwich we had all summer. Blackened grouper sandwich and the Chesapeake Bay Benedict not far behind. Things we weren't crazy about: the lobster frittata and the burger. Excellent desserts.

Maggie's, 2709 Dune Drive, Avalon; (609) 368-7422. French toast a cinnamony delight. Not sure what was Philly about the Philly Plate — fried oysters, turkey salad, tomatoes and cucumbers — but the oysters perfectly done. Average grilled cheese sandwich, decent omelet.

Maui's Dog House, 806 New Jersey Ave., North Wildwood; (609) 846-0444. The draw at this doggy stand is the creative — if kooky — range of toppings and choice of traditional hot dog or "Whitey," made of veal. Salty Balls, fresh small potatoes cooked in a brine of salt and spices, are addictive.

Original Fudge Kitchen, 4120 Boardwalk at Roberts Avenue, Wildwood; (609) 522-4396. Excellent fudge, and the shop is a chocoholic's vision of heaven. Great place to pick up souvenirs for family and friends back home.

Original Hot Spot #1, 3421 Boardwalk and Cedar Avenue, Wildwood; (609) 522-4500. Open-air boardwalk stand/Greek diner. Great people-watching spot.

Primo Pizza, 832 Boardwalk, Ocean City; (609) 525-0022. A worthy contender to Mack and Manco, the king of boardwalk thin-crust pizza. Slices hit all the right notes — thin, crispy and just-so greasy. The perfect Jersey Shore dessert, if you ask us.

Schooner American Lobster House, 906 Schellengers Landing, Lower Twp.; (609) 884-8296. The Lobster House is a seafood Disneyland, with its indoor restaurant, outdoor cafe, various raw bars and fish market. On the Schooner, you can enjoy steamed shrimp, shrimp cocktail and other light fare.

Sea Shell Ice Cream, 300 E. Rio Grande Ave., Wildwood; (609) 522-7822. The Banana Moo (three kinds of ice cream, three kinds of toppings and three mix-ins, plus a banana, whipped cream, nuts and cherries) is outrageous and good.

Steel's Fudge, 1000 Boardwalk and 10th Street, Ocean City; (609) 398-2383. Elizabeth Steel opened her fudge shop on the Atlantic City boardwalk in 1919. Today, no visit to either Atlantic City or Ocean City is complete without a stop at Steel's.

Cumberland

The Bait Box, 30 Hancock Harbor Road, Greenwich; (856) 455-2610. A way out-of-the-way place with scenic views over the Cohansey River and excellent seafood. One must: the sauteed soft shell crabs.

Essex

3 Guys Pizzeria and Ristorante, 366 Franklin Ave., Belleville; (973) 751-4602. The sausage and mushroom pie is greasy-good, although you'd better like cheese because there's loads of it. Interesting twist: You can ask for canned or fresh mushrooms.

Algieri's Pizza, 502 Union Ave., Belleville; (973) 751-3577. Good enough sausage pie, but the plain pie seemed too cheesy, too greasy. Munchers split on the crust. "A little cardboardy," said one. "Better crust than we've had all day," said another.

Anthony's Homemade Cheesecakes/Lunch Box Deli, 176 Broad St., Bloomfield; (973) 566-0154. Co-owner Anthony Lauro was working a computer data entry job seven years ago when he made a cheesecake from his mother's recipe and brought it to the office. Ditch the data entry, open a cheesecake shop. New York-style cheesecake "absolutely superb," according to one Muncher.

Arturo's, 180 Maplewood Ave., Maplewood; (973) 378-5800. Dan Richer does Italian differently than your local restaurant. Pasta are prepared in pans, cooked in a wood-burning oven and topped with parmesan reggiano, which isn't cheap. The margherita pizza may have been the summer's best pie.

Bagel Box, 642 Eagle Rock Ave., West Orange; (973) 731-4985. Home of the Russian Bomb, a pumpernickel, onion and sesame bagel. Egg and cinnamon raisin bagels also good. Excellent, unique cream cheeses, including salsa and horseradish.

Bangkok Kitchen, 391 Bloomfield Ave., Caldwell; (973) 618-9975. Welcome retreat from the highway's hubbub. Coconut juice here the perfect summer tonic. Spring roll: good, crispy shell, but predictable ingredients. Peanut sauce, a curry, cinnamon and coconut-flavored paste, a winner. Fatty ribs, and the Penang seafood dish skimped on the seafood. But the lemongrass shrimp soup, sweet and spicy, might have been the best item we sampled all day.

Belmont Tavern, 12 Bloomfield Ave., Belleville; (973) 759-9609. Joe DiMaggio ate here — twice. Signature dish is the vinegar-laced chicken Savoy. Pork chop dried out, but both pastas — ziti with pot cheese, and side of linguine — cooked just right. Nothing we sampled outstanding, but food consistently good.

Bloomfield Steak and Seafood House, 409 Franklin St., Bloomfield; (973) 680-4500. A 22-ounce porterhouse's off-putting smell was noticed by everyone at the table except the waiter. Its replacement turned out to be quite tasty. And the pan-seared filet mignon with port wine reduction is outstanding.

Boi Na Brasa, Store #4, 70 Adams St., Newark; (973) 589-6069. Charming little hideaway, seemingly miles from frenetic Ferry Street. Nice rodizio; the best meat is the beef tenderloin, terrifically chewy. Leave room for the slices of cinnammon-dusted grilled pineapple afterwards.

Brasilia, 132 Ferry St., Newark; (973) 465-1227. Not a rodizio for beginners; the first round of meat is chicken hearts. Fried bananas — fat and squishy — best of our five-restaurant bunch. Plump, tender chicken, but the pork loin on the salty side, and the fist-sized beef short ribs, while tender, lacked flavor. Terrific turkey wrapped in bacon.

Cafe Tartufo, 1049 Broad St., Bloomfield; (973) 893-0655. Cool little cafe/restaurant, with peach-colored walls and mirrored glass. Peanut butter chocolate-chip gelato features strong, heady bite. The strawberry drew raves. Coconut gelato a good choice for those who like coconut but don't want a strong aftertaste.

Cait and Abby's Daily Bread, 15 Sloan St., South Orange; (973) 763-2229. Warning, chocolate lovers! This place may test your limits: chocolate shortcake, chocolate fudge cake and Truly Chocolate Cheesecake among offerings.

Calandra's, 244 Route 46, Fairfield; (973) 227-5008. Probably the best-recognized name in the fresh bread business in New Jersey. The Newark store opened in 1960, the bigger Fairfield store in 1992. The bread did not quite reach the lofty level as Il Forno or Nicolo's, but the long lines here over the holidays testify to the pull of the Calandra name.

Calandra's, 201 First Ave., Newark; (973) 484-5598. "Hot Bread Every Hour Until 9 p.m.," says neon sign. Great jelly doughnuts, delightfully chewy twist bread. A Newark institution.

Caldwell Diner, 332 Bloomfield Ave., Caldwell; (973) 228-2855. The Munchers loved the pancakes, but they seemed average at best. There was no disagreement over the fine French toast, though.

Caldwell Seafood Market and Cafe, 390 Bloomfield Ave., Caldwell; (973) 226-2031. Appetizer heaven: the calamari balsamico. Several thought the grilled rainbow trout, with Cajun seasoning, the day's best fish dish. Skip the lobster bisque and New England clam chowder.

Caribbean Cuisine, 5 Winans St., East Orange; (973) 674-2992. Owner Mario Lall credits Indian, Creole, Chinese and Spanish influences on his "Trinidad-style" cuisine. There's some fire in his food; if you order the jerk chicken, have a pitcher of water nearby. Plaintains soft and squishy good. Also recommended: the stewed chicken, oxtail and curry shrimp.

Casa Filippo, 373 Bloomfield Ave., Caldwell; (973) 364-9999. It's like dining in someone's home — one perched above the tumult of Bloomfield Avenue. All the appetizers scored high. Recommended entrees include stuffed shrimp and sole, the snapper oreganato and the Calabrese fish stew. Great place for a company party; we've had a few there.

Casa Nova, 262 Ferry St., Newark; (973) 817-8712. May look more like a pub than a restaurant, but the spit above the charcoal pit never rests. Sausage, while greasy, the spiciest of those sampled. Chicken boasts a juicy, crackly skin. Great top sirloin, but the short ribs are fatty, the turkey wrapped in bacon dried out and the pork loin salty.

Casa Vasca, 141 Elm St., Newark; (973) 465-1350. Cozy, beautiful little hideaway amidst the Ironbound's hustle and bustle. Menu reflects owner's Spanish-Basque background. Rabbit stew — tender but not gamey meat in a silky brown sauce — first-rate. Baked red snapper head resting proudly on the plate, skin crisp and crackly — a near work of art, and delicious besides.

Charlie Brown's Steakhouse, 35 Main St., Millburn; (973) 376-1724. The Farmers' Market salad bar at your local Charlie Brown's is a model salad bar: two cavernous bowls of fresh lettuce and rows of tomatoes, cucumbers, olives, green peppers, radishes and other salad bar essentials. Tasty toppings: raisins, crispy noodles, granola. Good clam chowder, too.

China Gourmet Restaurant, 468 Eagle Rock Ave., West Orange; (973) 731-6411. Much of the dim sum cooked on a portable grill around the corner from the tables. Try the flaky, mildly sweet pork triangle; the sesame bun is another late-morning marvel. Great pork buns — baked, not steamed, with an irresistible glazy coat.

Chris' Red Hots, Heller Parkway, Newark. Raves all around for the hot onions. Excellent mustard, but ordinary dog, a Sabrett's all-beef.

Ciccone's Italian Deli, 658 Bloomfield Ave., West Caldwell; (973) 228-4070. The prosciutto di Parma, roasted red peppers and mozzarella sub at this diner-like, tiled-floored deli is terrific. Several Munchers thought the grilled chicken sub with mozzarella and roasted peppers was even better.

Cloverleaf Tavern and Restaurant, 395 Bloomfield Ave., Caldwell; (973) 226-9812. Smallest brunch of those sampled. Stuffed sole "to die for," according to one reader. Pork tenderloin, Swedish meatballs and macaroni and cheese all better than average. Standard omelet and French toast.

Cooper's Deli, 594 Orange St., Newark; (973) 482-0316. Lottery to the left, liverwurst to the right at this funky neighborhood hangout. Walk up the ramp and give your order to whomever's behind the counter. Sandwiches are loaded; just when you think they're done layering the meat, they'll throw on some more.

Cosimo's Trattoria, 194 Broad St., Bloomfield; (973) 429-0558. The small, lively dining room is owned by Cosimo Pensiero, a former lunch truck operator. Two super salads: the special salad with mango, and the seafood salad, in a wondrous lemon and olive oil dressing. The quattro stagione pizza is outstanding; the linguine alio e olio does that traditional Italian pasta proud. The filet mignon — just okay — seemed to come from a different kitchen.

Coutinho's, 88 Wilson Ave., Newark; (973) 589-9316. The custard cups here an Ironbound tradition. But there's much more to like, including bread, turnovers and an egg/sugar doughnut known as a bola de berlim. Dynamite espresso.

Crockett's Fish Fry, 162 Bloomfield Ave., Montclair; (973) 746-2114. Marine-minimalist decor: white tile floors, peach walls, lone fan. But marvelous mac and cheese and slices of whole grain bread instead of the usual white bread are the prelude to a fried fish feast. The seafood combo overpriced at $9.95, but everything else sampled a winner. Catfish sandwich featured five hefty chunks of fish, crisp and crunchy. Excellent potato salad, sweet and creamy.

Cucina Calandra, 216-234 Route 46 East, Fairfield; (973) 575-7720. High quality, reasonable prices. Forget boring fried calamari and try the grilled calamari over arugula here. Great mussels fra diavolo, and the zuppa di pesce is one of the best anywhere.

Dairy Queen, 1123 Stuyvesant Ave., Irvington; (973) 372-7952. Local cop's tip: the frozen bananas dipped in chocolate and rolled in peanuts. The coldest of all the ice creams sampled.

Di Paolo Brothers Bakery, 399 Bloomfield Ave., Newark; (973) 485-6737. Any bakery that makes pizza — and an excellent one at that — is a bakery worth putting on your speed-dial. Start with the prosciutto-stuffed biscuits; you may have trouble stopping, they're that good. First-rate bread; the pane casareccio, super-crusty, tastes great right out of the bag. Good brownies, and pignoli. But the black-and-white cake seemed ordinary.

Dickie Dee's, 380 Bloomfield Ave., Newark; (973) 483-9396. "Please keep your feet on dee floor," reads a sign at this legendary hot dog haven, open since 1958. Decorated with pictures of various saints and one piece of artwork — a still life of hot dogs and potatoes. The Italian hot dog is good but the sausage sandwich better. Brave? Try the Ulcer Special, an all-cheese sandwich.

DiPietro Foods, 1701 Springfield Ave., Maplewood; (973) 762-4077. Started in Livingston 40 years ago, moved to Maplewood in 1975. Creamier ravioli than those at Florence Ravioli. Manicotti even creamier, if that is possible, but the stuffed shells not as good. Try the homemade sausage.

Divina Ristorante, 461 Bloomfield Ave., Caldwell; (973) 228-5228. Try the Linguine Marechiara, Chicken with Mushrooms and Pizza Napolotano. Everything's good.

Donnie's Dogs, Fairmount Cemetary, Newark. Excellent hot relish and sauerkraut. Judged state's best dirty-water dog by the S.W.A.T. Dog team.

Eder's BBQ, 301 S. Orange Ave., Newark; (973) 621-0808. Lively little hole-in-the-wall delivers good ribs and chicken. They use 100 percent natural wood charcoal. The chicken is marinated in lemon, vinegar, garlic, salt and other spices. The ribs are greasy, fatty and oh-so-good. And don't forget to try the rice and beans, the tostones and some of the homemade hot sauce.

El Bandido, 548 Main St., Orange; (973) 678-8631. Restaurant a series of artful nooks and crannies, brought to stunning life with brightly colored murals. Beef burrito not as chunky or chewy as others sampled. Creamy-good refried beans. Savory salsa — on the syrupy side, but spicy and flavorful. Best item: the camarones Acapulco, cheese-stuffed, bacon-wrapped shrimp with a piquant green sauce.

Eppes Essen, 105 E. Mt. Pleasant Ave., Livingston; (973) 994-1120. Excellent pastrami. Reubens, like buffalo wings, suffer from a depressing sameness; Eppes Essen's version boasts a dare-to-be-different Russian dressing. The Bubbie is da bomb; it's a great, gooey sandwich with brisket, fried onions, Muenster and Russian dressing. The electric-green cabbage slaw looks weird, but is quite good.

Essex Grand Buffet, Essex Green Mall, 326 Prospect Ave., West Orange; (973) 325-8898. "Grand" does not do this place justice; more than 200 items available, including mountains of crawfish, 10 kinds of chicken, plus noodle bar, soup bar, sushi bar and salad bar. Good, viscous egg drop soup. Broccoli fresh and crunchy. Excellent salmon. Rubbery salt-and-pepper squid. Greasy chicken teriyaki. Best buffet sampled.

Fatima's, 487 Bloomfield Ave., Newark; (973) 482-2811. Old-time Italian market-deli; brawny construction workers and old men in tattered T-shirts enjoy sausage and peppers, broccoli rabe and other items. Have them make you a fresh mozzarella, tomatoes and roasted red peppers sandwich.

Fernandes Steak House, 158 Fleming Ave., Newark; (973) 589-4344. Bank-turned-restaurant. The broiled seafood combination is a boatload of marine munch. Better-than-average filet mignon, served smoking and sizzling on a cylindrical stone. The blue sangria is smooth and seductive. Anyone who makes Windex jokes should be shown the door.

Fornos of Spain, 47 Ferry St., Newark; (973) 589-4767. Ferry Street fixture is a suave, stylish gathering place. Portions the day's biggest, and in the Ironbound, that's saying something. Roasted lamb shank — three mammoth hunks of meat in peppery, tomato-ey sauce — excellent. So is the filet mignon, menacing and meaty.

Forte Pizzeria and Ristorante, 182 Bloomfield Ave., Caldwell; (973) 403-9411. Excellent pasta and pizzas; you'll love the fresh, feisty bruschetta pizza with mozzarella, basil, arugula and a seeming bushel-load of fresh tomatoes on top.

Frankie D's, 227 Centre St., Nutley; (973) 6674700. Outstanding mustard, average dog, below-average roll.

Franklin Steak House, 522 Franklin Ave., Nutley; (973) 667-1755. "Cheers"-like atmosphere. Friendly bartenders. First-rate filet mignon and other steaks.

Gaslight Brewery and Restaurant, 15 South Orange Ave., South Orange; (973) 762-7077. Attractive, dartboard-decorated hangout. Wide-ranging menu. Must-try: the beer cheese soup. Good ribs, pretty good Roquefort and roasted pear salad, great cilantro shrimp. Best brews: the Pirate Ale, tangy and captivating, and Abbey Normal.

Gencarelli's, 446 Broad St., Bloomfield; (973) 743-1480. Cheese-cake to live and die for. Cannoli made to order. Huge turnovers. Good Italian loaf bread.

Gimmee Jimmy's Cookies, 23 Church St., Montclair; (973) 325-0917. There are 18 varieties of cookies; start with the double chocolate walnut and see if you can stay away from the other 17. Owner Jimmy Libman and many of his employees are deaf.

Gina's Bakery, 110 Walnut St., Montclair; (973) 233-1010. Tiny bakery offered some big hits, including the oatmeal raisin cookies and chocolate-covered strawberries. Decent scones; brownies merely OK.

Gone with the Wings, 236 Franklin Ave., Nutley; (973) 661-9464. "Frankly, my dear, we do give a damn" is the slogan at this takeout joint. Hot wings, while meaty enough, coated with unremarkable Buf-falo wing sauce. Medium wings tastier. Barbecue wings, basted with a tangy, tomato-ey sauce, among day's best.

Greek Delights, 14 Park St., Montclair; (973) 783-9100. A real Greek diner — the menu features moussaka, dolmades, spanakopita and other Greek treats. The Greek salad will make the one at your local diner look weak by comparison. Other winners: the stuffed cabbage; chicken and lamb kebabs, and the cinnamon-scented pastichio. A must-try: the fries, sprinkled with garlic and lemon. Best fries we had all summer.

Green Jade, 227 Franklin Ave., Nutley; (973) 284-1222. The all-you-can-eat lunchtime buffet offers a staggering variety of food, including five-flavor pork, egg rolls .. and zeppoles. OK, so not all of it is Chinese.

Hamburgao, 288 Lafayette St., Newark; (973) 465-1776. Broaden your hamburger horizons and try a burger here; it might include chicken breast, ham, bacon, mozzarella, egg, corn, potato sticks, let-tuce, tomato and mayo. Enroladinho de presunto e queijo (fried pastry filled with ham and cheese), irresistible little treats, as are the coxinha catupiry, Brazilian cheese-filled fried chicken balls.

Harris Diner, 21 N. Park St., East Orange; (973) 675-9703. Tums commercials filmed here, but that's no reflection on the food, which is always good. My favorite Jersey diner breakfast: two eggs sunnyside up, bacon, grits, whole wheat toast and coffee at the Harris.

Havana Sandwich Cafe, 17 Franklin St., Bloomfield; (973) 429-3303. It's hard to imagine a better Cubano sandwich than the one served here. We also loved the Cuban tamale. The roasted pork skins are irresistible, the mamey shake delicious.

Holsten's, 1063 Broad St., Bloomfield; (973) 338-7091. Started as Strubie's in 1939. Classic ice cream parlor/luncheonette. The last scene in the last episode of "The Sopranos" was filmed here.

It's A Wrap, 9 Village Plaza, South Orange; (973) 762-7474. Run by a couple originally from South Africa, Elaine and Russ Gordon, who got tired of the corporate rat race and decided to open a wrap/smoothie joint. Their hummina hummina wrap is a humdinger, filled with hummus, romaine, carrot, tomato and spinach. We also loved the rare roast beef and curry chicken breast wraps.

Je's, 260 Halsey St., Newark; (973) 623-8848. The heart of Newark's soul food scene. Shaquille O'Neil among the celebs who have found their way here. The meat loaf here is better than Mom's, trust us.

Jimmy Buff's, 60 Washington St., West Orange; (973) 325-9897. Buff's invented the Italian hot dog — Jersey's contribution to cholesterol naughtiness or nirvana, depending on how you look at it. Good sausage, too. "An awesome greasy hot dog," one of our S.W.A.T. Dog team members raved. A must-stop.

JJ's Truck, Bloomfield Avenue, Newark. Silver truck a Bloomfield Avenue fixture. Nice kick to the chili, but the Sabrett's all-beef just OK.

John's Place, 24 Wright St., Newark; (973) 824-9233. The thick pork chops are deep-fried to near-perfection. Waffles-and-chicken on menu.

John's Texas Weiners, 63 Branford Place, Newark; (973) 643-6133. Small dog — "looks like something they served in the Depression," one Muncher noted. Good chopped-pork sandwich and cheesesteak.

Johnny's on the Green, 440 Parsonage Hill Road, Short Hills; (973) 467-8882. (Formerly Fore Seasons Restaurant.) Sit outside, next to the putting green. Start with the eggplant rollettes, nice and creamy, filled with ricotta, topped with mozzarella. The bar pie is a decided improvement over bar pies you may have known and not loved. Excellent chicken parm, but the salmon in the spinach/salmon salad dried out.

JR's, Franklin Avenue and Carolyn Street, Belleville. Nice spicy chili at Ralph Caruso's orange-and-white striped truck. Get the "sweet works"

(mustard, kraut, relish) or the "hot works" (mustard, kraut and red onions). Uses Sabrett's hot dogs.

The Landmark, 259 W. Mount Pleasant Ave., Livingston; (973) 533-9787. Former Colonial stagecoach stop now cozy bar/restaurant. Good burgers; decent pizza.

Laughing Burrito, 392 Bloomfield Ave., Caldwell; (973) 618-9600. Tiny takeout specializes in not-so-ordinary dishes; strawberry melon soup, Southwest style spaghetti squash and frozen margarita mousse pie among selections. Salsas here the freshest-tasting of all those sampled. Tropical fruit salsa sweet and sensational. Excellent chili, rich and spicy.

Lenny and John's Subs, 161 Bloomfield Ave., Bloomfield; (973) 429-1736. No-frills neighborhood sub shop. The tuna sub seemed too mayonnaisey, and the roast beef sub just ok, but the subs are loaded with meat, and they use good bread.

Libretti's, 554 Nassau St., Orange; (973) 673-5155. Start by dipping the pizza bread — crunchy on the outside, sensationally soft on the inside — in imported olive oil. The linguini with red clam sauce might have been the best meal of our spaghetti-and-meatballs excursion. Other pastas not far behind.

Livingston Bagel and Deli, 37 E. Northfield Road, Livingston; (973) 994-1915. Heavenly chocolate babka, delicious minced nova, chewy egg bagels in full-service deli.

Lombardi's, 597F Pompton Ave., Cedar Grove; (973) 239-6600. Pizzeria as sports shrine; photos and magazine covers of athletes fill every available inch of wall space. The cheese pie placed in the middle of our ranking, but the sausage is super — big chunks of not-too-sweet, not fennel-overpowered meat (from Appetito in Union City). It's so good you may find yourself picking off chunks as you're driving down the parkway, as the Big Dog's driver did.

Los Tapatios, 10 Main St., West Orange; (973) 736-8869. Good salsa, real good huevos rancheros, superb guacamole. You'll even love the refried beans.

Lou's/World's First Italian Style Hot Dogs, 202 14th Ave., Newark; (973) 621-9468. Jimmy Buff's, creator of the first Italian hot dog, started right here, and the current owners serve up an authentic, drippy-greasy dog.

Luigi's, 561 Bloomfield Ave., Newark; (973) 481-9696. Popular neighborhood spot. Rice balls and spiedini made for promising start, but many of the entrees, while super-sized, are over-sauced. The veal saltimbocca swimming — make that drowning — in its wine sauce, and the Chicken Savoy overwhelmed by balsamic. One dish we liked: Chicken Murphy.

MaDear's, 39 Glenridge Ave., Montclair; (973) 746-5600. Small, spare place delivers big-time; the smothered pork chops, fried chicken and yams all are memorable. Breakfast sandwiches daily, and fish and grits on Saturday.

Mangia Questa, 558 Bloomfield Ave., Verona; (973) 239-7444. Owner Janet Tedesco appeared in an episode of "The Sopranos;" several of the stars have eaten in her restaurant. Nice meatballs. Good, thick prosciutto and honey maple ham sandwich. Tedesco's sauce, enlivened by red peppers and fennel, well worth a dip. Best item sampled: the broccoli rabe, wonderfully crunchy.

Mark and Julie's, 476 Pleasant Valley Way, West Orange; (973) 731-6011. Owners Mark and Julie Orenstein make their own hard ice cream, 52 flavors in all in their immaculate, white-walled shop. Chocolate milkshake thick as molasses and delicious.

Meema's Country Desserts, 107 Pine St., Montclair; (973) 783-0100. The vanilla cheesecake — light, luscious — is first-rate. We made quick work of the powdered-sugar-topped pignoli and the chocolate pecan tart, but the pies had bland, powdery crusts.

Mexicali Rose, 10 Park St., Montclair; (973) 746-9005. Chicken Problema and Lindy's Backyard Steak among dishes. Nonalcoholic pina coladas smooth and delicious.

Michael's Roscommon House, 531 Joralemon St., Belleville; (973)-759-0060. Neighborhood bar with better-than-average food. Best burger of trip found here, the kind that doesn't need any fancy toppings. Advertises "the world's best chocolate fudge layer cake." It's nowhere near that good.

Millburn Deli, 328 Millburn Ave., Millburn; (973) 379-5800. Don't be alarmed by the loud, honking horn; it just means someone has ordered a Gobbler, a yummy turkey, stuffing and cranberry sauce-stuffed sandwich. We loved the breads here, and the Sloppy Joe. Pastrami not as good as the Evergreen's, though.

Nasto's Olde World Desserts, 236-40 Jefferson St., Newark; (973) 589-3333. The Ironbound and ice cream can only mean one thing: Nasto's. Opened in 1939, Nasto's supplies ice cream to 700 restaurants, hotels and caterers; you can buy it in the spotless, blue-awninged retail store. They do the basics — vanilla, chocolate and strawberry — well.

Nauna's Bella Casa, 151 Valley Road, Montclair; (973) 744-3232. "Grandma's Beautiful House." Try the sundried tomato-and-artichoke hearts pizza.

Nicolo's, 6 Baldwin St., Montclair; (973) 746-1398. Plenty of Italian specialties, including chicken cutlet, and escarole and beans. Standout breads: the thick, crusty ciabatta, and the softer, more rounded panella. One word for any of the breads dipped into Nicolo's homemade marinara: bellissimo. Best loaf here may be the sausage- and mozzarella-stuffed bread.

Nubian Flavor Restaurant, 410 Springfield Ave., Newark; (973) 242-2238. Down-home diner on stretch of Springfield Avenue that is slowly coming to life. Thirteen stools, time-warp wooden booths and faded tile floor add to charm. Terrific turkey sausage, alone worth the trip. Recommended: the waffles; French toast, nice and cinnamon-y; the fresh-tasting eggs; and the salmon croquettes.

O'Reilly's Bar and Grill, 2208 Millburn Ave., Maplewood; (973) 378-9774. Hammerhead shark, caught off Key West, prowls the airspace above the bar. Cajun wings greasy but good, with a faint Caribbean jerk-like coating. The five-alarm wings more like one-alarm, and there is a world of pain between the mildly spicy "suicide" wings here and the fire-eater wings at Cluck-U.

Ocha, 403 Bloomfield Ave., Caldwell; (973) 228-8856. This cool, casual haunt rated Top Dog on our sushi trip. The scallops carpacchio look, and taste, great. An absolute must: the sushi pizza, with tomato, seaweed, scallion, onion and a spicy barbecue sauce. Yum.

The Original Pancake House, 817 Bloomfield Ave., West Caldwell; (973) 575-9161. The Dutch Baby a cross between French toast and pie; the Apple Pancake — a gooey, globby gargantuan pancake — is better. The bacon — thick, crisp, hickory-smoked slices from Oregon — deserves a spot in the Bacon Hall of Fame.

Otto's, 392 Bloomfield Ave., Caldwell; (973) 228-9555. Nearly-cold dogs not a good introduction. Bland chili. Decent Italian hot dog.

Pal's Cabin, 265 Prospect Ave., West Orange; (973) 731-4000. A Jersey food institution. Started as a 10-by-12 hot dog stand in 1932 in the midst of the Depression. Today, it's a seemingly never-ending, multi-level restaurant. Burgers the real deal, fat and juicy. Good, salty fries, but below-average onion rings. "Famous" cheesecake seriously overrated.

People's Choice, 63 Central Ave., East Orange; (973) 674-8260. Cramped, neon-lit storefront can get busy on weekends. Best dish: the stew beef. Wimpy jerk chicken, though.

The Petite Cafe, 231 Franklin Ave., Nutley; (973) 667-7778. Traditional morning favorites updated and redefined. The French toast is stuffed with sweet cream cheese, and you can get egg-white omelets, steel-cut Irish oatmeal and a fresh fruit yogurt parfait. Breakfast burrito not as perky as expected; cheesesteak egg wrap tasty but salty.

Pilgrim Diner, 82 Pompton Ave., Cedar Grove; (973) 239-2900. Fresh blueberries in the blueberry pancakes, and the bananas artfully blended into the banana pancakes. Good, honest buttermilk pancakes.

The Priory Restaurant, 233 W. Market St., Newark; (973) 242-8012. Ever want to eat in church? You can, at the Priory. Nice lunchtime buffet, reasonably-priced.

Raymond's, 28 Church St., Montclair; (973) 744-9263. Stylish breakfast/brunch spot, reminiscent of a train station waiting room. The French toast — towers of baguette bread — is a work of art, but unfulfilling. The corn batter cakes and spinach, tomato and goat cheese omelet, though, are outstanding.

Red Hawk Diner, Montclair State University, 1 Normal Ave., Montclair; (973) 655-4057. The nation's first on-campus diner, the shiny red Red Hawk is named after the school's mascot. It's a stylish, stainless hangout, but the food could have been better. Excellent onion rings, good fries. But the greens in the salad are wilted and the jerk chicken breast overwhelmed with cheese. Decent pastrami.

Reservoir Pizza, 106 W. South Orange Ave., South Orange; (973) 762-9795. The original Reservoir opened in Newark's North Ward in 1935. The unofficial motto here: good food, and plenty of it.

Ritz Diner, 72 E. Mount Pleasant Ave., Livingston; (973) 533-1213. Abandon all diner-pie stereotypes when you enter here. The open-face blueberry pie, with a tractor load of berries, screams to be served chilled. The cherry crumb pie a mountainous, thick-crumbed — maybe too thick — creation, but the cherries are sweet and delicious.

Scuttlebutts Pub, 400 Centre St., Nutley; (973) 661-2026. Badges from every conceivable police department, or so it seems, on display. But the wings, coated with that cliched sauce, are mediocre. The hot wings had a bit of a bite, at least.

Seabra's Rodizio, 1034 McCarter Highway, Newark; (973) 622-6221. Staggering salad bar, stocked with 40-plus items, with a selection of olive oils and vinegars from Spain, Portugal and Italy. Great thick, crunchy bread, from Teixeira's. Dried-out ribs, but juicy chicken. Dynamite top sirloin, but the alligator, filet mignon, pork loin, turkey wrapped in bacon and other meats suffer from too much salt or too much time on the motorized spit.

Smokey's American BBQ, 312 Orange Road, Montclair; (973) 233-0087. We liked the fried salmon and crab cakes more than the ribs and roasted chicken. The sweet potato salad, flecked with cucumber, the day's best side.

Solar do Minho, 15 Cleveland St., Belleville; (973) 844-0500. Best rodizio sampled. One can't-miss appetizer: the octopus (polvo a Feira),

the most tender of its kind we've ever tasted. Sirloin stuffed with cheese, onions, carrots and peppers a first-round rodizio knockout. Salty, overdone spare ribs; average sausage. But turkey wrapped in bacon, sirloin in garlic sauce, and the pork loin all outstanding.

Sonny's, 123 South Orange Ave., South Orange; (973) 763-9634. "Hot Bagels," proclaims the red neon sign in window of this tiny shop, opened by Sonny Amster in 1970. Are plain bagels boring bagels? You won't think so after trying one out of the oven here.

Spanish Sangria, 157 Magazine St., Newark; (973) 344-9286. Away from the Ferry Street hubbub. Start with the sausage, blackened on the edges. The swordfish a monstrous piece of fish, but slightly dried out. Standout: the bacalao (dried codfish): flaky and succulent.

St. James Gate Publick House, 167 Maplewood Ave., Maplewood; (973) 378-2222. Cool Irish pub in village of Maplewood, with picture windows and a century-old bar. Terrific, juicy burger. A must-try: the Publick House chips: browned, super-crispy and altogether addictive, although the quality can vary.

Star Tavern, 400 High St., Orange; (973) 675-3336. American flags on the wall, a poster of a maniacally grinning Jack Nicholson from "The Shining" behind the bar. Sausage pie not top-of-the-line, but the cheese pie is gloriously, but not overly, greasy, the crust slightly — and nicely — burned at the edges. The Star makes star-quality thin-crust.

Starlite Restaurant and Pizzeria, 993 Pleasant Valley Way, West Orange; (973) 736-9440. Neighborhood institution; opened in 1961. Not on same level as, say, the Star Tavern, but still a good pie.

Stretch's Italian Restaurant, 18 E. Mount Pleasant Ave., Livingston; (973) 994-4043. Stretch's salad — mozzarella, roasted peppers, black olives, red onions, tomatoes and balsamic vinegar — drew raves from Federico Castelluccio of "The Sopranos." Don't dare leave without trying the Chicken Savoy.

Supreme Bakery, 40 Main St., West Orange; (973) 736-1732. Thomas Edison may have been in the middle of eating a Supreme Bakery doughnut when he invented the light bulb. That's according to Supreme's website, anyway. The chocolate cheesecake tasted almost sour. But the New York-style cheesecake an instant hit: soft and creamy, although the strawberries on top could have been fresher. Skip the peach cobbler and the dry brownies.

Sweet Potato and Pecan, 103 Forest St., Montclair; (973) 746-3444. Jamaican-born cook serves up a savory storm of soul, Southern and Jamaican food. Start with the homemade iced tea/lemonade and proceed to the barbecue ribs, oxtails, grilled salmon or other entrees. And don't forget the sweet potato pie!

Teixeira's Bakery, 184 Ferry St., Newark; (973) 589-8875. This Ferry Street fixture supplies bread to many Ironbound restaurants. Nondescript French bread, but the Portuguese roll, with its trademark hard, coned shell and soft, chewy interior, is excellent. You'll love the custard cups. Good coffee and espresso. Great place to spend a rainy day.

Thai Chef, 664 Bloomfield Ave., Montclair; (973) 783-4994. Many dishes — wild mushroom soup, fried squid green curry, pan fried scallops — not ordinarily found at Thai restaurants. Chicken curry puff mushy and a bit overdone, but the steamed Thai ravioli, meltingly soft and bathing in Worcestershire sauce, probably the day's best appetizer. Adventurous? Try the frog legs green curry.

Tinga Taqueria, 321 Millburn Ave., Millburn; (973) 218-9500. Busy, happy, hip place, with the most adventurous menu of the places visited. Build your nachos out of everything from creamy black beans to fresh sauteed spinach. Nachos nothing special. Chips nowhere near as good as those at Lupe's Cancun, but the overall ingredients fresher. Good sauces. Standard guacamole — we didn't find really good guacamole at any stop.

Tony Da Caneca, 72 Elm Road, Newark; (973) 589-6882. There was a Tony but never a Caneca at this Ironbound haunt; caneca is Portuguese for the clay jars wine was kept in. Chorizo set on fire at your table. Excellent steaks and seafood, especially the formidable grilled prawns.

Tony's Specialized Hot Dogs, Branch Brook Park, Lake Street and Park Avenue, Newark. Parked in same spot for the past 40 years. Among the best hot dog wagons in the state. His hot onions are fiery. The Super Dog — chili, kraut, cheese, mustard, relish, hot onions — may have been my favorite dog of the S.W.A.T. Dog summer.

Toro Loco Mexican Restaurant, 23 Valley St., South Orange; (973) 761-1515. Looking for a nice quiet romantic Mexican dinner? This is not the place. Tables set close together, and it can get noisy. The guacamole is strictly assembly-line stuff. Recommended: the queso fundido, chimichangas and mixiotes Veracruz (chicken or pork marinated in Mexican chilies, herbs, olives and butter and wrapped in plantain leaves and steamed).

Town Hall Deli, 60 Valley St., South Orange; (973) 762-4900. Bills itself as the birthplace of the Sloppy Joe, although Sloppy Joe's in Key West, among others, disagree. Town Hall's classic version is a monstrous ham, tongue and Swiss cheese sandwich with homemade Russian dressing and cole slaw, cut into eight squares.

Watchung Delicatessen, 117 Watchung Ave., Montclair; (973) 744-1452. Busy, bustling deli. The Angry Dwarf — turkey, melted Muenster, tomato, onions and mayo — is marvelous. So is the "The" Sandwich

— peppered turkey, bacon, melted cheddar and Russian dressing on a toasted roll.

Zen, 277 Eisenhower Parkway, Livingston; (973) 533-6828. Elegant but not stuffy atmosphere. The toro (fatty tuna) is near-perfect: thin, luscious and lovely. Not far behind: the Heat Wave (spicy tuna, spicy salmon and asparagus) and the Fuji-apple-filled Maccabee Roll.

Gloucester

Joe's Pizza, 108 Swedesboro Road, Mullica Hill; (856) 223-9921. Voted best pizza in Gloucester County, but your neighborhood pizzeria will be better.

Hudson

Amanda's, 908 Washington St., Hoboken; (201) 798-0101. Cool digs; housed in former private residence. Good brunch. Favorites: the roasted sweet pepper omelet with herb cream cheese; poached eggs with crab hash and orange hollandaise sauce; grilled steak and eggs. The Jack Benny — eggs Benedict — nearly stole the show.

Benanti's Italian Delicatessen, 16 W. 22nd St., Bayonne; (201) 437-5525. Choose your bread from one of the cardboard boxes by the window, take it to the counter, and tell Charlie Benanti or one of his crew what you want on it. Great, old-school Italian deli.

Boulevard Drinks, 48 Journal Square, Jersey City; (201) 656-1855. Belongs in the New Jersey Fast Food Hall of Fame, if there were one. Bright, blinding-yellow walls; bright-green menu; fitful, flickering neon sign and better-than-expected hot dogs make for a one-of-a-kind stop.

Broadway Diner, 1081 Broadway, Bayonne; (201) 437-7336. "World Famous Pancakes" served here and in sister location in Summit, but you'll find better elsewhere.

Brothers Quality Bakery and Deli, 365 Kearny Ave., Kearny; (201) 991-4364. The cream puff tower is a nearly foot-high construction of cake, cherries, whipped cream and cream puffs. You'll like the apple-raisin streusel, cherry danish, the brownies, and the bread.

Carlo's City Hall Bake Shop, 95 Washington St., Hoboken; (201) 659-3671. Patty Hearst has bought crumbcake here; what more do you need to know? The owner, Mary Valastro, is a charmer. The sfogliatelle, or lobster tail, with its superb, flaky crust, is a must. So are the pignoli. And quasimal, a nutty, slighty sweet cookie. Good, creamy cannoli. One disappointment: the chocolate cheesecake.

Chart House Restaurant, Lincoln Harbor/Pier D-T, Weehawken; (201) 348-6628. For pure dining drama, the Chart House may be unparalleled in New Jersey. Tables offer an Imax-like sweep of the Manhattan skyline. Seared ahi tuna, with a lemon-mustard sauce, is fresh and fabulous. Spicy kick to the lobster bisque. Linguine served in a sassy, sensational tomato-basil sauce.

El Unico Restaurant, 4211 Park Ave., Union City; (201) 867-9801. For sheer value, the hands-down winner on Munchmobile 2001. Great range of soda, a United Nations of sweet, sugary sensations. Pork with rice, beans and black cassava undistinguished, but the grilled chicken breast, with rice and firm, flavorful beans, a standout.

Feed Your Soul, 520 Jersey Ave., Jersey City; (646) 498-8432. Mya Jacobson left her job as a trader on the New York Stock Exchange to open a cookie factory/store in downtown Jersey City. Her chocolate brownie chunk cookie, topped with white chocolate morsels, is fabulous.

Feelgood Cafe, 1309 Paterson Pike Road, Secaucus; (201) 223-5670. Former car repair garage now an attractive restaurant. You must try the oxtail, enlivened by a puckish, peppery sauce. The chicken fricassee almost as good, although we were underwhelmed by the pork spare ribs. Chocoholics: Don't you dare leave without trying some of the incredible triple-chocolate cake.

Gina's Pizza and Restaurant, 503 Frank Rodgers Blvd., Harrison; (973) 482-4883. The absolute biggest slices in New Jersey next to the Sawmill in Seaside Park, which does, after all, claim to have the world's largest slice.

Ibby's Famous Falafel, 303 Grove St., Jersey City; (201) 432-2400. Tiny, atmospheric storefront. The falafel may be famous, but the baba ghanoush and hummus are better. The tabouli, a mixture of cracked wheat with fresh vegetables, is a minced marvel. Try the homemade desserts, especially the warm apple-pie-like kanafe.

La Isla Restaurant, 104 Washington St., Hoboken; (201) 659-8197. Omar Giner's Cuban restaurant bridges the gap between neighborhood Spanish restaurants in North Jersey and Nuevo Latino restaurants in the city. His Cuban sandwich takes the usual ingredients — pork, ham, Swiss cheese — and tops them with a garlic sauce.

Laico's, 67 Terhune Ave., Jersey City; (201) 434-4115. Great neighborhood restaurant/hangout ruled by Louie Laico. Good pasta fagioli.

Lee Sims, 743 Bergen Ave., Jersey City; (201) 433-1308. Tiny, fluorescent-lit candy shop squished between a discount store and clothing shop. Runaway group hit: the honeycomb-like sponge pillows, sweet and crackly. Great dark chocolate coffee beans and dark chocolate breakaway.

Magic Fountain, 907 Broadway, Bayonne; (201) 823-1114. Classic walk-up ice cream stand on Bayonne's main drag. Marvelous soft ice cream here — soft, smooth, not too sugary, no cloying aftertaste. Try the vanilla with fresh bananas and hot fudge.

Mr. Nino's, 442 Bergen St., Harrison; (973) 484-5770. Looks like your typical strip mall pizzeria, but Nino D'Angelo's Sicilian pie is the model Sicilian: a crust both chewy and crunchy, super sauce, good cheese and quality, not-out-of-the-jar toppings. His margarita and plain pies are nice.

Petridis, 546 Broadway, Bayonne; (201) 436-0974. Started as hot dog cart in 1923. Not a memorable hot dog, but we fancied the fries.

Piccolo's Clam Bar, 92 Clinton St., Hoboken; (201) 653-0564. Sparky Spaccavento started the business in 1955 at age 17. Once famous as a clam bar, but they haven't served them since 1968.

Spanish Pavillion Restaurant, 31 Harrison Ave., Harrison; (973) 485-7750. Convivial atmosphere; dig the deer and bull heads in the bar. Try the camarones provencial: shrimp sauteed in white wine, brandy, garlic and lemon. Good flan.

Stewart's Root Beer, 938 Passaic Ave., Kearny; (201) 998-0600. One of the vanishing breed of Stewart's with carhop service. Nothing better than a frosted mug of root beer on a hot day. Hot dog chili one of the meatier ones anywhere, but the dog itself, a Haydu, merely ordinary.

Subs Galore, 327 Kearny Ave., Kearny; (201) 998-7827. Unusual items: deep-fried breaded ravioli, onion rings dipped in beer batter. Try the turkey melt sub, with mozzarella, roasted peppers and honey mustard. Great chicken at sister store next door.

Tops Diner, 500 Passaic Ave., East Newark; (973) 481-0490. Ever-busy diner just across the river from downtown Newark. Dependable dinners, better breakfasts.

Torico Homemade Ice Cream Parlor, 20 Erie St., Jersey City; (201) 432-9458. Flavors reflect Jersey City's diverse populace — mamey, lychee, ube (an Asian purple yam) among the more unusual offerings. They do chocolate well here; the chocolate-chocolate chunk and chocolate marshmallow are highly recommended.

White Mana, 470 Tonnelle Ave., Jersey City; (201) 963-1441. The first diner to go worldwide through its DinerCam. Atmospheric spot; owner Mario Costa says the White Mana was at the 1939 New York World's Fair. Good burgers.

Hunterdon

Annandale Deli, 55 Beaver Ave., Annandale; (908) 735-5232. Nice touch: choice of five kinds of bread for your sub. Pastrami, piled high on Portuguese roll with mustard, pretty close to hoagie heaven.

Baker's Treat, 42 Route 12, Flemington; (908) 782-3458. Owner Nancy Baron donates 100 percent of her profits to programs for women in early recovery from alcohol and substance abuse. Two super salads: the bowtie pasta salad with olives, tomatoes, peppers and a dusting of cheese, and the Mediterranean tuna nicoise. Standout desserts: the trail mix cookie and the raspberry oat square.

Basil Bandwagon Natural Market, 276 Route 31/202, Raritan Township; (908) 788-5737. Sprawling health food market. The hummus sandwich a smooth sprout-and-red-onion-dotted operator. The falafel didn't come off well, and neither did the cucumber lemonade. But Vegas Elvis — a sandwich with organic bananas, granola, honey, peanut butter and Bacuns bits on multigrain bread — saved the day.

Blue Fish Grill, 9 Central Ave., Flemington; (908) 237-4528. Call this unprepossessing restaurant fast food fish-style. But it's more than fried shrimp and fish and chips; we really liked the grouper po' boy sandwich, fish taco, and orange roughy in pineapple juice.

Bridge Street Dog Pound, 10 Bridge St., Milford; (908) 995-7750. Creative, crazy combos. Recommended: the River Rat, with fried peppers, barbecue sauce, onions and mustard.

The Brownie Express, P.O. Box 49, Pittstown; (908) 735-6799. Big, bold brownies, bursting with chocolate, nut and fudge goodness. Available by mail order or Internet only

The Cafe at Rosemont, 88 Kingwood-Stockton Road, Rosemont; (609) 397-4097. This country luncheonette, with hardwood floors and creaky front porch, is a ride from just about anywhere, but worth it. Good breakfasts; some pricey. Each Wednesday night, they host a dinner featuring the cuisine of a different country or region.

California Grill, Kitchen Expo Plaza, 1 Route 31, Flemington; (908) 806-7141. Salad names — Never Once Gave a Thought to Landing, Just Jump, All Across the Horizon and others — reflect a near-fatal helicopter crash endured by owner. The Strawberry Masquerade looks great, tastes better — baby spinach, arugula, endive, hearts of palm, toasted walnuts, goat cheese, cucumber and dried strawberries.

Country Pride Restaurant, TravelCenters of America Truck Stop, Route 78, Exit 7, Bloomsbury; (908) 479-4136. Gift shop offers one-stop-shopping for the travelin' man and woman. Immense, surprisingly good pancakes. Throw in some biscuits, you'll have plenty of fuel for the road.

Cracker Barrel, 6 Frontage Drive, Franklin Twp.; (908) 713-9205. One chain that does it right. Country-store atmosphere; good, hearty breakfasts. Grits slightly on the watery side, but delicious sourdough French toast and thick, crisp bacon.

The Fudge Shoppe, 461 Route 202, Raritan Twp.; (908) 782-7123. Atmospheric, hardwood-floored candy store once a state police barracks. Love the chocolate-covered strawberries and blueberries; the nonpareils may be without equal.

Full Moon, 23 Bridge St., Lambertville; (609) 397-1096. Airy, high-ceilinged cafe has carved out a nice little niche on the breakfast/lunch front. Goat cheese salad best of those sampled. The house ranch dressing is smooth and sensational; the honey Dijon, strong and assertive.

Gronsky's Milk House, 125 W. Main St., High Bridge; (908) 638-6030. Local landmark nestled picturesquely on the riverside. We stopped for for ice cream, but you'll want to go for the breakfasts, fine and filling.

Hot Rod's, 2113 Route 31, Glen Gardner; (908) 537-7022. Bland dog, but one Muncher called the chili one of the summer's best.

JR's Bakery, 19 Commerce St., Raritan Twp.; (908) 806-3904. It's a one-stop sugar stop; the sticky buns, loaded with big juicy raisins, are sensationally, sinfully caramel-sticky. Nice jelly and cream doughnuts. Skip the Long Johns, though.

Mangia Bella Pizza, 3568 Route 22 West, Whitehouse Station; (908) 823-1873. Chicken Pasquale simmers in a delectable butter-and-wine sauce. The ravioli alla Aragosta will make a convert of anyone turned off by standard vodka sauce. The gnocchi swam in a savory tomato sauce.

Mark Koppe's General Store, 39 Church St., Bloomsbury; (908) 479-6100. Pancakes and frozen bait: What more could you want? Small grill, huge pancakes, great atmosphere.

Market Roost, 65 Main St., Flemington; (908) 788-4949. Country-store setting. No buffet line; order from menu. Super sticky buns. Memorable eggs Benedict. Also recommended: English muffin, Kahlua French toast, grilled focaccia.

Melick's Town Farm, 170 Oldwick Road, Oldwick; (908) 439-2955. The best pies of the roadside markets, none of which actually made their own. The apple pie a sweet success, with its sugary latticed crust and cinnamon-laced fruit. The Very Berry is lovely and luscious, a near-perfect blend of tart and sweet.

Miller's, 2 Beaver Ave., Annandale; (908) 735-9915. More road-house than restaurant, with its pool table and neon beer signs. Right off Routes 22 and 78. Terrific thin-crust, crackly good, not too greasy. Either the plain pie or the sausage pie would make it on the favorites list of every Muncher except one.

Mom's Restaurant, 36 John Ringo Road, Ringoes; (908) 782-8025. Breakfast served until 2 p.m. in this cozy, drape-decorated restaurant. Elvis is in the building — the peanut butter and banana French toast is a delight. Excellent home fries, crisp and salty. Good eggs Benedict, buttermilk pancakes, and Polynesian French toast — three slices layered with fresh bananas and topped with toasted coconut and powdered sugar.

Peaceful Valley Orchards, 150 Pittstown Road, Union Township; (908) 730-7748. Open-air market stocks fruit, vegetables, even fresh and frozen pork. And pies. Best of the bunch: the red raspberry. The strawberry rhubarb judged the day's best rhubarb. Good cherry pie.

Pizza Como, 5 Old Highway 22, Clinton; (908) 735-9250. The Munchmobile's driver lived on this pizza when he lived in town eons ago; it's still good. Fresh mushrooms, chewy crust and good sauce add up to a nice pie.

Polar Cub, 380 Route 22 West, Whitehouse; (908) 534-4401. One of the state's classic roadside ice cream stands, the Polar Cub provides good ice cream and shakes in a rural, shaded setting. Not as good as Cliff's in Ledgewood, but plenty good enough.

Ship Inn, 61 Bridge St., Milford; (908) 995-0188. New Jersey's first brew pub; opened in January 1995. This is the place for good, authen-tic bangers and mash, or steak and mushroom pie. Excellent hickory shrimp, wrapped in bacon, enlivened with horseradish and glazed with an Irish stout-laced barbecue sauce. First-rate fish 'n' chips. Best brews: Golden Wheat Light, mellow and yellow, and ESB, Ship Inn's flagship brew.

Siam Restaurant, 61 N. Main St., Lambertville; (609) 397-8128. High-ceilinged, low-key restaurant feels right at home in artsy Lam-bertville. Kai thom soup rich and heady, with big chunks of chicken. Nua nam tok is terrific — peppery, almost fiery strips of tender beef intertwined with onions. Yam wun sen: slithery vermicelli with shrimp, ground pork and lime juice and spiked with hot pepper.

Sky Manor Airport Restaurant, 48 Sky Manor Road, Pittstown; (908) 996-3442. Neat spot for a getaway, in more ways than one; country-like kitchen looks out over this Hunterdon County airfield. The Super Glassair III burger, named after a plane, is mammoth and meaty. Crunchy onion rings, but standard fries. Top it off with a piece of good cherry pie.

Stewart's Drive-In, 235 Route 22 East, Lebanon; (908) 236-2303. Maybe the most beautifully landscaped Stewart's anywhere. Foot-long chili dog, with great homemade chili, worth the hike.

Stockton Inn, 1 Main St., Stockton; (609) 397-1250. Hotel and wishing-well out back inspired the Richard Rodgers-Lorenz Hart song "There's a Small Hotel." Several items had us nearly breaking into song — the homemade potato chips; the salmon BLT with applewood bacon, roasted tomatoes and jalapeno mayo; and the Max and Me Crabcake.

Verducci's Gourmet Food and Grocery, 176 Route 202 North, Raritan Township; (908) 788-7750. Resistance to the baked goods here is futile. The chocolate caramel pyramid deserves mention as a wonder of the bakery world. The chocolate truffle mousse may have been better. Lemon drops a "disaster," according to one Muncher, but the chocolate espresso cookie may have been the best cookie we tried all summer.

Viva Mexico, 117 Broad St., Flemington; (908) 788-0744. Casual, colorful restaurant features food from Mexico's Oaxaca region. First-rate salsa and chips. Excellent tortilla soup. The Texas burrito is fat and gooey without being mushy. The huevos con chorizo are OK, nothing more. The bunuelos — thin, fried, cinnamon-dusted dough with ice cream — among the summer's top desserts.

Ye Old Sub Base, 29 Main St., Clinton; (908) 735-8870. Day's best tuna — chunks of tuna, easy on the mayo — found here. The best bread, too. Recommended: the Bowzer, with turkey, roast beef, Russian dressing, lettuce and tomato.

Mercer

Americana Diner, 359 Route 130 North, East Windsor; (609) 448-4477. The Americana — dig the 1940s retro-chic look — is one of the state's most stylish diners. One difference with the omelets here — they are first cooked in a pan, then baked in the oven. The result: nice puffy omelets.

The Bent Spoon, 35 Palmer Square West, Princeton; (609) 924-2368. One of the state's best ice cream stops. You won't find plain old vanilla here; the daily lineup might include organic coconut streak; organic blueberry and dark chocolate habanero, heady and intense. High-end ice cream, worth the higher price tag.

Chuck's Spring Street Cafe, 16 Spring St., Princeton; (609) 921-0027. Crunchiest of the wings sampled. Subtly spicy sauce stands out from the formulaic stuff found at most takeout places.

DeLorenzo's Tomato Pies, 530 Hudson St., Trenton; (609) 695-9534. Best pizza in New Jersey? Some think so. It's a one-of-a-kind place, with wooden booths, old-time cash register and glasses right out of grandma's attic. Unforgettable.

Hoagie Heaven, 242 Nassau St., Princeton; (609) 921-7723. You will probably not find a cheaper sub anywhere, and they'll fill you up. Roast beef could have been fresher; it was taken out of a Tupperware-like container. Mushy tomatoes. Better bet: the No. 1 sub (provolone, cappacola, boiled ham, salami), the most popular sub here.

Olives, 22 Witherspoon St., Princeton; (609) 921-1569. Gourmet food store in downtown Princeton. The Munchers raved about the Rocky Road brownie, the chocolate muffin and chocolate brownie. Chocolate chip cookie nothing to write home about.

Passage to India, 2495 Business Route 1 South, Lawrence Twp.; (609) 637-0800. Overall, the best of the five Indian restaurants visited on our Indian road trip. Loved the murg chettinad, chicken tenders cooked in spices and enough crushed black pepper to require a separate ship at Port Newark.

PJ's Pancake House, 154 Nassau St., Princeton; (609) 924-1353. Popular Princeton University hangout, but judging from our visit, can't understand why. The "famous" pancakes were insubstantial, spongy. French toast fared much better. Two winners: the chocolate waffle and the raspberry crepe. The "mashed browns" should have been called "mushed browns."

Porfirio's Italian Foods and Cafe, 320 Anderson St., Trenton; (609) 393-4116. You can't do Italian in New Jersey without doing Chambersburg, and Porfirio's, in the 'Burg, is a great place to buy fresh pasta and other items.

Small World Coffee, 14 Witherspoon St., Princeton; (609) 924-4377. Popular college hangout uses "East Coast roast," darker than a full-city, lighter than a French roast. Eclectic, healthy menu — where else can you get slow-cooked, steel-cut Irish oats with maple syrup, organic banana and nutty granola? Or sweet potato and cilantro soup? The organic Sumatran coffee is sensational.

Terhune Orchards, 330 Cold Soil Road, Lawrence Twp.; (609) 924-2310. Excellent red raspberry pie, pretty good blueberry. Average apple pie; the coconut custard pie, much better. The apple cider slush, available year-round, is cold, sludgy, sweet and sensational.

Triumph Brewing Company, 138 Nassau St., Princeton; (609) 924-7855. Probably the state's grandest, most stylish brew pub, with brick walls and vaulted ceiling. Ambrosia salad — with Napa cabbage, bok choy, red onion, shaved carrot, avocado, goat cheese and pineapple — a nice, summery mix. Fine, flaky fish 'n' chips. Best brews: Honey Wheat, subtly sweet, and the Pale Ale.

Middlesex

Anthony's Chicken and Grill, 56 Obert St., South River; (732) 257-2259. The extra, extra hot wings live up to their billing. "My tongue is on the floor," one Muncher moaned. Better-than-average Buffalo wing sauce. The barbecue sauce was way too sweet.

Aposto Pizzeria and Restaurant, 76 Raritan Ave., Highland Park; (732) 745-9011. Looks like a neighborhood pizzeria, but the two Greek sisters who run this place know their way around a kitchen. Wonderful salads, accented with a luscious lemon vinaigrette. The margherita pizza is smooth, saucy and loaded with tomatoes. Meaty mussels, in pleasing marinara and white wine sauces.

Arthur's Tavern, 644 Georges Road, North Brunswick; (732) 828-1117. Mention "steak" and "New Jersey," and many people will reply with one word: Arthur's. The Double — 48 ounces of prime Delmonico — is daunting; but we liked the 24-ounce Delmonico better. "Famous" potatoes anything but.

Bagel Boys, 1898 Route 130, North Brunswick; (732) 422-8700. Strawberry bagel not very strawberry-ish, but the super cinnamon raisin and other bagels rated high with several Munchers. Owner Elie Machalany makes a "mystery" bagel every week.

Bien Hoa, 2090 Route 27, Edison; (732) 287-9500. Roasted quails crackly good if overly greasy. Same could be said of the Vietnamese crepe with shrimp and pork. But the Vietnamese beef stew, substantial and savory, was a group favorite. Vietnamese egg rolls also recommended, as is the house papaya salad.

Big Ed's BBQ, 305 Route 34, Old Bridge; (732) 583-2626. Roadhouse atmosphere, good ribs and chicken. Try the Pulled Baby on a Bun!

Birnn Chocolate, 314 Cleveland Ave., Highland Park; (732) 545-4400. A respected name in candy since 1932, when Birnn's opened across the river in New Brunswick. Creative truffles — mango French chocolate, amaretto French chocolate, among others. Good cordials, superior butter crunch and hall-of-fame nonpareils.

Blue Water Seafood Company, 1126 Route 18 North, East Brunswick; (732) 967-9220. Ignore the highway location and prepare to enjoy creatively-prepared seafood. Tasty homemade cheddar biscuits. Average crab cakes, and the buffalo scallops sounded better than they tasted. But several dishes excelled: sashimi tuna, the grilled whole red snapper Mediterranean style, the Maryland soft shell crabs and the mesquite-grilled Cajun catfish.

Brasi-Luso, 344 Washington St., Perth Amboy; (732) 376-9555. No-frills storefront, with plenty of soccer memorabilia. Picanha fatiada —

sliced steak — a group favorite. Clear winner: the sirloin (bife de vaca sem osso), bursting with grilled goodness and a great bargain besides.

Buzzy's, 200 Stelton Road, Piscataway; (732) 752-2229. Nachos here all about the cheese, and there's plenty of it. Three kinds used — Monterey jack, Swiss and cheddar. Crispy light chips, "and they don't skimp on the stuff," one Muncher observed. Better than average.

Caribbean Cafe, 85 Bayard St., New Brunswick; (732) 846-2620. Doesn't look like much outside or inside, but this subterranean spot serves up good grub: nice squishy plantains, a beautifully cooked whole red snapper, and excellent fruit shakes.

Chicken Holiday, 390 North Ave., Dunellen; (732) 968-1666. Spare interior — two benches for takeout customers, cactus tied to a post — but serves up nice, fiery wings.

Chicken Holiday, 1803 Route 27, Edison; (732) 985-2130. A chain that does it right. Chicken made to order in a pressure cooker, not the conventional deep fryer. That translates to more natural juices retained, and less fat than conventional frying. The juiciest chicken of the day; oily pools gathered on our paper plates.

Colonia Dairy Maid, 1075 St. Georges Ave., Woodbridge; (732) 634-5885. A roadside stop for 50-plus years. Thirty flavors of soft ice cream available; the banana strawberry is highly recommended, a creamy, extra-thick combination of two summery flavors. You'll need to work that straw!

Colonial Restaurant, 366 New Brunswick Ave., Woodbridge; (732) 738-0554. Long, narrow luncheonette. Mediocre pork roll sandwich. Better: the bacon and egg, with sturdy, smoky bacon. Good French toast, surprisingly good waffles.

Country Cow Creamery, 523 Inman Ave., Woodbridge; (732) 882-1234. Weird, wonderful flavors of hard ice cream here, including German streusel and sweet potato. The soft chocolate and vanilla drew raves from the Munch crew. Shared Top Dog honors with the now-closed Custardthing! in Westwood.

Crown Fried Chicken, 109 Smith St., Perth Amboy; (732) 442-7789. Downtown storefront offers juicy but not otherwise distinguished chicken; the wings are a better bet.

D'Italia Restaurant, 1500 St. Georges Ave., Woodbridge; (732) 574-1120. Some of Jersey's best cooking is done in strip malls; D'Italia, sequestered in a complex of medical offices, is proof. Several appetizers — lobster bisque, bruschetta, clams — turned out subpar, but the entrees wowed us. The lasagna is creamy smooth, just like your Italian grandmother made it. Lovely eggplant rollatini, stuffed with prosciutto and ricotta. You may not find a better calzone in Middlesex County.

Dairy Quick, 615 Bound Brook Road, Dunellen; (732) 752-1695. Owner Laszlo Barta makes his own homemade hard ice cream; try the rum raisin and black raspberry. His banana soft ice cream "knocks your socks off," according to one regular. We agree. The chocolate not as distinctive as the Magic Fountain's, but the vanilla better than most.

Dick's Dock, 452 Main St., Metuchen; (732) 744-1274. Good seafood in Metuchen? Sure, at Robert and Sandy Dick's place. Thick New England clam chowder; tangy steamed littleneck clams and Prince Edward Island mussels; ultra-rich, milky-smooth crabmeat bisque.

Dunellen BBQ, 626 Bound Brook Road, Dunellen; (732) 968-3200. The barbecue chicken, in a huge rice-and-French-fry-filled pan, is a winner. The steak sandwich is a great value, and tasty besides.

East Hana, 275 Route 18, East Brunswick; (732) 257-1088. Cute little restaurant located across from Hong Kong Supermarket, a celebration of Asian food. The yasai gyoza — steamed vegetable dumplings — are superb. Highlight: Chirasi, a bounteous, kaleidoscopic assortment of sashimi.

Edison Diner, 101 Route 1, Edison; (732) 985-3335. Diversified menu that draws from different ethnic cuisines. Munchers found the bacon "thick and meaty."

Edo, 68 Easton Ave., New Brunswick; (732) 514-0700. Owner Jun Kim also doubles as the sushi chef. Big Mac roll a tantalizing mix of yellowtail, salmon and avocado. Sashimi deluxe a boatload of tuna, yellowtail, eel, salmon, octopus, giant clam and red snapper. The succulent white tuna, ordered as sushi, easily one of day's standouts.

European Provisions, 301 Old Bridge Turnpike, East Brunswick; (732) 254-7156. Brick-walled exterior belies shiny, well-stocked interior. We liked the litewska kielbasa, the spicy Hungarian kielbasa, the goosewurst, Polish meatloaf, apple strudel, hazelnut cookies and Russian salad. We liked a lot of things here.

Harold's New York Deli, Holiday Inn, 3050 Woodbridge Ave., Edison; (732) 661-9100. Softball-sized matzo balls, hubcap-sized pancakes, lampshade-sized carrot cakes. A monument to wonderful excess.

Headquarters, 647 Georges Road, North Brunswick; (732) 247-5454. Smooth, smoky baba ghanoush; you're either going to love it or hate it. Fatoosh — cucumbers, tomatoes, salad greens and parsley in an oil-and-lemon base — is excellent. Adventurous? Try the fhool, a soup-like fava bean salad. Inside tip: Ask for your pita bread toasted.

J and G Texas Weiners, 238 North Ave., Dunellen; (732) 968-4343. Luncheonette/hot dog stand short on looks, but long on atmosphere. I'm not a fan of their chili, but many people swear by it.

Jack Cooper's Celebrity Deli, Tano Mall, 1199 Amboy Ave., Edison; (732) 549-4580. It all started with Morris Cooper, who ran a series of candy stores and sandwich places in Irvington and Newark in the '40s and '50s. In 1970, one son, Jack, opened the Broadway Deli in East Brunswick and five years later opened Jack Cooper's Celebrity Deli in Edison.

Joe's Meat Market, 437 Smith St., Perth Amboy; (732) 442-4660. Old-timey market, with kielbasa suspended from hooks and formidable hunks of smoked ham and other meats on the counter. The pork tenderloin is thick and juicy. The wiejska kielbasa is moist, garlicky and assertive, and the mysliwska or hunter kielbasa makes for a hearty snack or meal.

La Bonbonniere, 2062 Route 27, Edison; (732) 287-1313. Busy bakery opened in 1952; there are four locations in New Jersey. Good chocolate cheesecake, creamy and subtle. So-so crumbcake. The New York-style cheesecake is mushy, bland. First-rate chocolate cupcakes, seriously fudgy. Nice linzer tart.

The Landmark Tavern, 117 N. Broadway, South Amboy; (732) 721-6812. Sports bar with restaurant-length menu. Curly fries wonderfully crisp, almost onion ring-like in texture. Big, juicy 10-ounce burger, spilling from a poppy seed roll. Delicious deal: get two burgers, normally $5.25 each, for $7.50 on Tuesdays.

Le Peep Restaurant, Wick Plaza, 561 Route 1 South, Edison; (732) 819-7666. Cheery, friendly place with children's drawings splashed on the walls. Good coffee. Two omelets sampled were exemplary — the salmon, with smoked salmon, cream cheese, onions and dill; and the Spanish omelet, with cheese, salsa, onions, green chilies, sour cream and chives.

Makeda, 338 George St., New Brunswick; (732) 545-5115. One of New Jersey's few Ethiopian restaurants is housed in a stylish, almost sensuous space. The kefta, or Moroccan meatballs, are a first-rate appetizer — finely-ground beef, herbs, spices, onions and red peppers. Several entrees, though, were almost buried under heavy-handed sauces and ingredients. But we liked the collard greens (gomen wat), sauteed in onions, garlic, ginger and Ethiopian spices.

Martini's, 3602 Route 35 North, South Amboy; (732) 727-9466. Only in New Jersey: a cherub-decorated romantic hideaway, a former nun's retreat, next door to a gentleman's club. Recommended: the broccoli rabe; the grilled veal chop served in a porcini cognac sauce; and the yellow tuna, pan-seared in a creamy grappa sauce.

Mendokers' Quality Bakery, 34 W. Railroad Ave., Jamesburg; (732) 521-0056. Amazing array of cakes, pies and cookies in this longtime business. Well-built cheesecake — soft but not mushy inside, with a firm but not hard shell.

Menlo Park Diner, 1475 Route 1 South, Edison; (732) 494-1760. Face it: Most diners serve standard, or sub-standard, fare. This one is well above the pack. Loved the corn beef hash, the Tayor ham and egg, waffles and pancakes.

Mie Thai, 34 Main St., Woodbridge; 732 596-9400. Tom kha soup — coconut milk, lemongrass, fresh chili, galanga or Thai ginger, mushrooms, lime leaves — is excellent. Good spring and summer rolls, the latter a rice paper-wrapped combo of pork, shrimp, greens and rice noodles. Excellent pad mie thai, with sauteed thin rice noodles, shrimp, chicken, onions, tofu, ground peanuts and eggs.

Milltown Ice Cream Depot, 87 Washington Ave., Milltown; (732) 545-1177. Classic walk-up ice cream stand, with decent ice cream. Favorites: the classic chocolate, and peanut butter ripple.

Moghul Express, 1670 Oak Tree Road, Edison; (732) 549-6222. Pink-and-green neon-lit fast food stop features selection of 50 different sweets. "No place in America has the variety we do," a manager told us.

Mr. Dee's, 3 Johnson Lane, Parlin; (732) 525-8300. Clean, well-lit store, but small dog, mushy chili. Italian hot dog ordinary-tasting. The Italian potatoes — parboiled, then deep-fried — will transport you to spud heaven.

Mr. Pi's, 257 Central Ave., Metuchen; (732) 494-8686. This hardwood-floored restaurant was the most casual of the sushi places visited. Start with the Tako Sunomono (sliced octopus with vinegar sauce) and proceed to either the Spider Roll, with beautiful bits of soft-shell crab, or the Lobster Tail Roll. The mochi (ice cream inside egg-like rice dough shells) and the fried banana are top-notch.

Old Man Rafferty, 106 Albany St., New Brunswick; (732) 846-6153. The takeout side of the New Brunswick restaurant is a good stop for sandwiches, salads and desserts. Items come from 10 or so bakers, including Junior's, which supplies the cheesecake. Best dessert sampled: the raspberry cheesecake, light and luscious. The New York-style cheesecake just passable. We flipped over the frutti di bosci, a custard-filled and raspberry, blueberry and blackberry-topped cookie shell. Skip the Black Forest cake and the chocolate mud pie.

Pho 99, 3600 Park Ave., South Plainfield; (908) 791-9880. Spare, attractive storefront, but needs work to reach the level of Little Saigon or Bien Hoa. Nice firm wonton in the egg noodle soup, but middling broth. Durian is often called the world's stinkiest fruit, but you won't turn up your nose at the durian shake here; try it, you'll like it!

Piquant Bread Bar and Grill, 349A George St., New Brunswick; (732) 246-2468. Butter chicken — tandoori chicken in a delightful tomato butter and fenugreek sauce — one of the Munchmobile driver's favorite dishes of the summer. Loved the tandoori pizza and the chilled mango soup.

Portuguese Manor, 310 Elm St., Perth Amboy; (732) 826-2233. Clams Portuguese Manor, in a rich, musky brown sauce, among group favorites. Blackened chicken delicious. Melon sorbet sensationally light and fruity.

Reo Diner Restaurant, 392 Amboy Ave., Woodbridge; (732) 634-9200. Who doesn't known the Reo? Long-time gathering spot for local pols; Bob Grant used to host his radio show here. Munchers made note of the "perfect" pancakes and an "outstanding" Florentine omelet.

Roscoe's, 725 Georges Road, North Brunswick; (732) 249-2491. The Hawaiian Delight — orange, pineapple and coconut — a highlight, but the mint chocolate chip ranked as the day's worst flavor.

Rutgers University Grease Trucks, College Avenue and Hamilton Street, New Brunswick. How are the burgers? Let's put it this way: The more partying you do beforehand, the better they'll taste.

Sahara Restaurant, 165 Easton Ave., New Brunswick; (732) 246-3020. Attractive, mural-decorated space, with an outdoor patio. The menu spans the Middle East. Several knockout dishes, including the pizza feta toast, spiced ezme and the Combination Kebab.

Sciortino's Harbor Lights, 132 S. Broadway, South Amboy; (732) 721-8788. Legendary Perth Amboy pizzeria moved to South Amboy in 2004. Pizza's still good — nice and tomato-ey.

Seabra's Armory, 200 Front St., Perth Amboy; (732) 826-6000. Rodizio here markedly better than sister restaurant in Newark, and great waterfront views to boot. Incomparably soft, chewy bread. Recommended appetizer: mushroom caps with cheese and spinach. Turkey wrapped in bacon: super. Pork ribs best of the five sampled. But shish kebob overdone, and chicken too fatty.

Skylark Fine Diner and Lounge, 17 Wooding Ave., Edison; (732) 777-7878. Part airport lounge, part sci-fi fantasy, the Skylark is a dazzling addition to the Jersey diner scene. You'll keep reaching for the basket of bread and mini-muffins. Skip the bruschetta, order the Mediterranean salad. You won't find a better diner omelet.

Stuff Yer Face, 49 Easton Ave., New Brunswick; (732) 247-1727. Rutgers University institution, founded in 1977, famous for its stromb-olis, known here as "bolis." Standard Buffalo wings; they might as well come from Boise or Baltimore. Decent pizza. The garden burger over-cooked and nearly tasteless. But we liked the barbecue boli and the Laura boli, with spinach, ricotta, tomato, eggplant and cheddar cheese.

Sub Place Better, 166 Main St., Metuchen; (732) 906-1262. Excellent tuna sub. The cheesesteak didn't look promising and wasn't. The Crimefighter (chicken, cappicola, Swiss, barbecue sauce and ranch dressing) is a winner, and so is the Nassau (roast beef, corned beef and Swiss).

Sun Glo Bakery, 606 Main St., Sayreville; (732) 257-1132. Neighborhood bakery with top-notch crullers, sturdy and firm. The cream in the eclair and Boston creme doughnuts not up to Munch standards. Nice sugar doughnut.

Sunny Palace, 1069 Route 18 South, East Brunswick; (732) 651-8668. Great pork buns; the sugary-sweet fried shells made them special. One Muncher loved the pork and shrimp dumplings' "bold" taste. Excellent won ton soup; the dumplings are doused in a scallion-laced broth tableside.

Thai Chili, 210 Summerhill Road, Spotswood; (732) 723-0600. Its strip mall location and soft-pink lighting may not sound enticing, but Thai Chili serves up good, reasonably-priced Thai. Standard summer rolls, but the tom yum gai, a clear chicken soup with lemon grass, chiles, mushrooms and lime juice, is sweet and near-sensational. Recommended dishes: Siam duck, chili chicken, soft shell crabs, honey salmon.

Thomas Sweet, 55 Easton Ave., New Brunswick; (732) 828-3855. Known for creative flavors — the shop has created more than 100 — and blend-ins. Oreos and cream ice cream sundae, topped with fresh strawberries, is excellent.

Tido 'n His Junkyard Dogs, 139 Easton Ave., New Brunswick; (732) 246-8980. Best fries of the summer, but the dog — salty, but otherwise bland — received a universal thumbs-down.

Tommy's Hot Dogs, 117 Grant Ave., Carteret; (732) 541-8409. Low-rent, colorful place, with a comprehensive menu and scenic view of tank farms down the street.

Tumulty's, 361 George St., New Brunswick; (732) 545-6205. Popular Rutgers University haunt. First-rate burgers, especially the Black Angus burger, but lackluster sides — onion rings, fries, cole slaw, potato skins. Death by Chocolate? Here you can get Death by Burger — two 10-ounce burgers, your choice of two toppings.

Uncle Petey's Weenies, Lunch truck on St. Georges Avenue, Woodbridge. Catchy name, but "wimpy" dog. Nice onions, and the Italian hot dog featured good bread.

White Rose System, 154 Woodbridge Ave., Highland Park; (732) 777-1881. What's The System? Let the cooks explain it to you. Late-night hangout for thousands of Rutgers students over the years.

Woojeon Restaurant, 411 Route 1, Edison; (732) 572-6100. You'll never go hungry on Route 1; this Korean-Japanese restaurant is one of the highway's better Asian stops. Waiter initially stuffy, but he warmed up. Outstanding kimchee. Irresistible black beans. Skip the shredded raw fish marinated with vegetables and go with the shredded pork with mixed vegetables and spicy sauce.

Zia Lisa Pizzeria and Restaurant, 242 Plainfield Ave., Edison; (732) 985-3531. The bread — crusty, warm semolina — is outstanding. Good, albeit salty, calamari. Decent veal scallopini marsala. Linguine pescatore fully stocked with fish, but would have benefited from lighter red sauce. Best dish: baked mussels oreganato, soaking in pleasingly pungent white wine sauce.

Monmouth

10th Ave. Burrito Co., 702 10th Ave., Belmar; (732) 280-1515. Grinning skulls and other Day-of-the-Dead-like kitsch welcome you at this tiny taco/burrito joint. The burritos are California-style: lots of lettuce, easy on the salsa. Burritos heavy and gummy, and the chili seemed a long way from the "soon to be famous" tag on the menu. But we liked the fish tacos, the chipotle shrimp and portobello quesadilla.

Allenwood General Store, 3208 Allenwood-Lakewood Road, Allenwood; (732) 223-4747. Both general store and antique shop: You can get both pancakes and those back issues of Boys' Life magazine you've been trying to find for years. The pancakes are first-rate, and the pork roll, egg and cheese sandwich may be the Jersey Shore's best.

Amy's Omelette House, 444 Ocean Blvd., Long Branch; (732) 222-1206. The Maryland Benedict — crabmeat patties, poached eggs and an oh-wow hollandaise sauce — the first indication breakfast is done right here. Fried whiting and eggs a good choice for those who want something different. Nice French toast; not-so-nice pancakes.

Bahrs, 2 Bay Ave., Highlands; (732) 872-1245. John Bahr, who ran a necktie business in Newark, opened this Jersey Shore institution in 1917, serving eggs, fried eels and buckwheat pancakes to local fishermen. Lobster bisque silky-smooth. Yummy homemade potato chips and good powdery warm biscuits. Crab cake — delicately fried, incredibly soft and moist — is outstanding.

The Baker Boys, 69 Main Ave., Ocean Grove; (732) 775-0052. Bright, airy store with open kitchen. One bite of the German chocolate icing and you'll surrender to its creamy, dreamy goodness. Also liked the Kitchen Sink cookies, with oatmeal, raisins, chocolate chips and nuts.

Barnacle Bill's, 1 First St., Rumson; (732) 747-8396. Great spot for drinks or dinner at sundown. Very good, beefy-tasting burgers. Try the Brownie a la Mode.

Basil T's, 183 Riverside Ave., Red Bank; (732) 842-5990. Best food of all brew pubs visited; the Chatham Cod and margarita pizza are top notch, and the rotisserie lemon chicken, amazingly tender and moist, is the best chicken we've had in years. Best brews: Maxwell's Dry Stout; the Rocket Red Ale; and Light Summer Ale, clean and refreshing.

Battleview Orchards, 91 Wemrock Road, Freehold Township; (732) 462-0756. Roadside cornucopia filled with fruit, produce, baked goods. Lemon Krunch pie the best of those sampled. The Very Berry pie bursting with berries, but strangely lacked much of a berry flavor. Apple pie judged too sweet.

Black Forest Restaurant, 42 S. Main St., Allentown; (609) 259-3197. Housed in a circa 1700 mill, probably the closest thing in New Jersey to a Bavarian country inn restaurant. Sauerbraten here the tangiest and most distinctive of those sampled. Wiener schnitzel, first-rate; the red cabbage, enlivened with cloves, bay leaf, vinegar, salt and sugar, is terrific.

Blue Rock Cafe, 522 Amboy Ave., Cliffwood Beach; (732) 583-7699. Lively roadhouse/sports bar. View from deck: limitless expanse of marsh and reeds, Manhattan skyline. New England clam chowder could have been hotter; try the Manhattan clam chowder, awash with clams, instead. Huge, wondrously greasy burgers.

Chilango's, 272 Bay Ave., Highlands; (732) 708-0505. This bayside restaurant would be a cozy port in any storm, with lit plastic chilies strung around the entrance and a cozy bar. Pork wings — think tangy barbecued pork on a stick — a great little appetizer. Chicken taco OK, but the chorizo taco — spicy, a little greasy — is dynamite. The fajitas mariscada, with shrimp, scallops, mussels and sauteed onions and peppers, didn't seem worth the trouble or expense.

Chocolate Carousel, 2510 Belmar Blvd., No. 8, Wall; (732) 280-0606. Slightly-off-the-beaten path ice cream/candy store. Their fudge-chunk-filled chocolate carousel ice cream one of the day's best chocolates. Zesty key lime ice cream, but nobody got excited about the creamsicle flavor. Good, authentic banana and a smooth hazelnut chip.

Circus Drive-In, 1861 Route 35, Wall; (732) 449-2650. Look for the splendid, neon clown sign. Owned by the same man, Richard Friedel, since 1954. Soft-shelled crabs popular here; menu items are circus-themed (Wild Animal Special, Bareback Betsy, etc.). Real good chicken, excellent pink lemonade.

Cluck-U Chicken, 15 Route 36, Eatontown; (732) 389-2888. Purple-shuttered, neon-lit chicken hut. The honey/hickory wings — nice and meaty — are a good choice for those hankering for down-home traditional barbecue sauce.

Crown Palace, 8 N. Main St., Marlboro; (732) 780-8882. The garden behind the Crown Palace, with its temple-like gate, foot paths and pond, is one of the more tranquil spots in New Jersey restaurant land. Good egg rolls. Entrees fair if formulaic; many lathered with a been-there-eaten-that brown sauce.

Day's Ice Cream, 48 Pitman Ave., Ocean Grove; (732) 988-1007. They don't make their own, but don't hold it against them. Some of the day's best flavors found here. It's a Goody, with vanilla, peanut butter swirl and chocolate chips, lived up to the name. Peppermint stick, hazelnut truffle latte, black raspberry chip and the dulce de leche all first-rate.

Dearborn Farms, 2170 Route 35, Holmdel; (732) 264-0256. Plain-Jane crusts no match for the fabulously flaky crusts at Delicious Orchards, but the apple raspberry is a tart, winning combination. The cherries in the cherry pie described as "boring" by one Muncher, but the five fruits of the forest pie made it on several Munchers' favorites list.

Delicious Orchards, 36 Route 34 South, Colts Neck; (732) 462-1989. Five hundred pies a day sold in this sprawling market. Apple pie — bulging with fresh, sweet fruit — is excellent. Close behind: the peach and blueberry. One Muncher described the pecan pie as "stellar." I love their trolley buns.

Dixie Lee Bakery, 303 Main St., Keansburg; (732) 787-0674. Bill Baker has been a baker here for 45 years. Best-selling items include buttercream cakes, apple crumb cake and old-fashioned kaiser rolls.

El Meson Cafe, 40 W. Main St., Freehold Borough; (732) 308-9494. Ordinary chips. Below-average combination tacos — lots of parsley and celery but not much else. Marinated grilled lamb: huge portion, but overcooked. Taco salad a flaky volcano bursting with mushrooms, guacamole, olives, cheese and other ingredients. Guacamole — fresh, cool and chunky- the day's best.

Espresso Joe's, 50 W. Front St., Keyport; (732) 203-9499. Keyport? For coffee? Why not? This Internet-accessed coffeehouse is a slice of SoHo near the shore. Smooth-as-silk latte; the house coffee a blend of Viennese and French roasts. Better-than-expected panini here; the turkey with sun-dried tomatoes and spicy cheese is a standout.

Frank's Deli and Restaurant, 1406 Main St., Asbury Park; (732) 775-6682. Spacious shore hangout with booths and stools. Mammoth, but not especially memorable, pork roll sandwich. Bacon and egg sandwich contains a heart-stopping amount of bacon, but it's not otherwise special.

Fred and Murry's Deli Restaurant, 4345 Route 9 North, Freehold Twp.; (732) 462-3343. Strip mall storefront. Good sandwiches and tongue. Really.

Fritzy's, 2200 Route 9 South, Howell; (732) 845-1500. Forget the strip mall location; Fritzy's offers some of the best German this side of Munich. The kassler ripchen — center cut pork chops — are outstanding. The wiener schnitzel is tender and crunchy. Good spaetzle and potato pancakes.

G and G Hot Dog Truck, Shrewsbury Avenue and the railroad tracks, Red Bank. Dogs with nice, crispy snap. Good homemade chili, but not enough on dog. Can't beat the price, though.

Hey Daddy Bagels, 949 Route 36, Leonardo; (732) 872-7170. Owner Geoffrey Steneck calls his salt bagel "the closest thing to a New York City salt bagel outside New York City." Terrific cinnamon buns, too.

Ice Cream on 9, 2300 Route 9 South, Howell; (732) 780-2020. A chocoholic's vision of heaven — 10 of the 29 flavors of hard ice cream are variations of chocolate. You have a problem with that?

Ice Hut, 101 Route 71, Spring Lake Heights; (732) 974-8837. First Ice Hut opened in Nutley. They mix ice and fruit immediately, rather than churning them to mix the flavors. Specialty is the Creamsicle effect — layering vanilla ice cream with orange ice, or any other fruit flavor.

Inlet Cafe, 3 Cornwall St., Highlands; (732) 872-9764. Waterfront restaurant with views of Sandy Hook and New York skyline. Sesame-crust ahi tuna, with a side of delicious seaweed salad, one of the summer's most memorable dishes. The Inlet scallops are melt-in-your-mouth good.

Jack's Rib and Ale House, 149 Brighton Ave., Long Branch; (732) 870-8800. "Friendliest place in town" serves decent barbecue. Ordinary potato salad: too creamy and gloppy. Pulled pork sandwich: dried-out, coarse-textured. Okay ribs. Best item: the barbecue rib sandwich, thin, charcoal-grilled slabs of pork on a good, soft roll.

Jake's Cree-Mee Freeze, 619 Route 33, Millstone; (732) 446-5305. Classic roadside ice cream stand. Orange sherbet nice and creamy, vanilla soft ice cream okay, nothing more. "Dairy Queen-like, but very good," one Muncher said. Scene in "Sex and the City" filmed here.

Jameson's, 652 Route 35, Neptune; (732) 775-4699. This storefront not in the same league as the others, but we liked the deep-fried pork chop, short ribs and oxtails. Disappointments: the cornbread, barbecue sauce and deep-fried catfish.

Jersey Freeze, 120 Manalapan Ave., Freehold; (732) 462-3008. Roadside institution. Soft-serve only, and while it can't compare with artisanal makers like The Bent Spoon, Jersey Freeze will melt the hardest heart. The nonfat gourmet chocolate didn't live up to its billing, but we loved the juicy strawberry and the grape — soda in a cone, only better.

Jersey Joe's, 712 Port Monmouth Road, Port Monmouth; (732) 787-5779. Joe Lopomo started selling Italian hot dogs 40 years ago here in what was little more than a shack. The Italian dog comes with the usual specs — pizza bread crammed with potatoes and onions — but you can get better at any number of doggy dives in and around Newark. Best part about going here: tables and decks across the street, overlooking Raritan Bay.

Jim's Burger Haven, 1215 Route 36, Hazlet; (732) 264-6990. Breakfast-and-burger joint with faded food photos straight out of a drive-in-movie snack bar. Dependable food; good bacon and egg sandwich.

Kelly's, 43 Laird Road (Route 35 South), Neptune City; (732) 775-9517. Popular shore bar/restaurant bathed in eerie, and strangely soothing, red glow. Plenty of food choices — Maine steamers, fisherman's pie, grilled chicken breast, among others. The Large Reuben is a molten behemoth, the Swiss cheese browned on top, the corned beef, kraut and Russian dressing hidden within.

Klein's Waterside Cafe, 708 River Road, Belmar; (732) 681-1177. Overlooks marina. Recommended: the king crab legs, and the seafood diablo, a heaping plate of shrimp, scallops, clams and a half lobster over a bed of linguine, topped by spicy tomato sauce.

Manalapan Diner, 48 Route 9 North, Manalapan; (732) 462-7165. Fresh-squeezed orange juice. The crew admired the salmon and onion omelet, and a just-out-of-the-oven danish.

Maria's Italian Cuisine, 165 Main St., Manasquan; (732) 223-2033. Quality thin-crust pizza. Middling marinara, and overcooked ravioli. One Muncher described the osso buco as "all right." The tortellini verde drew raves, though. And you'll love the lima beans.

Mariner's Cove, 712 Union Ave., Brielle; (732) 528-6023. For sheer omelet extravagance, you can't beat Mariner's Cove, with 220 omelets. Catchy names, including the Sweetie Pie (jam, cream cheese, potato) and the Italian Heartburn (ham, salami, hot peppers, pepperoni, potato, mozzarella). Not sure what is Cajun about the Cajun omelet, but it's a fine, filling dish. "Zero flavor" to the hash browns and corned beef hash, according to one Muncher. But good grits.

Max's Hot Dogs, 25 Matilda Terrace, Long Branch; (732) 571-0248. Photos of celebrity patrons — Bruce Springsteen known to eat here — decorate walls of this seaside hot dog shrine. Great homemade

chili; super cheesecake, too, made by owner Celia Maybaum. And beer on tap.

My Two Sons, Englishtown Auction Sales, 90 Wilson Ave., Manalapan; (732) 786-1900. Ignore the simple surroundings and chow down. The plump and juicy fried catfish sandwich alone will have you coming back. Top-notch potato salad and cole slaw, and the homemade tartar sauce is not the usual white glop you find everywhere else.

No Joe's Cafe, 51 Broad St., Red Bank; (732) 530-4040. You can order everything from a Girl Scout Cookie (espresso, chocolate, steamed milk, frosted mint and whipped cream) to a Van Halen (espresso, vanilla, hazelnut, steamed milk). Self-serve coffees range from the dark-roasted Sledgehammer to the peanut butter-flavored Lunch with Elvis.

Off the Hook, 1 Navesink Ave., Highlands; (732) 872-2006. The deck, overlooking Sandy Hook Bay and the Atlantic Ocean, is a great place to while away an afternoon. The baby back ribs — thick and juicy — are special. Good buffalo shrimp, too.

Old Heidelberg Inn, 20 Boardwalk, Keansburg; (732) 787-3131. Atmospheric Shore haunt, with its tilted floor, boardwalk setting and a one-item menu — hot dogs and more hot dogs. Decent chili; you don't come here for the food, but for a fun time. Don't forget to stop at Ann's Zeppoles just down the boardwalk.

Pete and Elda's, 96 Woodland Ave. (Route 35 South), Neptune City; (732) 774-6010. Jersey Shore's best-known thin-crust pizza. Welcome sign: "No cell phone use while in dining room." Sausage pie not up to Lombardi's level, but the plain pie shot up nearly to the top of our cheesy charts. Crunchy, crackly crust, more seasoned than the others. A pie with attitude.

Peter's Fishery, 921 Route 34, Matawan; (732) 583-5666. Seafood joint dressed up as a diner. Manhattan clam chowder did not distinguish itself, but the lobster bisque a standout. Parmesan-crusted halibut a bit overcooked. One Muncher's evaluation of the fried haddock: "not good, not bad." The fried catfish sandwich — soft, tender, lightly and deftly fried — saved the day.

Pirate's Cove, 901 Port Monmouth Road, Belford; (732) 787-6600. Seafood restaurant, with an outdoor deck, nestled amidst the boats at the Belford Seafood Co-Op. Nice New England clam chowder; other soups didn't rate as well. Day's best crab cake. Excellent seared sea scallops.

Polar Bear, 128 Route 36, Middletown; (732) 291-9589. A giant vanilla cone sits on the roof of this roadside ice cream stand. Big appetite? Try the Ocean Liner — a double banana boat.

Potato Bar, Boardwalk, Keansburg. A fry stand with history, opening more than 50 years ago. Service sometimes indifferent, but fries — try to get them hot out of the fryer — a treat. Don't forget the salt and vinegar!

Princess Maria Diner and Restaurant, 2044 Route 35 North, Wall; (732) 282-1722. Open around the clock, and a good place to cap off a night at the Jersey Shore. Good Greek salad. Dependable, but not especially noteworthy, food.

Ray's Cafe, 523 Washington Blvd., Sea Girt; (732) 449-1717. Pork roll sandwich here a near-perfect blend of tasty meat, drippy cheese and chewy roll. Very good onion rings — crispy and crunchy. Okay burger, but good French toast, steak sandwich and chicken salad.

Re-Juice-a-Nation, 99 Main St., Manasquan; (732) 223-2222. Looks like George Jetson's living room, with retro, space-agey chairs. Excellent drinks and smoothies, and surprisingly good homemade sandwiches. There's another store in Hoboken.

River's Edge Cafe, 35 Broad St., Red Bank; (732) 741-7198. Omelets billed as "gourmet omelets," but several fell shy of that mark. The Rubusto Omelet featured good sausage, but there's no evidence of any marinara sauce, and the omelet is dried out. Best one is the simplest: the three-cheese, a marvelous, molten combination of Monterey jack, Swiss and cheddar.

Rooney's Ocean Crab House, 100 Ocean Ave., Long Branch; (732) 870-1200. Can't beat the views at this oceanfront restaurant. Emerald Cove oysters, fresh and near-fabulous, with eye-opening ginger lime and chipotle pepper dipping sauces. The steamed snow crab clusters and the 2-pound steamed Dungeness will please the most finicky crab lover. The Key West crab salad is super.

Saigon II, 650 E. Newman Springs Road, Lincroft; (732) 933-1964. Terrific banana shake. Grilled marinated beef dried out, but the charbroiled pork balls tender and juicy. Standouts: the Vietnamese spicy and sour prawn soup, with jumbo shrimp, pineapple, tomato, vegetables and tamarind; and the whole red snapper, seared crisp and topped with spicy and sour sauce. A real show-stopper.

Something Fishy, 140 Ocean Ave., Sea Bright; (732) 747-8340. Soggy, limp french fries, but the hot baked bread a welcome change to the usual bland restaurant rolls. Overcooked crab cake, but the Alaskan king crab legs made it on several Munchers' favorites-of-the-day list. The lemon sherbet one of the best desserts of the entire Munch summer.

Strollo's Lighthouse, 65 New Ocean Ave., Long Branch; (732) 222-1222. "High quality" ice at this Jersey Shore fixture, located across

the street from Seven Presidents Park. Other stores in Belmar and Red Bank.

Sunsets, 302 S. Concourse Ave., Neptune City; (732) 775-9911. Marina setting makes for an atmospheric dinner-and-drinks hangout. The oysters and Prince Edward Island mussels could have been fresher, but the lobster gazpacho is clean, light and luscious. So-so crab cakes, and mediocre Po' Boy, but the grilled swordfish steak and king crab legs are hits.

Tony's Family Restaurant, 228 Morris Ave., Long Branch; (732) 222-3535. Cozy hangout; popcorn machine on the bar, plants everywhere. The plain pie is more tomato-ey than cheesy, and the crust is more substantial than the others. The flat sauce didn't have much in the way of tart or tang. Good sausage, but still not as good as Lombardi's.

Twisted Tree Cafe, 609 Cookman Ave., Asbury Park; (732) 775-2633. This is the former Be Green, with much of the original menu carried over. The foccacia melt — roasted red peppers, artichokes, olives and vegan pesto on homemade bread — is a winner. So is the soy chicken salad sandwich.

Vic's Italian Restaurant, 60 Main St., Bradley Beach; (732) 774-8225. Fun, friendly, family place. Italian for beginners: ordinary pasta and sauces; the marinara recommended over the tomato sauce. Meatballs not in the same league as Libretti's. Can't go wrong with the pizza, though.

Whispers, 200 Monmouth Ave., Spring Lake; (732) 974-9755. Few Shore towns are as romantic as Spring Lake, and Whispers, in the Hewitt-Wellington Hotel, is a perfect, if pricey, getaway. Salad takes a creative turn with the grilled romaine heart with Caesar dressing, sun-dried tomatoes, pine nuts and red pepper.

Wilson's, 444 Ocean Blvd., Long Branch; (732) 229-5500. Classic ice cream parlor with weakest, least memorable ice cream of the trip. The strawberry and amaretto shakes the best of an average bunch.

The Windmill, 586 Ocean Ave., Long Branch; (732) 229-9863. Max's or the Windmill? There are devoted followers of each. Spicier dogs than Max's, plus a lively group of employees. And you can't beat the red windmill on the rooftop deck, with its view of the ocean.

Ye Olde Pie Shoppe, 74 Oceanport Ave., Little Silver; (732) 530-3337. Good Key lime pie; owner Tom Caruso uses Key West lime juice. Scones, muffins, other baked goods available. The banana cream pie — soft, pillowy, and jammed with bananas — is pie nirvana.

Zebu Forno Old World Bakery, 20 Broad St., Red Bank; (732) 936-9330. Good breads, bagels and scones. Twelve kinds of gelati

in summer. The peach burst with sweet, juicy flavor. The chocolate, a group favorite, is near-perfect, not too sweet, with nary an aftertaste. Also recommended: the stracciatella, with its subtly minty taste.

Morris

Alexis Diner Restaurant, 3130 Route 10 West, Denville; (973) 361-8000. The Alexis and the Jefferson Diner each describes itself as Morris County's number-one diner; we'll give the nod to the Alexis. The Reuben may be better than the one at your favorite deli. The patty melt the summer's best hamburger. Good French toast, too.

A and A Fine Foods, 191 Main St., Lincoln Park; (973) 633-7878. Classic Italian deli-specialty store where the TV is tuned to the Food Network. As if you need any motivation or appetite. Display case filled with fresh grilled artichoke hearts; hand-rolled peppers with prosciutto and provolone; rosemary herb-seasoned stuffed chicken breast and other items.

Anthony's Pizza and Pasta, 47 S. Park Place, Morristown; (973) 285-5464. First-rate sausage and mushroom pie, even if the sausage seemed of the assembly-line variety. Margarita pizza nice, but it could have used more flavor and feistiness.

Applegate Farm, 134 Ridgedale Ave., East Hanover; (973) 884-0222. Call it an ice cream palace: a towering white building with a winding walk leading to the cold creamy treasure inside. You can literally buy the Farm here — it's a 16-scoop sundae, with four toppings and two bananas.

Arthur's Tavern, 700 Speedwell Ave, Morris Plains; (973) 455-9705. A museum of beer, with giant plastic bottles hanging from the ceiling. Good Delmonico steak — 48 ounces, only $25.95. Bring lots of cash; they don't take credit cards.

Attilio's Tavern, 80 E. McFarlan St., Dover; (973) 328-1100. Formerly located in Denville, Attilio's continues to serve high-quality Italian food.

Bagels of Parsippany, 294 Route 46 West, Parsippany-Troy Hills; (973) 575-4380. Owner Mo Shaltout's Black Russian bagel is a sumptuous, sinewy combination of pumpernickel and cinnamon raisin. His homemade salads, especially the tuna and chicken, really got the Munch Team's attention.

Best Little Luncheonette, 233 Main St., Chatham; (973) 635-8949. Best pancakes in the county? The mozzarella/provolone omelet nice and gooey. Good sausage links. Scrapple, an acquired taste if there ever was one, available here.

Big D's, Crescent Park, Dover. Truck offers standard-issue Sabrett. We liked the hot onions, though.

Boonton Diner, 909 Main St., Boonton; (973) 335-4897. Classic small-town diner. Vintage Coke machines and AMI jukeboxes provide the retro decor. We liked the Sloppy Joe, the Sloppy Joe chili dog, and the French toast.

Bosphorus Restaurant, 32 N. Beverwyck Road, Lake Hiawatha; (973) 335-9690. The lamb chops in the mixed grill (karisik izgara) dried out, although the chicken kebab in the same dish featured subtly seasoned chicken. Chalky hummus, but delicious baba ghanoush. Best baklava of the day found here. Turkish coffee muddy, murky and marvelous.

Branda's Italian Grill, 1 Mount Olive Road, Budd Lake; (973) 448-0300. Food not on the same level as D'Italia or Cosimo's, but there are still things to like, including the spiedini, eggplant lasagna and the stracciatella. Middle-of-the-road pasta fagioli and pizza, but the roasted pepper and mozzarella ravioli might get your attention.

Caffé Buono, 215 Newark-Pompton Turnpike, Pequannock; (973) 406-4081. Attractive, spacious cafe, but the desserts not on the same level as other stops on this trip. Carrot cake had a split personality — good cake, so-so icing. The regular cheesecake and blackout cake both tasted as if they were past their expiration date. Ordinary rugelach. Not-bad peach pie. Best item: the made-on-premises croissants, thick and chewy.

Calaloo Cafe, 190 South St., Morristown; (973) 993-1100. Cool atmosphere: fish-mural bar, outdoor patio engulfed by tropical plants. Chicken with garlic dried out; turkey breast and seafood pasta much better. Huevos rancheros and Italian frittata, on special brunch menu, both recommended.

Casa Maya, 615 Meyersville Road, Meyersville; (908) 580-0799. In the middle of nowhere, but worth the trip. Excellent gazpacho. Adventurous? Try the Cactus Enchiladas.

Chand Palace, 257 Littleton Road, Parsippany; (973) 334-5444. Start with the garlic nan, from the tandoor oven. The mulligatawny, with lentil and tomatoes, and the tomato soup, with a hint of black pepper, both smooth and subtle. Favorite entree: sabzi vindaloo, mixed vegetables swimming in a spicy, tomato-ey sauce.

Chatham Bakery, 463 Main St., Chatham; (973) 635-1960. Quintessential small-town bakery is home to the "patty cake," a 5-inch pie. The plain cheesecake may have been the creamiest of all those sampled, but the chocolate cheesecake, with its almost pudding-like filling, came as a slight disappointment. But several Munchers ranked the fresh fruit cheesecake among the day's favorites.

Chili Willie's, 702 Main St., Boonton; (973) 299-8775. The menu at this cozy, pastel-walled restaurant is Mexican, with a dose of the Do-

minican, reflecting the owners' backgrounds. Average salsa and chips, but most of the entrees are first-rate, including the pulled pork, queso flameado con chorizo, chicken enchilada with chipotle sauce, and especially the pork chops Durango, a rousing, garlic-spiced delight.

Circle Grill, 134 Route 46 East, Netcong; (973) 347-9090. Replaced the late, great Cozy Drive-In. Chili looked good, tasted OK. Standard dog, but better-than-average toppings.

Cliff's Dairy Maid, 1475 Route 46, Ledgewood; (973) 584-9721. Best roadside ice cream stop in the state, as far as I'm concerned. If the Double Dark Chocolate Fudge Crunch doesn't satisfy your chocolate craving, nothing will.

Cluck-U Chicken, 64 Morris St., Morristown; (973) 540-0186. The summer's hottest experience: the fire eater wings here. Have plenty of water nearby; the clucker bees — cornbread bits — make a good palliative. Honey barbecue wings not particularly distinctive. Nuclear wings won't set off any alarms at the White House or your house. Best wing: the thermo, slathered with a thick, peppery sauce.

Collins Bar and Restaurant, 688 Speedwell Ave., Morris Plains; (973) 455-9831. Huge burgers in Irish pub/sports bar setting.

Cornerstone Cafe and Deli, 65 Indian Road, Denville; (973) 625-5320. Hungry? Try the 3/4 pound Mega Burger at this homey luncheonette on Indian Lake. Good Colby Jack cheeseburger and veggie burger, too.

Country Pie Factory, 67 E. Mill Road, Long Valley; (908) 876-8500. Sally Vilardi's strip-mall pie store is country cute — black and white tile floors, sunshiny-yellow walls. I loved her powdered sugar and crumble-topped peach pie, and her tart-like blueberry Diane is a delight.

Davy's Dogs, 14 Howard Blvd., Mount Arlington; (973) 770-3289. Swiss chalet-like hot dog stand. The tiny Sabrett's dog seemed lost in the big roll, but the dog is spicy and flavorful.

Denville Dairy, 34A Broadway, Denville; (973) 627-4214. Does a big business in ice cream cakes year-round. About 25 flavors of hard ice cream are available; we loved the Panda Paws, with coconut and fudge chips; the Party Cake, made with real cake mix; and Oreos and cream. Excellent extra-thick shakes. The mango ice bursts with flavor; the passion fruit ice is much less intense.

Denville Seafood, 61 Broadway, Denville; (973) 627-2987. Clean, brightly-lit market and adjacent restaurant. Super soups: a thick, savory seafood gumbo; a smooth shrimp bisque; a tuna-and-salmon-stocked bouillabaisse, but the clam chowder could have been better. Also recommended: the crab cake sandwich and the smoked fish salad.

Don Jose Mexican Restaurant, 200 Route 10 West, East Hanover; (973) 781-0155. Spectacular, vivid mural — fruit stands, cantinas, flamenco dancers — wraps around the walls. Chili-studded salsa the spiciest we encountered. Excellent cheese taco, oozing Muenster. Steak chimichanga: greasy shell, but succulent steak. Recommended appetizer: shrimp el Dorado — juicy, bacon-wrapped shrimp.

Donut Towne, 370 N. Main St., Wharton; (973) 361-6887. Doughnuts fried in soy oil, which means less transfat. Big, distinctive doughnuts here, including a Frisbee-sized coffee roll. The mixed-jelly doughnut, with its swirl of boysenberry, grape and blackberry, amounts to sweet surrender.

The Dover Grill, 240 Route 46 East, Dover; (973) 989-4007. Dynamite chili — a tomato-ey, slightly spicy mix. The Texas weiner sauce is nowhere as good. First-rate hot onions.

Enjou, 8 DeHart St., Morristown; (973) 993-9090. You name it; the folks at Enjou will make it out of chocolate. One customer ordered a set of solid chocolate noses for her doctor, who had done her nose job. Chocolate-covered popcorn an immediate hit. Dark almond bar is chunky, chewy, terrific.

Falls View Grill, 25 Newton-Pompton Turnpike, Pequannock; (973) 872-2299. "Famous" hot dog turned out to be "skinless, tasteless, useless," according to one of our hot dog panelists.

Florham Park Deli, 182 Ridgedale Ave., Florham Park; (973) 301-2000. Owner Mary Venturi makes surprisingly good homemade mozzarella and excellent iced tea. Different: the Manny sandwich, with a chicken cutlet, bacon, cheese and mashed potatoes.

The Great Wazu, 33 Ridgedale Ave., East Hanover; (973) 386-1114. We found most of the subs here lacking. Two we liked: the Paisano (prosciutto, sharp provolone, mozzarella, roasted peppers, red onions and arugula) and the roast beef sub, with excellent, juicy-red meat.

Health Shoppe, 66 Morris St., Morristown; (973) 538-9131. Talk about choices; this health food supermarket is located next to a Burger King. The chicken curry salad is subtle and satisfying. Standouts: the New Yorker (roast beef with horseradish and Russian dressing on rye) and the Mastermind (Genoa salami, provolone and balsamic vinegar on Tuscan hero roll).

Heritage Grill, 18 Broadway, Denville; (973) 983-9600. Hardwood floors and early American furniture make for pleasing, patriotic atmosphere. Four salads sampled all contained abundant, tender meat and fish, but paltry greens. Great grilled steak in the Wyoming Ranchers Salad deserved better than the so-so greens.

Hot Rods Real Pit BBQ, 19 N. Main St., Wharton; (973) 361-5050. Owner Anthony Sibona makes some meaty music here. Ribs nice and thick. Thick, husky barbecue sauce. Memorable baked beans, with a strong, almost smoky flavor. Crisp corn on the cob, and cornbread with apple butter. Good hush puppies, too.

J. Emanuel, 57 Main St., Chester; (888) 536-2683. Upscale chocolate shop. Nearly 40 kinds of truffles, including Bailey's Irish Cream and dark French Bordeaux. Trademark treat is Chester Crunch, in milk or dark chocolate, bursting with a great, nutty, chocolatey taste. Expensive but worth it.

Jefferson Dairy, 741 Route 15 South, Jefferson; (973) 663-1750. Popular roadside ice cream stop. Chocolate chip ice cream sundae with hot fudge sauce: outstanding.

The Jefferson Diner, Pathmark Shopping Center, 5 Bowling Green (Route 15), Jefferson; (973) 663-0233. The Jefferson did some items — pancakes, hash browns, omelets — better than rival Alexis. Real syrup: That's always a plus. The Greek salad needs work.

Jeremiah's, 44 N. Beverwyck Road, Lake Hiawatha; (973) 334-2004. Frogs — frolicking on lily pads, flying through the air — make for a colorful cafe. Owner Theresa Navarro named the cafe after her brother, Jeremy Giordano, one of two pizza deliverymen murdered in Sussex County in 1997. Great salad: the Salad Theresa, a sweet summery mix of candied walnuts, grilled onions, mixed greens, tomatoes and tender chicken. My vote for salad of the year. Salad Valerie — strips of delicious grilled prosciutto, chicken and Parmesan over greens — is merely terrific.

Jimmy Buff's, 354 Route 10 West, East Hanover; (973) 463-0099. Buff's invented the Italian hot dog — Jersey's contribution to cholesterol naughtiness or nirvana, depending on how you look at it. Good sausage, too.

Kabab Paradise, 76 N. Beverwyck Road, Lake Hiawatha; (973) 334-7900. This Morris County community has become a United Nations of food, with the Afghan-centric Kabab Paradise fitting right in. Start with the wondrous flatbread and the tangy, cilantro-peppy green sauce. Loved the leek dumplings and borani banjan (eggplant), but much of the food seemed heavy and/or bland.

Lin's Palace, 40 Speedwell Ave., Morristown; (973) 993-8668. Formerly known as Mr. Lin's, this is a big step up from your neighborhood Chinese takeout place. Creative dishes; the various sauces are a revelation.

Long Valley Pub and Brewery, 1 Fairmount Road, Long Valley; (908) 876-1122. Housed in a 200-year-old barn in picturesque Long Valley. Go with the sesame wings instead of the hot wings. Filet mignon nicely cooked, and the mahi-mahi flaky and tender. Surprisingly good angel hair with shrimp and tomatoes. Best brews: German Valley Amber, distinct and delightful, and the Lazy Jake Porter, smooth and friendly.

Maggie Moo's, 50 Route 10 West, East Hanover; (973) 599-0010. The Banana Moo (three kinds of ice cream, three kinds of toppings and three mix-ins, plus a banana, whipped cream, nuts and cherries) is a creamy wonder.

Mara's Country Desserts, 281 Speedwell Ave., Morristown; (973) 682-9200. Best cheesecakes in the state, period. Standouts: almond brownie chocolate cheesecake, baked atop a chocolate cookie crust, studded with brownie chunks and topped with chocolate ganache and toasted almonds; the strawberry swirl cheesecake, with fruit blended in; and caramel apple streusel, with a great crumbly crust.

Maria's, 49 N. Main St., Wharton; (973) 366-4790. Neighborhood hangout didn't surprise or disappoint. Go for the pizza, with a chewy/crunchy crust and agreeable sauce.

McCool's Ice Cream Parlour, 26 Main St., Madison; (973) 301-0303. Shakes offered a nice balance of flavor and consistency. Big winner: the outrageous oatmeal cookie shake. Both the chocolate and vanilla shakes are creamy-smooth. The rainbow sherbet shake a cool, colorful treat.

Minuteman Restaurant and Pie Shop, 990 Route 202 at Bailey's Mill Road, Harding; (973) 425-9798. Sells about 25,000 pies a year. Apple pie not as good as counterparts at Delicious Orchards or Best's Fruit Farm, but the harvest pie is a bewitching blend of cranberry, pecans and awesome apple crumb. Good cherry pie, too.

Mr. B's Grill, 84 Speedwell Ave., Morristown; (973) 451-0141. Plain cheesesteak seemed a little light on the cheese, but the meat is tender, and the roll soft and chewy. Chicken cheesesteak better. Best steak sampled: the Billy B, with stewed tomatoes and hot peppers.

Mrs. Erb's Good Food, 20 First Ave., Denville; (973) 627-5440. Store shelves stocked with vitamins, drinks, organic honey cake, peanut butter brownie cupcakes and other items. Excellent salads, especially the hearts of palm in an oh-so-light dressing of extra virgin olive oil and lemon juice, and the delicious kale slaw, with organically grown kale, carrots, onions, parsley, apple cider vinegar, sea salt and pepper.

Nikko, 881 Route 10 East, Whippany; (973) 428-0787. Spicy tuna tataki consists of succulent slivers of tuna atop crisp, translucent-green seaweed. Homemade coconut juice — thick, sweet, ice-cold — is outstanding. Also good: the gyoza or shrimp dumplings; lobster roll; yakitori (skewered chunks of chicken) and naruto roll.

Old Mill Tavern, 55 Route 24, Chester Twp.; (908) 879-9815. The bar's "suicidal" wings are terrific, but they may have you calling for the local fire department, if not a team of paramedics. Outstanding blue cheese dressing!

Pop's, 42 Lincoln Place, Madison; (973) 301-0101. A storefront with funk; there's a skeleton-topped walking stick in the corner. Not your typical takeout; specials include apple-smoked prime rib, apple smoked brisket and wagon wheel mac and cheese. Ribs here the best of those sampled — spicy, juicy, pull-apart good. Great seasoned collard greens.

Portofino's, 29 Mills St., Morristown; (973) 540-0026. Big portions. The seafood marecharia, an avalanche of shrimp, clams, mussels, scungilli and calamari with pasta of your choice, will give you enough fuel to run several marathons.

Pub 199, 199 Howard Blvd., Mount Arlington; (973) 398-7454. Deer, bear, mountain goat, wild turkey and other animals are mounted on the walls of the antler-chandeliered dining room. Disappointing fries. But we liked the thick slabs of bacon in the bacon burger.

Reservoir Tavern, 90 Parsippany Blvd., Parsippany; (973) 334-5708. Far from thin-crust, as several readers claimed, but a good pie nevertheless. It's a very saucy pie, with a strong tomato-ey taste. One Muncher thought the sauce overwhelmed the cheese, but another thought the crust near-perfect — crunchy and chewy at the same time. Not thin-crust, but a pizza with purpose.

Ruth's Chris Steak House, Parsippany Hilton, 1 Hilton Court, Parsippany; (973) 889-1400. Great appetizers (seared ahi tuna and carpaccio tenderloin), killer desserts (creme brulee and cheesecake).

Sergio and Company, 28 Broadway, Denville; (973) 627-1043. "Friendliest person on earth" one customer said of Sergio Sciancalepore, owner of this Italian specialty shop. We can't argue with that. The well-stocked store is fragrant with the smell of mozzarella, peppers, semolina and focaccia. Excellent sandwiches.

Soho 33, 33 Main St., Madison; (973) 822-2600. "World comfort cuisine" is the motto here, although it's not always carried off successfully. First-rate salad: the arugula salad, with spiced walnuts, roasted pears, blue cheese and greens. The roasted pears were so good we wished we could have ordered a gallon to go.

South Street Creamery, 146 South St., Morristown; (973) 267-8887. The sweet cream ice cream here is smooth, creamy, light, refreshing. You can get your ice cream straight or have items swirled together on a marble slab. They also have homemade baked goods; the double chocolate brownies are first-rate.

Stewart's Root Beer, 449 Route 46, Rockaway; (973) 328-0070. "Crushingly ordinary" hot dog, according to S.W.A.T. Dog team member. Average chili.

Sun High Orchards, 19 Canfield Ave., Randolph; (973) 584-4734. Pies, made by a supplier in Ohio, are temptingly eclectic. The cherry rhubarb a delicious combination of two highly compatible fruits; the light, flaky crust the equal of any of the homemade crusts sampled. Good apple raspberry, too.

Taylor's Ice Cream Parlor, 18 E. Main St., Chester; (908) 879-5363. Take your cone out on the porch and enjoy Chester's classic small-town atmosphere. Death by Chocolate among the day's best chocolates, and the cotton candy ice cream is a carnival of delights.

Thai Thai, 1168 Valley Road, Stirling; (908) 903-0790. Tom kha gai, the traditional Thai coconut milk soup, is excellent — smooth and silky, with lemongrass, lime leaves, chiles and mushrooms. Entrees sampled not in the same class, though.

Veggie Heaven, 1119 Route 46 East, Parsippany; (973) 335-9876. May not be for everyone, but it is different. Meat dishes made from blends of bean curd, taro root, wheat gluten, mushrooms and other vegetables. Good juices.

Venturini's Super Deli, 802 Main St., Boonton; (973) 335-1642. Classic small-town deli, with some of the biggest sandwiches you'll find anywhere. Super Sloppy Joe. The subs are a bit oily; you may want to ask them to go easy.

Viking Bakery, 34 First Ave., Denville; (973) 627-7333. Oversize chunks in the chunky chip cookie. Good chocolate eclairs, and a monstrous, memorable sugar doughnut. "Great" white chocolate chunk cookie, according to one Muncher. A few things didn't float our boat, including the bowtie, black-and-white cookie and brownie.

Wightman's Farms, 1111 Mount Kemble Road, Harding; (973) 425-9819. Average apple and blueberry pies. The coconut custard pie is nicely constructed, but the filling is inferior. The lemon crunch pie probably the best of those sampled.

Ocean

Beach Haven Fishery, 2115 Long Beach Blvd., Spray Beach; (609) 492-4388. "Best meal of the year," News12 reporter Tony Caputo raved after our stop. King crab legs; grilled swordfish on a bed of arugula with portabello mushrooms sauteed in garlic butter; and the grilled tuna with crushed tomato bruschetta and fresh arugula in balsamic vinegar, all first-rate.

Berkeley Clam Bar, 1808 Boardwalk, Seaside Park; (732) 793-8833. Raw bar on the fabled — some say tawdry — Seaside boardwalk. Slurp up a dozen oysters, then head over to the nearby Sawmill for a slice of "The World's Largest Pizza."

Broadway Bar and Grill, 106 Randall Ave., Point Pleasant Beach; (732) 899-3272. Trick here is finding a parking spot at happy hour in the summer. The building, with its houseboat-like interior, housed Nealy's Long Bar for 50-plus years. The wings — fat, crispy, slightly blackened on top, with a smooth, tangy, tomato-tinged sauce — the best in the state, as far as the Big Dog's driver is concerned.

Bum Rogers, 2207 S.W. Central Ave., Seaside Park; (732) 830-2770. Located at entrance to Island Beach State Park. We're sweet on Jean LaFeet, Bum's name for its "oven-blasted" zesty-spiced garlic crabs. Crabs arrabiatta — garlic crabs baked in a marinara-like Cajun spicy sauce — didn't know whether it wanted to be Cajun, Italian or something else entirely.

Charlie's Cafe, 491 Route 35, Normandy Beach; (732) 793-3300. They should call this place Cheesecake Charlie's. The farm market/cafe makes 5,000 cheesecakes a summer, and just on Mondays and Tuesdays, although you can buy them any day. The regular cheesecake is so light it practically floats above the plate. The chocolate cheesecake, nearly mousse-like and topped with chocolate bits, may be even better.

The Chicken or the Egg, 207 N. Bay Ave., Beach Haven; (609) 492-3695. Decor runs from a Norman Rockwell or two to crab traps and a giant Swatch watch. Good combo: apple cobbler pancakes and fresh-squeezed orange juice. Chicken wings come in 14 sauces, from mild to ludicrous. Don't try the ludicrous unless you feel really stupid.

Chicken Town, 2791 Hooper Ave., Brick; (732) 920-3870. The deep-fried wings here are tender and meaty, but the Buffalo sauce is one we've tasted hundreds of times before. The barbecue wings, though, really take flight: super-crisp but not overcooked, coated with a tangy, slightly sweet sauce. Excellent apple fritters: crunchy and juicy.

Colonial Bakery, 1906 Grand Central Ave., Lavallette; (732) 854-9500. The jelly doughnuts alone make the trip down the Parkway worthwhile. Tasty sugar twists and other doughnuts. The coffee's surprisingly good.

The Cottage, 35 Broadway, Point Pleasant Beach; (732) 892-9513. You've got to play by the rules here — no French toast before 8 a.m., for example — but the frequent weekend waits are worth it, for good, honest dockside breakfasts. Walk inside, give your name and wait in the parking lot. You'll be called when your table is ready.

Country Kettle Chowda, 830 N. Bay Ave., Beach Haven; (609) 492-2858. Chowderfest is a big deal on Long Beach Island, and Country

Kettle has won the New England clam chowder competition three times. Its New England is nicely seasoned; we liked it much better than the Manhattan clam chowder, which seemed familiar, formulaic. Best of the bunch: the lobster bisque, smooth and creamy.

The Crab's Claw Inn, 601 Route 35 North, Lavallette; (732) 793-4447. Shore institution, and weekend hot spot. Homemade crab cake is recommended — fine, fried texture and a soft but not mealy filling. Dungeness crab, steamed in beer, does this crustacean proud. Seafood lasagna too cheesy. Double fudge chocolate ice cream cake is delicious.

Donuts Plus, 3173 Route 35 North, Ocean Beach; (732) 793-8646. Apple turnover, light and puffy, markedly better than the leaden one at your local diner. Excellent Boston cream doughnut, and the almond delight is a streusel-topped wonder. Pretty good pork roll, egg and cheese sandwich, too.

Emery's Berry Patch, 346 Long Swamp Road, New Egypt; (609) 758-8514. Homemade pie heaven. The peach berry, fragrant with peaches, cherries and blueberries, is outstanding. The berries in the blueberry pie, the freshest of all those sampled; you almost expect to find a "just picked" tag.

Exit 63 Seafood Corner, 747 E. Bay Ave., Manahawkin; (609) 978-3474. Some of the best sides sampled all year; too bad the main courses are not on the same level. Outstanding fries, good onion rings, excellent crab bisque. Swordfish sandwich, juicy, but the tuna sandwich, mediocre. Fish and chips, a nice surprise. Skip the scrod.

Forked River Butcher Shop, 109 Lacey Road, Forked River; (609) 693-7100. Wolfgang Barsch runs this spacious deli-butcher shop, with a smokehouse next door. They'll deliver a roasted whole pig right to your door. Lovely liverwurst, thick and juicy. The schnitzel is tender and tasty, and the apple strudel is delicious.

Gregory's Seafood Market and Restaurant, 2064 Route 37 West, Manchester; (732) 323-9105. Sit outside, like we did, on canopy-covered benches. Average oysters, but a nice New England clam chowder. Mediocre crab cakes. Salmon Michelangelo a beautifully tender piece of fish atop scalloped potatoes.

Harvey Cedars Shellfish Co., 7904 Long Beach Blvd., Harvey Cedars; (609) 494-7112. Louisiana crawdads, with spiced shells and Cajun dipping sauce, make for a great start. Sauteed clams and mussels in ambrosial white wine, garlic, butter, herb and Parmesan cheese sauce. Clams marinara did not live up to the menu's "hot and spicy" billing.

Harvey Cedars Shellfish Co. Clam Bar, 506 Centre St., Beach Haven; (609) 492-2459. Give your name to the waitress, drop your beer or wine in the iced bucket, and wait outside for your name to be called. Cocktail sauce, with Worcestershire sauce, lemon juice and horseradish, packs a punch. Excellent New England clam chowder. Crispy fries, maybe the summer's best. Mussels with white wine outstanding.

Hoffman's Ice Cream, 800 Richmond Ave., Point Pleasant Beach; (732) 892-0270. A Shore tradition. The chocolate chocolate chip, rich and velvety smooth, probably the best of all the chocolates sampled.

Jeff's Cotton Candy, Casino Pier, Seaside Heights. Watch the man spin a bundle of sugary fun onto a paper cone. "I prefer pink because it's the more stereotypical cotton candy, but the blue was fine," one Muncher said. "Actually, it was great."

Joe Leone's, 400 Route 35 South, Point Pleasant Beach; (732) 701-0001. You can buy a $200 bottle of balsamic vinegar here (for sipping), but you'll more likely settle for the aromatic array of gourmet salads, hot entrees, imported pastas, fresh mozzarella, delicious potato and rice balls, homemade bread and other items.

Kelly's Old Barney Restaurant, Third Avenue and Broadway, Barnegat Light; (609) 494-5115. Dependable restaurant in shadow of Old Barney. Good Manhattan clam chowder. Crisp, sweet corn on the cob. Tuna in the tuna sandwich overcooked, but French fries a beautiful golden brown. Best appetizer: potato skin with broccoli and homemade cheese sauce.

Kohr's Frozen Custard, Grant and Boardwalk, Seaside Heights; (732) 793-4343. No better late-night treat than a Kohr's soft ice cream cone. Family business can be traced to 1919, when five brothers named Kohr opened an ice cream stand on Coney Island.

Lainie's Ice Cream Porch, 811 Bay Ave., Beach Haven; (609) 207-0777. Pink-awninged ice cream stand across the street from a brilliantly-lit Ferris wheel. We loved the chocolate shake, fat-free vanilla yogurt and the pistachio ice cream.

M and M Steam Bar, 13301 Long Beach Blvd., Beach Haven Terrace; (609) 492-9106. It's a Munchmobile kind of place: Sit at the open-air bar and order from the seemingly endless menu. Great soups. The blackened swordfish one of the summer's best fish entrees. You'll find better crab cakes elsewhere.

Mario's Italian Market, 1905 Long Beach Blvd., Surf City; (609) 361-2500. Surfside Italian deli crammed with meats, bread, cheese, pastries, homemade sausage and enough prepared food to shame many restaurants. Good olives, decent mozzarella. Cappellini cakes disappointing, but the fried ravioli a wicked, wonderful treat.

Martell's Shrimp Bar, 310 Boardwalk, Point Pleasant Beach; (732) 295-2526. Not to be confused with the raw bar, this stand is just in-

side the boardwalk entrance of Martell's. Try the blackened tuna bites, seared in an iron pan. Or the Atlantic grouper sandwich, topped with a mango and mandarin orange salsa. I ran into a couple from Riverdale who make two trips a year just for the shrimp gumbo.

Martell's Tiki Bar, 308 Boardwalk, Point Pleasant Beach; (732) 892-0131. Martell's Tiki Bar is a Jersey Shore institution. About 1,500 oysters and clams each are shucked on a typical summer weekend at the outdoor raw bar, where you can also get fresh-squeezed orange juice.

Maruca's Tomato Pies, Boardwalk and Porter Avenue, Seaside Park; (732) 793-0707. The best pizza on any Jersey boardwalk. Don't you dare try to tell me otherwise.

Mrs. Walker's Ice Cream, 132 S. Main St., Forked River; (609) 693-9500. An hard ice cream lover's vision of paradise, with 35 flavors, including Swiss chocolate almond and banana fudge. Good, not great, chocolate shake. The highlight: a strawberry sundae with vanilla custard, the latter sensationally smooth.

Mud City Crab House, 1185 E. Bay Ave., Manahawkin; (609) 978-3660. Food ranged from good to near-great. New England clam chowder tasted like it had stopped at Boston; could have used more pep. The Maryland clam chowder, with fat chunks of tomatoes, a group favorite. Garlic crabs: too many bread crumbs, not enough garlic and butter. Outstanding entrees: blackened grilled salmon, blackened tuna and marinated tuna. Made every Muncher's top-10 list for the summer.

Mueller's Bakery, 80 Bridge Ave., Bay Head; (732) 892-0442. Known for its crumb buns, but we found them OK, at best. Loved the chocolate doughnuts and the jelly doughnuts, oozing liquidy sweetness.

Mustache Bill's, Broadway and Eighth Street, Barnegat Light; (609) 494-0155. Classic 1950s diner within walking distance of Old Barney. Omelets, overall, are terrific — eggy, fluffy, fresh. Real good grits, served in a big bowl with melted butter. Good potato salad and cole slaw.

Ob-Co's Donuts, 547 Fischer Blvd., Toms River; (732) 270-3882. Doughnuts from 6:30 a.m. on, and once they run out, that's it. The "croissant doughnut" bears little resemblance to a croissant; it's a cinnamony-twisty creation that is the best doughnut I've had in years. The apple fritters are enormous, and the chocolate and cream doughnuts are superb. You're going to love this shack.

Off The Hook, 1905 Bayview Ave. and 20th Street, Barnegat Light; (609) 361-8900. At the far north end of LBI and worth the ride. Takeout only, but you can sit at one of the tables at adjacent Viking Village, a series of fishing shacks-turned-gift shops. Don't you dare leave without trying the scallops. The fried soft shell crab and tuna teriyaki first-rate. The Manhattan clam chowder should be better.

Pinky Shrimp's, 8211 Long Beach Blvd., Beach Haven Crest; (609) 492-0706. Sit on benches outside and feast away. Great Manhattan and New England clam chowders. Famous Fish Kebabs are excellent.

Primo Hoagies, 500 Brick Blvd., Brick; (732) 920-2334. Gets my vote for best subs down the Shore. It all starts with good bread, from Liscio's in Glassboro. Good meat — they use Thumann's — and loads of it. No vinegar is used unless you ask for it; it curdles the meat, they say.

Red's Lobster Pot Restaurant, 57 Inlet Drive, Point Pleasant Beach; (732) 295-6622. Colorful waterfront haunt, with boats docked outside. Terrific linguine in white clam sauce and Pasta Posilippo. Lobster doesn't get any fresher. Outdoor bar, too.

Sawmill Cafe, 1809 Boardwalk, Seaside Park; (732) 793-1990. The World's Largest Slice of Pizza can be found at this famous boardwalk bar. It's not bad, considering the state of most boardwalk pizza.

Shore Fresh Seafood Market, 703-707 Bridge Ave., Point Pleasant; (732) 899-1300. Fresh fish and shellfish glisten on plastic sheet-covered mounds of ice. Fried flounder sandwich, blackened tuna bites and fried halibut sandwich among hits. Forgettable: the cole slaw and tartar sauce.

Shrimp Box, 75 Inlet Drive, Point Pleasant Beach; (732) 899-1634. Fresh, juicy oysters. Blackened salmon seemed overcooked, but one Muncher loved it. Excellent king crab legs. Very good New England clam chowder. Nearby is Red's Lobster Pot, a highly recommended Munch stop.

Skeeter's Crazy Water Cafe, 120 W. Main St., Tuckerton; (609) 296-4163. Fishing reels and 25-foot-long bamboo outriggers provide the decor. The Skeeters Special, with crab, clams and shrimp, is a good start. Highly recommended: the shrimp gumbo, she-crab soup, and beer-battered soft-shell crabs. Skeeters is located at Tuckerton Seaport, well worth a visit on its own.

Slice of Heaven, 610 N. Bay Ave., Beach Haven; (609) 492-1900. It may sound yucky, but the cheesesteak-stuffed pizza here is the stuff of Munch legend. Think the best cheesesteak you've ever had, minus the roll and grease, inside a first-rate Sicilian pie. Tips the scale at an astounding six pounds. Unforgettable.

Spike's Fish Market Restaurant, 415 Broadway, Point Pleasant Beach; (732) 295-9400. Classic Jersey Shore seafood shack. Don't feel like waiting an hour or two? Place a takeout order, like we did; it

was filled in 20 minutes. Homemade desserts, including a killer Key Lime pie.

Steaks Unlimited, 21 Ocean Terrace, Seaside Heights; (732) 830-8830. Nothing like a fat, greasy cheesesteak at 4 or 5 in the morning. Or so say the late-night denizens of this open-air, block-from-the-boardwalk stand. Chicken cheesesteak drew oohs and ahhs from the Munchers, but it's not on Chick's lofty level.

Sunny Hunny by the Sea, 1907 Route 35 North, Ortley Beach; (732) 793-3717. Popular Shore breakfast spot. Lukewarm coffee, so-so buttermilk pancakes, dry Canadian bacon. But good hash browns, creamed chipped beef and eggs Benedict.

Surf Taco, 1300 Richmond Ave., Point Pleasant Beach; (732) 701-9000. Catch a wave and then some tacos. Surfboard-decorated shop serves no-surprises Mexican. Self-serve salsa bar a nice touch. You'll find better beans elsewhere. Try the steak tacos, chicken enchilada. Fun place; food could be better.

Uncle Bill's, 2112 Asbury Ave., Ocean City; (609) 398-7393. Part of popular Shore minichain. Spongy pancakes, but good cinnamon-dusted French toast. Maybe the biggest hunk of scrapple you'll ever see, for whatever that's worth. Customers have been known to put syrup on it. Yum!

Passaic

A and S Pork Store, 281 Browertown Road, West Paterson; (908) 735-5232. Old-style Italian deli. Friendly, funny staff. Great subs, including the Godfather (ham, prosciutto, cappicola and mozzarella) and the Goodfella (mortadella and fresh mozzarella).

Bethwood, 38 Lackawanna Ave., Totowa; (973) 256-8316. Best dessert spread of all the brunches. Try the apple-filled French toast. Lasagna Bolognese marred by mealy meat filling. Sausage croute, beef Portuguesa, chicken Normandy filled with artichoke salsa among unusual offerings.

Big Daddy's Hot Dogs, 62 Main St., Little Falls; (973) 785-0206. Eat 12 dogs, become member of Ed Borne's Dirty Dozen Club. Staggering selection of sauces, some of them staggeringly hot, to go with pushcart-style dogs.

E and V Ristorante, 322 Chamberlain Ave., Paterson; (973) 942-8080. Maybe the biggest servings of Italian food anywhere. Try the filet mignon bruschetta and the "assorted specialty" as appetizers; proceed to the gnocchi or the fusilli with sun-dried tomatoes and pesto. No credit cards.

El Sol De Cuba Restaurant, 161 Passaic St., Passaic; (973) 472-4400. Mamey shake, named after peach-shaped West Indian fruit, the perfect tonic for a hot day. Biftec Sol de Cuba, a savory strip steak, and biftec de pollo (chicken steak) equally tender and delicious. The pollo assado al vino (baked chicken in wine) among the day's favorites.

Goffle Grill, 1140 Goffle Road, Hawthorne; (201) 423-0881. Legendary Passaic County hot dog stand. The chili more of the nutmeg or cinnamon-flavored variety common to Passaic. Excellent shakes. "Uninspiring" dog, according to one Muncher.

Guernsey Crest Ice Cream Co., 134 19th Ave., Paterson; (973) 742-4620. Ignore the graffiti-streaked facade, and the fact that the ceiling looks as if it's about to collapse. Step up to the heavy duty plastic-sheeted front counter — is this an ice cream stand or check-cashing service? — and pick up a cone or shake. All the shakes have a smooth, silky consistency.

Hot Dog Hut, 126 Mountainview Blvd., Wayne. Dozens of sauces line the shelves. The meaty chili rocks. But inferior dog.

Hot Grill, 669 Lexington Ave., Clifton; (201) 772-6000. Our S.W.A.T. Doggers split on the deep-fried dog — one called it "average," another a "classic." Your call.

Jimmy Geez, 436 Belmont Ave., Haledon; (973) 790-9729. Wings come swaddled in foil-wrapped baskets, with crunchy carrots that would make Bugs Bunny happy. B and B wing is a creative mix of hot sauce, barbecue sauce and honey mustard, but none of the ingredients really step forward. Buffalo fingers boast a delicious, crispy skin. "Wimpy" wings-straight wings, no sauce — will please wing purists.

King of Shish Kabob, 932 McBride Ave, West Paterson; (973) 812-9888. The King is Syrian-born Michael Ibrahim. Syrian olives, pleasantly bitter, are an irresistible treat. The grape leaves and tabboule rated high. The kabobs, though, seemed dry and too chewy.

Kingdom's Sea and Soul, 136 Vreeland Ave., Paterson; (973) 569-2900. You may not find a livelier duo than sisters Kathy and Betty Dixon, who run Kingdom's. The Munch jury split on their Soul Rolls, a Southern take on Asian rolls, but we drooled over the fried catfish. Dynamite desserts, especially the coconut pineapple cream cake and banana ginger snap pudding.

Krause's Homemade Candy, 203 McLean Blvd., Paterson; (973) 345-4606. Yellow-shingled, red-awninged house, a roadside confection. Lots of bark — almond, hazelnut, raisin, cashew, pecan, among others. Excellent chocolate-covered strawberries, slightly chilled. Amaretto balls and butter crunch are standouts.

Libby's Lunch, 98 McBride Ave., Paterson; (973) 278-8718. Hot dog joint with history galore. Texas weiners the house specialty. Walk across the street for one of New Jersey's great scenic wonders: the Great Falls.

Maria's Homemade Ravioli, 190 Route 23 North, Wayne; (973) 256-9006. Watch ravioli and other pasta being made on the other side of a floor-to-ceiling glass partition. Cheese ravioli excellent, second only to Casa di Trevi. The cheese and roasted red pepper ravioli didn't rock our world, but the cheese and spinach ravioli — near-perfect pasta, extra-fine filling — easily among the day's best. Take-home meals, sauces, meatballs and other items available.

Mario's, 710 Van Houten Ave., Clifton; (973) 777-1559. Opened in 1945, uses "same recipe, same oven" today, according to Gianni Bellini, grandson of founder Mario Barilari. About 1,300 pies are made here every week. Good, no-nonsense thin-crust, nice and crispy. Thumbs-up on the sausage and pepperoni.

McCobb's, 2391 Hamburg Turnpike, Wayne; (973) 835-0858. Everyone hated the tomato-ey chili except me. It's different, to say the least. The dog itself, nothing to get excited about.

New Corral, 499 Hazel St., Clifton; (973) 772-0941. A Jekyll-and-Hyde dog; one S.W.A.T. Dog member described it as "bland and tasteless," another said it was "deep-fried to perfection."

Olympus, Wayne Towne Center, Route 23, Wayne; (973) 256-6438. Greek fast food; owner Zois Soumilas and his three helpers spin and twist in their confined quarters. Good salads. The spinach pie is dried out, and the Grecian Cave's dolmathes are better. But the souvlaki-on-a-stick is surprisingly good, with fat, juicy, seasoned chunks of meat. It may be the best mall meat you'll have all year.

Pappy's, 315 Union Blvd., Totowa; (973) 595-1701. One of the summer's top Texas weiners, although one S.W.A.T. member described it as "mediocre." Chili admirably spicy and sweet.

Park West Diner, 1400 Route 46 West, Little Falls; (973) 256-2767. Most diner salads are instantly forgettable; the Park West, with nearly 20 on the menu, takes them seriously. The mango salad is a towering tumble of arugula, radicchio, foccacia croutons and roasted walnuts, the mango slices ringing the plate like surfboards.

Riddles, 300 Wanaque Ave., Pompton Lakes; (973) 835-0999. The bar's nachos are an awesome construction of cheese and chips, gloriously gloppy. Not for the faint-hearted. Standard — not homemade — salsa. Other menu items include sliced pork sandwich, shrimp in lobster sauce and various pasta dishes.

Rock and Roll Pizza, 775 Hamburg Turnpike, Wayne; (973) 628-7939. Posters of rock 'n' roll legends decorate the walls. Decent pizza, but the fried Snickers and fried Oreos are terrific.

Rutt's Hut, 417 River Road, Clifton. One of the state's hot dog shrines. Rippers — deep-fried hot dogs, the skins ripped open — rule. The relish will get your attention.

Salah Edin, 995 Main St., Paterson; (973) 225-0575. Excellent baba ghanoush. Chicken kebab spicy and tender, but not on the same level as Uncle's Place. Highlight: the fata hummus — chickpeas and bread slices marinated in a special sauce. Think a big warm bowl of almond-topped oatmeal, or Middle Eastern comfort food.

Sharky's Wings and Raw Bar, 545 Highland Ave., Clifton; (973) 473-0713. Day's best barbecue wing sauce — smoky, not sweet — found here. And the Buffalo wing sauce, on the peppery side, at least tried to be different. Nice, meaty wings.

Teddy's Lunch, 693 Market St., Paterson; (973) 742-3435. Horseshoe-shaped counter, a TV with reception issues, LoveMeter machine in the corner. They don't make hot dog joints like this anymore. Snappy dog, so-so chili.

Tick Tock Diner, 281 Allwood Road (Route 3), Clifton; (973) 777-0511. Probably the best-known diner in North Jersey. "Eat Heavy" proclaims the outdoor sign; you won't go away hungry. Solid, dependable diner food; the club sandwiches are well-constructed.

Tomo's Cuisine Japanese Restaurant, 113 Route 23 South, Little Falls; (973) 837-1117. Tomonori Tanaka is a character, and his cozy restaurant is an improvement over his former South Orange storefront. He still serves first-rate Japanese, and a bit of friendly attitude.

Toros, 489 Hazel St., Clifton; (973) 772-8032. Paintings, ruffled curtains and ocher walls convey the look of a well-to-do Istanbul home, albeit one conveniently located near the Parkway. Hummus wondrously smooth and creamy. Shepherd's salad a perfect summertime — or anytime — treat. Dried-out meat in the chicken kabob. Two dynamite desserts: the baklava and the almond pudding.

Vinni's Pizzarama, 1025 Hamburg Turnpike, Wayne; (973) 628-1510. Looks like your basic pizzeria, but there are some surprises. Steak sandwich: good meat, great toasted roll (the bread is from Gian-

nelli's in Paterson). The pizza? Nice crust and taste. But the zeppole is greasy.

Ziegler's Town Tavern Country Inn, 673 Macopin Road, West Milford; (973) 697-8990. Christmas tree lights strung around the bar, dried wasps nests (minus the wasps) dangling from the ceiling — the decor at Ziegler's is country-funky. The prime rib — a monstrous, joyously juicy piece of meat — is worth the trip to this backroad restaurant-bar.

Salem

Hudock's Custard Stand, 544 Salem-Quinton Road, Quinton; (856) 935-5224. Best-known ice cream stand in Salem County. Good soft-serve, and if you're real hungry, you can take a stab at the Belly Buster, with its pancake-sized burger.

Somerset

Amazing Hot Dogs, 600 W. Union Ave, Bound Brook; (732) 469-0389. Serves up a supersize all-beef deep-fried Best's dog. Good fries, double-fried and nicely greasy.

Baja Fresh, 1595 Route 22, Watchung; (908) 322-0202. Brightly-lit, black-and-white-tile-floored restaurant, with self-serve salsa bar. Chicken and steak nachos, fresh and tasty, left one question unanswered: "Where's the beef?" And chicken. So-so guacamole, decent chips. But everyone liked the fish tacos, and the salsa verde was first-rate.

Bamboo Grille, Basking Ridge Country Club, 185 Madisonville Road, Bernards; (908) 766-8200. Best seafood we had all summer? Quite possibly the Malpeque oysters here. The macadamia-crusted brie is a recommended appetizer. The Jamaican jerk chicken stack is tasty, even if the chicken is nearly overwhelmed by the mountain of trimmings. Best entree: the Montreal rib eye, terrifically tender, with a just-off-the-grill flavor.

C.T.'s Bar-B-Que, 920 Hamilton St., Somerset; (732) 418-8889. Another strip mall discovery. The pulled pork sandwich is fat, flavorful and juicy. Beef ribs could have been better, but we loved the pork ribs and the collard greens, cooked with smoked turkey.

Caffe Piazza, 649 Route 206, No. 2, Hillsborough; (908) 359-9494. They make their own bread and sauce here. Recommended pasta dishes: the penne Stallone, in a vodka cream sauce; chicken puttanesca over linguine and the cavatelli Chaplin, with broccoli, sun-dried tomatoes, oil and garlic. The veal Sorrentina is bland, ordinary. Ask for a taste of the brisk, bracing homemade lemoncello.

Catered Affair, 424 Route 206, Hillsborough; (908) 874-7790. You'll love the roast beef, nice and juicy. And the New York New York, with hot corned beef and pastrami stacked triple-decker-style on rye. The bacon-cheddar potato salad one of the best sides we sampled all summer.

Chimney Rock Inn, 800 N. Thompson Ave., Bridgewater; (732) 469-4600. One of the state's highest-regarded thin-crust pizzas. We loved the Margarita pizza, with fresh plum tomatoes, mozzarella and basil. There is a sister location in Gillette.

CocoLuxe, 161 Main St., Peapack; (908) 781-5554. Colorful little slice of Paris, with its French-themed posters and European and American pastries, cakes, cookies and tarts. Underwhelming tiramisu. But the mango coconut and lime/blackberry tarts are excellent. Good traditional brownie. Top-shelf croissants. The sour cream coffee cake boasted a perfect sugary crown and soft, dense filling. Just-okay biscotti and scones.

The Coffee Shop, 23 Olcott Square, Bernardsville; (908) 766-6806. Tile-floored luncheonette serves a tasty sausage and egg, and bacon and egg sandwiches, but the pork roll sandwich not on same level as the one at the Allenwood General Store or Summit Diner.

Confectionally Yours, 3185 Route 27, Franklin Park; (732) 821-6863. Deck outside, water cooler inside: what more do you need? Flavors here did not pack the same punch of other stops, but we liked the key lime; the Candy Catastrophe, laden with peanut butter, malted milk balls, Snickers, M and Ms and other treats; and the cantaloupe, fruity and refreshing.

Country Fresh Restaurant, 145 W. Main St., Somerville; (908) 231-8090. Sunshiny orange walls dotted with flowers and vintage food signs. About 25 kinds of pancakes, all about the size of the nearby Somerville Circle. Intriguing combinations, including the Energy Booster (apples, raisins, nuts and cinnamon). Pancakes more firm than fluffy and nicely browned on top.

Culinary Creations, 434 Route 206 South, Hillsborough; (908) 281-3894. If the typical Jersey strip mall included more places like this, we would start liking strip malls. A creative, healthy take on breakfast and lunch in a casual setting. Good blueberry pancakes, topped with sliced bananas and powdered sugar. Crispy French toast comes as advertised. Excellent, crisp bacon. Recommended: the grilled vegetable and hummus club, and the arugula and mozzarella frittata.

De Island Breeze, 676 Franklin Blvd., Somerset; (732) 214-8611. The summer's most colorfully decorated restaurant, De Island Breeze offered satisfying if unsurprising Caribbean standards. Best dishes: the curry goat and curry chicken.

The Dessert Plate, 34 E. Main St., Somerville; (908) 722-9881. Ignore the spare surroundings and prepare to be pleased. Owners Megyn Craine and Kevin Gora use no preservatives, substitutes or mixes. Their scones, softer and fluffier than usual, are super. The almost Brie-like cheesecake is beyond creamy; you'll either love it or hate it. The flourless chocolate cake is another top-shelf item. The only disappointment: the walnut brownie, dry and lackluster.

Dynasty Restaurant, 100 Route 22 West, Green Brook; (732) 752-6363. Fronted by immense stone lions and housed in a high-ceilinged, porthole-windowed space. Top-drawer dim sum; the vegetarian dumpling, delicately stuffed with carrots, mushrooms, broccoli and bamboo shoots, the single best dim sum sampled on our trip.

Gabriel's Fountain, 1948 Washington Valley Road, No. 1, Martinsville; (732) 469-5800. Funkiest, most fun ice cream we had all summer. The peanut butter and jelly here is amazingly authentic. Cotton candy and SpongeBob ice cream sure kiddie-pleasers. Subtle peach, dazzling blue raspberry. The chocolate hash is smooth, rich and nutty.

Gary's Wine and Marketplace, 100 Morristown Road (Route 202), Bernardsville; (908) 766-6699. A wine-lover's vision of paradise; more than 5,000 kinds of wines available. Sandwiches with a savory twist include a duck rilette with radicchio and black truffle oil on seven-grain bread. Try the lobster salad, a seaworthy blend of fresh lobster and baby greens, and the caprese salad, with fresh mozzarella, basil and vine-ripe tomatoes over arugula with extra virgin olive oil.

Gina's Pastry Shop, 900 Easton Ave., Franklin Twp.; (732) 246-2929. We didn't find much to love here. One Muncher admired the "seriously fudgy and sugary" brownie," and we liked the cinnamon pastry, fine and filling. I liked the mini-cheesecakes, but I'm not sure anyone agreed with me.

Grub Hut, 307 N. Main Street, Manville; 908-203-8003. This casual, Southwestern-themed restaurant gets my vote for best barbecue in Central Jersey. Get your ribs one of four ways — dry, wet (dressed in barbecue sauce), flamed (straight from the pit, then grilled) or glazed (grilled, and dressed in sauce). The sassafras chicken is a must.

Hen Picked, 302 Routes 202/206 North, Pluckemin; (908) 306-0800. Good wings, outstanding sides: cranberry sauce, strawberry-apple sauce, mashed sweet potatoes, creamed spinach, macaroni salad.

Hillsborough Lobster Dock, The Boro Center, 424 Route 206 South, Hillsborough; (908) 874-3337. Owner Mike Drabich kept bragging about the seafood at his fish market/restaurant, but he backed it up. We started with tender, off-the-boat-fresh oysters. Diver sea scallops, pan-glazed with sherry, a sheer delight. More winners: the pecan-crusted swordfish, and jumbo shrimp, with a piquant, eye-opening cocktail sauce.

Hoagie Hut, 357 Union Ave., Bridgewater; (908) 722-4880. Popular lunchtime spot; good, thick subs. Excellent deep-fried potatoes.

House of Thai Cuisine, Sansone Plaza, 319 Route 22 East, Green Brook; (732) 968-0085. Tender chicken satay. Yum ped is yum yum — crispy duck in a spicy and sour marinade with ginger, pineapple, tomatoes, red onions, bell peppers and cashews. Outstanding green curry, creamy and three-alarm hot. Tom kha soup disappointing, but the mango ice cream, made in New York, is marvelous.

Joe's Meat Market, 28 Main St., South Bound Brook; (732) 356-4557. Once housed in spare, tiled-floored space down the street, now in a neat, spacious spot. Solid, stuffed subs; try the mozzarella-and-roasted-red-peppers sub.

La Piazza Ristorante, 1979 Washington Valley Road, Martinsville; (732) 563-1717. Looks like your neighborhood pizzeria, tastes like something quite different. Surprisingly good Italian, including lasagna, penne pesto, other pastas, and seafood.

Mediterraneo Bakery, 465 W. Union Ave., Bound Brook; (732) 356-6077. Friendly, small-town bakery. Come on, baby, let's do the twist; the twist bread, soft and chewy, is highly recommended. Good bastone and tea biscuits. Panella not as good as Nicolo's.

Monterey Gourmet, 167 Morristown Road (Route 202), Bernardsville; (908) 766-2000. Upscale deli/wine store. Highly recommended: the filet mignon with horseradish; the Greek salad; the Veggiewich, with peppers, zucchini, spinach and summer squash; and the cusabi, a cucumber wasabi.

Mr. Tod's Pie Factory, 1760 Easton Ave., Somerset; (732) 356-8900. This pie place is situated in one of the more dreary-looking strip malls anywhere, but the pies are so good you won't care. The Munchers raved about the Key lime pie. I'd go back for the cherry pie and especially the banana cream pie, a fluffy, puffy wonder.

Outback Steakhouse, 98 Route 22 West, Green Brook; (732) 424-0555. Sure, their steaks can't match those at the high-end places, but you can't beat the price. The sweet potato, doused with brown sugar, gives potatoes everywhere a good name.

Red Tower II, 864 Route 22 East, North Plainfield; (908) 754-0002. Looks like typical highway burger joint, but pleasant surprises on menu. Bounteous Greek salad. Spicy kick to chili dog. Onion rings fat and crispy. Potato salad dry but delicious.

Sukhothai Fine Thai Cuisine, 186 Orlando Drive, Raritan; (908) 707-4747. With teak tables, ornamental statuary and multi-colored lanterns fluttering in the breeze, Sukhothai one of the most atmospheric restaurants anywhere. Steamed mussels tender and delicious.

Good Thai egg rolls; lackluster curry puffs. Recommended entrees: Thai catfish, ped bai graprow (roasted duck) and pad phed pla doog (Thai catfish).

Tastee Sub Shop II, 3087 Route 27, Franklin Twp.; (732) 422-1212. Satellite location of original store, on Route 27 in Edison. Subs are simple — meat, shredded lettuce, tomatoes and onions — and good. The roast beef is juicy and rare, and the subs, overall, are great value. A whole sub is easily big enough for two.

Texas Weiner II, 150 Route 22 West, Green Brook; (732) 752-2882. Disappointing dogs. "Undercooked, undertaste, underwhelming," one Muncher noted. But decent chili.

Tsuru, 413 King George Road, Basking Ridge; (908) 580-1388. Try to grab a table in the quiet upstairs dining room. Marvelous black pepper tuna sashimi — a dish we would remember the rest of the summer. Loved the ice cream tempura and banana tempura.

Victor's Pizza Pasta Subs, 450 Amwell Road, Hillsborough; (908) 359-6364. Pizza Number 20 — mozzarella, olive oil, tomato sauce and basil — simply terrific. The sausage-and-mushroom Sicilian had an odd, off-putting aroma, and the sausage is no match for Mr. Nino's.

Warren Bagels and Deli, 125 Washington Valley Road, Warren Twp.; (732) 868-0565. Fattest bagels of the day; the sesame bagel weighed in at nearly half a pound. Standouts: cinnamon raisin crumb, egg and the power bagel. Maple walnut cream cheese way too sweet, but the vegetable cream cheese is delectable.

Sussex

Cafe Pierrot, 19 Sparta Ave., Sparta; (973) 729-0988. Hardwood floors, cozy dining room and porch make for a great escape. Excellent cakes, pastries, brownies, cookies and more. Sandwiches, wraps, salads available in restaurant.

Clove Brook Market, 800 Route 23, Sussex; (973) 875-5600. It's waaaay up there, 5 miles from High Point State Park, but Clove Brook and owner Kim Sytsema's baked goodies are worth the hike. Good sandwiches, especially the roast beef and the Little Italy (prosciutto, fresh mozzarella, roasted red peppers, oil and vinegar). Excellent muffins, scones and pies.

Dale's Market, 396 Route 206, Culvers Lake; (973) 948-3078. Super salads at this sprawling country market. Recommended: the tricolor pasta salad, with green and black olives, and the tortellini salad with perfectly cooked pasta. Cole slaw smooth and crunchy, with a delicious, just-made taste. Fried chicken another pleasant surprise.

The Elias Cole, Route 23 South, Colesville; (973) 875-3550. Colorful cross between log cabin and ski chalet. Good, honest country cooking. Monstrous meatloaf — two soft, moist chunks, on homemade, although ordinary, white bread. The open hot turkey and roast beef sandwiches looked magnificent. The Cole sells about 1,000 pies for Thanksgiving.

Euro Bakery, 302 Route 94, Vernon; (973) 764-7221. Excellent six-grain bread; on Fridays, you can get Kornbread, a mixture of whole wheat and rye.

Holland American Bakery, 246 Route 23, Sussex; (973) 875-5258. Mini-windmill marks 50-year-old bakery. Known for its cinnamon bread; try it at home, sliced thick and toasted, and you'll see why.

Krogh's Restaurant and Brew Pub, 23 White Deer Plaza, Sparta; (973) 729-8428. Brew pub as ski chalet, with woodsy, lacquered-beam interior and cozy little dining nooks. Chicken Cajun pizza — blackened and with a bite — a winner. Super desserts — the cookies 'n' cream mud pie, and the apple crisp. Best brews: Three Sisters Golden Wheat, and the Alpine Red, nice and mellow.

Lafayette House, 100 Route 94, Lafayette; (973) 579-3100. Brunch held in picturesque wood-beamed dining room. Better-than-average omelets, good eggs Benedict and waffles. Homemade whipped cream. Self-serve ice cream machine.

The Market Place Deli, 800 Canistear Road, Highland Lakes; (973) 764-5819. The wings, of the Rhode Island Red's brand, scored high marks for their size and tenderness. Skip the barbecue wings — the sauce is too sweet — and go for the honey lemon and hot wings instead.

Owen's Pub, Ballyowen Golf Club, 105-137 Wheatsworth Road, Hardyston; (973) 827-5996. Best views of any golf course restaurant we know — overlooks Ballyowen, a highly-acclaimed public golf course. The fish and chips are excellent; wish we had the recipe. The Bally burger, pastrami sandwich and herb-roasted chicken salad disappointments.

Perona Farms, 350 Andover-Sparta Road, Andover; (973) 729-6161. Grand room with silver service and revolving ice sculptures. Chilled shrimp, oysters on half shell, and prosciutto sliced on an antique slicer. Recommended: the steak Diane, grilled salmon, and chicken and apple sausage.

Sussex County Food Co-Op, 30 Moran St., Newton; (973) 579-1882. One-stop natural/organic food shopping in cozy country store. The beefless beef jerky may change your mind about jerky. The hummus is a hit, as are the Udon noodle salad and the various artisanal breads.

Yellow Cottage, 345 Route 206, Branchville; (973) 948-5149. Sussex County landmark noted for its brown derby, a towering strawberry and whipped cream-filled cake that earned high marks from one Muncher. Good napoleon, and peanut butter pie. But the cookies are generic bakery cookies, and the raspberry mango cheesecake sounded luscious but tasted dull and dry.

Zinga's Corn Patch, 640 Lafayette Road (Route 15), Sparta; (973) 383-6572. Call it country fast food, with everything from curly fries; the thoroughly addictive corn fritters; and Sloppy Joes to homemade muffins and 20-plus flavors of ice cream, including, appropriately enough, NJ Black Bear.

Union

Bagel Chateau, 223 South Ave. East, Westfield; (908) 232-1921. The manic counter scene and fluorescent lighting may have you thinking 33rd Street in New York rather than South Avenue in Westfield. We loved the whitefish salad and creamy, irresistible pickled herring; all the salads are top-notch. The Taylor ham and egg and cheese on a bagel — call it Jewish deli meets Jersey truck stop — is squishy-good. Raves for the Reuben, grease and guilt-free. Formulaic chicken soup.

Beana's, 988 St. Georges Ave., Rahway; (732) 381-3233. Colorful, festive storefront location. Good burritos, great bean dishes, friendly waitresses.

Big Stash's Restaurant, 1020 S. Wood Ave., Linden; (908) 862-6455. Restaurant named after original owner, who was six-foot-seven. The food is abundant and cheap, but not especially noteworthy.

Broadway Diner, 55 River Road, Summit; (908) 273-4353. "The world's best pancakes" can be found at the Broadway Diner, with locations in Summit, Red Bank and Bayonne. The buttermilk pancakes are soft, if a bit spongy, but seemed better than the thin, insubstantial ones sampled at the Broadway Diner in Bayonne. Real syrup.

Brummer's, 125 E. Broad St., Westfield; (908) 232-1904. Quintessential small-town chocolate shop. Wonderful, melt-in-your mouth-creamy fudge. Unremarkable coconut cream. But the raspberry cream is delicious. Good milk chocolate crunch. Lots of gift baskets and assorted knickknacks.

C and C Polish Delicatessen, 11 E. Price St., Linden; (908) 486-2860. Want to practice your Polish? Visit this narrow-aisled store, stocked with juices, candies, cookies, pickles and other items. Soups here definitely not subtle: the cucumber soup, doused with dill, evoked strong love/hate reactions. Hearty, savory goulash. Kielbasa not as good as its counterpart at Pulaski Meat Products, just around the corner.

Callaloo Cafe, 1401 Maple Ave., Hillside; (973) 391-1550. Owner Lemard Clarke is not interested in serving you sports-bar wings. He flavors his food, from wings to oxtails, with a dash of the Caribbean. His jerk wings, coated with a thickish, smoky sauce, are super. The hot, barbecue and plain wings are excellent. There's no trace anywhere of that annoying Buffalo wing sauce. Hallelujah.

Carmen's Italian Bakery, 609 Chestnut St., Union; (908) 686-2490. Old-fashioned bakery started on 15th Avenue in Newark 75 years ago; it's been in Union the past 25. Crunchy delight: the seeded twist bread. Our favorite: the scaletta, a loaf of thick Italian bread.

Casa di Trevi, 534 Westfield Ave., Roselle Park; (908) 259-9000. A stuffed pasta factory outlet: 25 kinds of ravioli, five kinds of manicotti, along with cavatelli, gnocchi, lasagna, sauces and other items. Best ravioli of the day, by far. Cheese ravioli deliciously smooth and creamy. Rest of the ravioli sampled ranged from good to terrific.

Charlie's, 18 S. Michigan Ave, Kenilworth; (908) 241-2627. Group verdict: Major league ingredients on minor league roll. Decent chili.

Charlie's Sons, 1030 Springfield Road, Union; (908) 686-0110. The better-than-average Italian dog — potatoes, peppers, onions and dog — is served in a soft, spacious pizza roll.

Cheeburger, Cheeburger, 251 North Ave., Westfield; (908) 389-1100. You don't need kids to have fun here, but it helps. Fun, busy burger joint, done up in pink-walled '50s chic. Advertises "America's biggest burgers." Good burgers; you can throw as many toppings as you want on them. Skip the onion rings and go right to the thick, yummy shakes.

Church's Kitchen, 2117 Springfield Ave., Union; (908) 810-1686. Good fried chicken available in former Vaux Hall post office. Chicken lightly breaded, but crispy and crunchy. Terrific potato salad and cinnamon-topped peach cobbler. What's in the potato salad? Maybe co-owner Judy Church will tell you; she wouldn't tell us!

Clark Bagels, 1045 Raritan Road, Clark; (732) 382-2435. Good bagels, better cream cheese, especially the scallion, vegetable and walnut raisin. Nice tuna salad.

Coppola Ristorante and Pizzeria, 590 Central Ave., New Providence; (908) 665-0266. Most distinctive cheesesteak in our exhaustive field trip found here. A cheesesteak with garlic and tomatoes somehow doesn't sound right, but it proved to be a grand slam of a sandwich.

Dee's Hut, Faitoute Avenue, Roselle Park. Delores Antonucci took over the spot in 1973. Good snap to her dogs; she keeps them in the water for "five, 10 minutes, no more." Hot Dog maven John Fox an admirer of Dee's.

DiCosmo's Homemade Italian Ice, 714 Fourth Ave., Elizabeth. Best Italian ice in Jersey? Right here, in Elizabeth's Peterstown section. The DiCosmos make 20 kinds of ice, but no more than three or four flavors are available at any one time. When they run out, you wait until the next batch is ready. It's worth it.

Dimaio Cucina, 468 Springfield Ave., Berkeley Heights; (908) 464-8585. Sal Passalacqua, a consultant on Emeril Lagasse's Food Network show, is the owner and executive chef. All the food sampled first-rate: grilled salmon, cheese ravioli, rigatoni alla serafino. Excellent bread, too.

Do Me a Flavor, 2195 Morris Ave., Union; (908) 686-8223. More than 30 kinds of hard ice cream. Favorite among women: strawberry. Among men: pistachio and chocolate swirl. Go figure.

Donna and Company, 19 Eastman St., Cranford; (908) 272-4380. Owner Diane Pinder uses Belgian, Venezuelan and Ecuadorian chocolate in her marvelous creations. The Martini is made with milk chocolate ganache flavored with Grey Goose vodka, dipped in milk chocolate and drizzled in dark chocolate. You get the idea.

Double Dipper Cafe, 38 A S. Martine Ave., Fanwood; (908) 490-0102. Looks like your typical neighborhood ice cream store, but there are nice surprises here, including the Cappuccino Explosion, which more than lived up to its name. Couldn't say the same for the Death by Chocolate.

El Palmar Restaurant, 523 Elizabeth Ave., Elizabeth; (908) 355-9621. Mamey shake did not pack the fruity punch of its counterpart at El Sol de Cuba, but the guava shake was lip-smackingly smooth. Try the white bean soup, Galician style. Pot roast, awash in a tangy tomato sauce, a nice surprise.

Evergreen Deli, 529 S. Springfield Ave., Springfield; (973) 376-6095. The knotty pine walls will either remind you of a 1950s Life magazine spread or an episode of "Twin Peaks." Great pastrami. The Sloppy Joe, with the right amount of Russian, Swiss, cole slaw, roast beef and turkey, is fat, creamy and delicious.

Father and Son Luncheonette, 10 E. Blancke St., Linden; (908) 486-9596. Oddest restaurant seating arrangement in New Jersey: The booths inside the wrap-around counter at Father and Son. Plain-Jane luncheonette opened about 1940. Signs on the wall advertise gift certificates (for chili dogs?). Good onion rings, better than those at Supreme Chicken and Ribs, not as good as Ray's. Nice snap to the dogs; smoky, spicy, slightly sweet chili.

Florence Ravioli Co., 1741 E. Second St., Scotch Plains; (908) 322-7222. Florence Losanno opened her store in Newark 60 years ago. Frozen dinners beckon — cavatelli and broccoli, chicken cacciatore, eggplant rolettes, tripe with sauce. Homemade sauce. Good, not great, ravioli.

Freshwaters Restaurant, 1442 South Ave., Plainfield; (908) 561-9099. Upscale setting, great food. We recommend the Southern fried chicken, filet of catfish, the baby back ribs — and everything else.

Frosty Freeze, 1 North Ave., Garwood; (908) 789-1110. Dependable ice cream stop. Chocolate standard-issue soft serve, slightly darker and richer than the others. Vanilla enlivened somewhat by the addition of chocolate chips.

Galloping Hill Inn, 325 Chestnut St., Union; (908) 686-2683. What Union County native has not been to this sprawling roadside stand? Made its reputation on hot dogs, but you can get burgers, fries, onion rings, salads — and beer.

Golden Palace, 504 Boulevard St., Kenilworth; (908) 276-8884. Best stop on a day-long Chinese food tour. Sizzling seafood soup is sizzlingly good. Outstanding duck sauce.

Goodman's, 180 Elmora Ave., Elizabeth; (908) 354-1802. Jewish deli in diner atmosphere. Friendly, frenzied atmosphere. Excellent rice pudding.

Grecian Cave, 1161 Elizabeth Ave., Elizabeth; (908) 351-4243. Tiny, blue-awningned downtown luncheonette. Nice pastichio, but we liked the dolmades — stuffed grape leaves — better. Good gyro, swaddled in plastic wrap like an oversize ice cream cone. Chicken in chicken gyro dry.

The Greek Store, 612 Boulevard, Kenilworth; (908) 272-2550. One-stop Greek shopping: cookies, wine, olive oil, Greek pasta, other items. Refrigerated and freezer cases filled with moussaka, seasoned kebobs, pastichio, octopus and squid. Olive lovers, this is your place. Recommended: koulourakia, the traditional Greek butter cookie.

Hershey's, 221 South Ave., Westfield; (908) 233-0430. The pepperoni and cheese sub, coated with oil and wine vinegar, a slippery delight. Overall, the bread is average, but we found the day's most consistent subs here. Distinctive, celery-flecked tuna.

Italian Village, 1304 South Ave., Plainfield; (908) 561-0031. Good fast food, Italian style. Wonderful salad, a mountainous tangle of shredded lettuce, tomatoes, black olives and hot peppers. Fat, flavorful meatballs, good pizza and garlic bread, a honest plate of spaghetti and meatballs.

Jerry's, 906 Second Ave., Elizabeth; (908) 355-4242. Classic open-air hot dog stand. Snappy all-beef Best's franks. Tommy's, another Elizabeth hot dog legend, several doors down. Try both and decide.

King Chef, Galloping Hill Mall, 1350 Galloping Hill Road, Union; (908) 810-8000. Adventurous selections: steak au poivre, lobster roll, cod with white wine and butter sauce. Good salad bar. Fair fried chicken, on undercooked side. Rare roast beef, but it showed the effects — picked apart, dried out — of sitting out too long. Recommended: the Seafood Delight, scallops, shrimp and lobster in a light butter sauce.

Lana's Fine Dining, Hyatt Hills Golf Complex, 1300 Raritan Road, Clark; (732) 669-9024. Handsome dining room, all dark wood and subdued lighting. Try the chorizo-laced Prince Edward Island mussels steamed in Brooklyn Lager. Nice antipasto, with Parma ham, caper berries, marinated artichoke hearts and white anchovies. Veal chops and roasted rack of lamb are standouts; the seafood didn't fare as well.

Manny's, 2580 Springfield Ave., Union. Snappy, if formulaic, dog, spicy chili. Extensive menu, though.

Maria's Restaurant, 381 Park Ave., Scotch Plains; (908) 322-2322. Short on charm, long on character. Turkish-born Mehmet "Mike" Reyhan is the sixth owner. Good pasta fagioli, with nary a hint of the cheesy overload that ruins many a pasta fagioli. You probably won't find bigger ravioli than the ones here but the cheese in several tasted off. The manicotti and stuffed shells, though, are fresh and filling.

Marino's Fine Foods, 905 Mountain Ave., Springfield; (973) 258-9009. Brazilian lobster shares space with Brooklyn's Best Ravioli. Calamari and shrimp salad a black olive-and-roasted red pepper-dotted delight. Okay calamari, but we all liked the rich red dipping sauce. Good, fresh mussels. Crab cake too sweet and lemony. Recommended: blackened swordfish, broiled combo, fried haddock sandwich, stuffed flounder.

Mario's Famous Pizzeria, 400A Amsterdam Ave., Roselle; (908) 259-9300. Verdict on broccoli rabe and sausage pizza: tasteless sausage, excellent broccoli rabe. Mexican pizza — green peppers, red onions, tomato salsa, American cheese, Cajun chicken — a hit.

Menger's Bake Shop, 342 Chestnut St., Union; (908) 686-8282. Plain-Jane place, but one bite of the sugar twist will teach you to trust your mouth, not eyes. Good chocolate eclairs. Above-average chocolate doughnuts, but not on the same level as those at Ob-Co's.

Merchants of Venice, 33 Westfield Ave., Clark; (732) 382-9222. Tuna and roast beef subs are middle-of-the-road, but you'll admire the Cardinal (prosciutto, wet mozarella and roasted peppers).

Monster Sushi and Steak, 395 Springfield Ave., Summit; (908) 598-1100. Godzilla's on the menu at this hip, attractive sushi stop. It's a roll with spicy tuna, avocado and flying fish roe. Big portions. Middling miso soup, but you'll like the soft shell crab or spider roll, and the dinosaur roll. Can't make up your mind? The chirashi-sushi, with 14-17 pieces, is a good intro to the world of sushi.

Mr. Apple Pie, 1524 Irving St., Rahway; (732) 388-0650. One of the cheesier grilled cheese sandwiches you'll find anywhere, but it's greasy. Subpar steak sandwich, the dried-out meat wasted on a good roll. Maybe we just caught them on a bad day.

Munce's, Rahway River Park at St. Georges Avenue, Rahway. Home-made chili — sweet and tomato-ey — is distinctive, but dogs not on same level as others. Points for parkside location, though.

Nancy's Towne House, 1453 Main St., Rahway; (732) 388-8100. Best way to warm up a cold slice of pizza: heat it in a skillet, a waitress here told us. Most distinctive crust of all those sampled: hollowed-out and potato chip-crackly. Excellent sausage: sweet, fresh and fennel-filled.

Natale's Summit Bakery, 185 Broad St., Summit; (908) 277- 2074. The flaky, layered chocolate horn — part pastry, part doughnut, alto-gether delicious — the day's most wonderful creation. Close behind are the poor man's pies, mini-pies of cherry and apple, with sugary crusts and tart, juicy fillings.

Neelam, 295 Springfield Ave., Berkeley Heights; (908) 665-2212. The lunchtime buffet popular among area workers. Tandoori chicken, marinated in yogurt and spices for at least 24 hours, a standout.

Nunzio's Pizza, 2387 Mountain Ave., Scotch Plains; (908) 889-4464. First-rate sausage on the sausage and mushroom Sicilian, but canned mushrooms. Several out-of-the-ordinary pizzas, including a creamed spinach pie; a cheesesteak pie with peppers and onions; and a "lite" pie with mozzarella, pesto, roasted peppers and no sauce.

Original Buffalo Wings, 101 E. Front St., Plainfield; (908) 755-8858. Downtown tile-floored storefront. Wings coated in a you've-had-it-a-thousand-times-before Buffalo wing sauce. Better: the chicken tenders. And the fries, coated with corn and spices, are thoroughly addictive.

Pierogi Palace, 713 W. Grand Ave., Rahway; (732) 499-8411. It's a far cry from a palace, but you may not find better pierogi. Jessica Avent and her workers turn out 250 dozen pierogi daily during the holidays. The sweet cabbage pierogi an instant hit. We also liked the plain potato and jalapeno/cheese potato pierogi.

Pinho's Bakery, 1027 Chestnut St., Roselle; (908) 245-4388. Brightly-lit display cases full of luscious-looking cakes, pies, cookies, pastries.

Most marvelous creation: the flower-shaped chocolate rose cake, topped by a beautiful white butterfly. Most popular loaf is the Bread Lover's, with a thin, crispy crust, but we found it bland. We loved the mission bread, a hearty, raisin-studded loaf; the olive/rosemary bread; and the rolls.

Pulaski Meat Products, 123 N. Wood Ave., Linden; (908) 925-5380. You may swoon at the sight of all the kielbasa in this sprawling, well-lit supermarket. The "noncountry" kielbasa, a smokier, heartier variety, one of the day's best kielbasa. Also recommended: the pork in cream sauce and the stuffed pork.

Rise-N-Shine, 375 Terrill Road, Scotch Plains; (908) 322-2666. Diner-length menu at this part luncheonette, part truck stop. Best dish: the Bird of Paradise, almond-embedded, cinnamon and fresh fruit-topped French toast.

Rockin Joe, 5 Eastman St., Cranford; (908) 276-0595. Instant karma's going to get you inside this cafe, formerly Cafe Rock, where walls are filled with albums from the psychedelic era. The regular coffee, good and rich, will jumpstart any morning. Excellent frozen blended vanilla latte. Good sandwiches, particularly the prosciutto, fresh mozzarella and tomato, and desserts.

Route 22 BBQ, 1607 Route 22 West, Union; (908) 687-9009. Buffalo wings on thin side, but good and spicy. Spare ribs big and meaty, but bland. Standouts: whole chicken (frango de churrasco), with nice crackly skin and tender meat; and the picanha, a beef sirloin steak.

Sal's Dog House, in the parking lot of American Legion Post 328, 78 Westfield Ave., Clark. Tasty dirty-water dog. The peppery chili is distinctive if not daring.

Santillo's Brick Oven Pizza, 639 S. Broad St., Elizabeth; (908) 354-1887. It's one of the more unlikely-looking pizzerias in the state — you walk down the driveway of a house to a side-door entrance — but Santillo's delivers, on all counts. The sauce — an often-overlooked ingredient when it comes to judging pizza — is smooth and tangy. One of the state's half dozen best pizzerias.

Scoops, 2014 Route 22, Scotch Plains; (908) 322-4550. Route 22 landmark offers middle-of-the-road ice cream. Likes: the lemon meringue, maple walnut, chocolate chocolate chip. Dislikes: Dutch apple, butter toffee.

Scoops 'n Scripts, 246 Mountain Ave., Springfield; (973) 912-9199. Once upon a time, drugstores had ice cream counters. Rich Libby brings the past back, with refreshing results. We loved the Key lime and chocolate brownie ice cream.

Scotchwood Diner, 1934 Route 22 East, Scotch Plains; (908) 322-4114. Seems like you can't go wrong with breakfast here. The pork roll and egg sandwich fat and filling. The fresh fruit cup served in a parfait dish. Best bet: the thick, cinnamon-topped French toast.

Shack's, 1160 E. Grand St., Elizabeth; (908) 436-0005. Photos of Negro League greats decorate the walls at Vonda McPherson's largely-takeout place. Rousing barbecue ribs, and model mac and cheese, moist and creamy. Super side: the tuna pasta salad.

Sisters of Soul Southern Cuisine, 1314 St. Georges Ave. (Route 27), Linden; (973) 449-5607. Cynthia Johnson, a former Union County police officer, owns this spare storefront with top-notch Southern food. Excellent fried whiting, smothered turkey wings, cornbread, Southern shrimp. And the yams were the best veggies we had all summer.

Spanish Tavern, 1239 Route 22, Mountainside; (908) 232-2171. The Spanish escargots, sauteed with leeks and vodka in a red pepper sauce, outstanding. One Muncher called the scallops "outrageous."

Spirito's Restaurant, 714 Third Ave., Elizabeth; (908) 351-5414. Legendary Italian restaurant with old wooden booths and laminated tables. Known for their pizza and homemade ravioli. Just down the street is DiCosmo's and the best Italian ice in New Jersey.

Star of India, 496 Boulevard, Kenilworth; (908) 272-6633. Vegetarian lunch a bewitching mixture of sag panir (spinach), bayngan bhurtha (eggplant) and dal special (lentils fried in butter with onions and tomatoes). Mango lassi (a rosewater-flavored drink) provides cool relief.

Stewart's Root Beer, 347 Jaques Ave., Rahway; (732) 388-2080. "Mediocre" deep-fried dogs, but we loved the bacon-and-chese dog. Good, meaty chili; wish it had more kick.

Summit Diner, 1 Union Place, Summit; (908) 277-3256. Hemingway ate here. You will, too, if you don't mind a moderate amount of grease in your diet. One of the more distinctive diners in the Diner State, the Summit is a wood-paneled wonder, with a grill out front, and the smell and sound of grease in the air. You haven't lived until you've tried the diner's signature sandwich, a Slider: Taylor ham, egg and cheese.

Sun Tavern, 600 W. Westfield Ave., Roselle Park; (908) 241-0190. Certainly among the upper echelon of Jersey thin-crust pizzerias. Their pizzas have been shipped as far as Japan. Other locations include Fanwood, Union and Mountainside.

Syrena Polish-American Delicatessen, 1117 W. St. Georges Ave., Linden; (908) 486-0677. Shelves jammed with goods from Poland, the Czech Republic and Germany. At the hot table, you can get a hearty meal — main course, two helpings of mashed potatoes and two side salads — for an amazingly low price. Pierogi greasy-good and substantial. The stuffed cabbage will leave you stuffed.

Teddy's, Central Avenue, Clark. Hot dog man Teddy Miller works out of a battered old, white camper in front of an abandoned Bradlee's. Good chili.

Texas Weiner, 100 Watchung Ave., Plainfield; (908) 756-5480. Claims to be the state's first Texas weiner establishment. Excellent grilled dogs. Spicy, kicking chili.

Tom the Green Grocer, 2305 South Ave., Scotch Plains; (908) 232-9216. Cappuccino chiffon, cranberry cream, sweet potato and Italian plum prune pie among intriguing selections. Peach pie featured a fine, latticed crust and gooey gobs of fresh peaches.

Tommy's, 900 Second Ave., Elizabeth; (908) 351-9831. Italian hot dogs don't get much better. Their potatoes the absolute best of all those sampled on our S.W.A.T. Dog travels.

Towne Liquors and Delicatessen, 810 Old Springfield Ave., New Providence; (908) 464-5400. Great cookies in unlikely setting — a liquor store/deli by the New Providence train station. They're huge, square, soft and chewy; get them right out of the oven and you're in cookie heaven.

Trap Rock Restaurant and Brewery, 279 Springfield Ave., Berkeley Heights; (908) 665-1755. We came for dessert, but enjoyed dinner more. Recommended: mixed grilled satays, oven roasted sea scallops, grilled basil marinated loin pork chop and the pan roasted beef tenderloin. Memorable Maine blueberry-filled napoleon. Excellent passion fruit and raspberry sorbet. Warm blueberry cake left us cold. Ditto for the apple tart tatin. But the warm chocolate cake a winner.

Union Plaza Diner and Restaurant, 2466 Route 22, Union; (908) 686-4403. Fresh-squeezed orange juice, a diner rarity, available. Above-average French toast. Recommended: the organic salad, with grilled salmon, sun-dried tomatoes, portobello mushrooms and mixed greens, and a tangy lemon vinaigrette.

The Waiting Room, 66 E. Cherry St., Rahway; (732) 382-0900. Healthy nachos are an oxymoron, but the nachos at the Waiting Room come close to the impossible. Tomatoes, onions, jalapeno and chili rest atop a bed of greens. The homemade salsa, tangy and tomato-ey, easily among the best of those sampled.

Westfield Diner-Restaurant, 309 North Ave., Westfield; (908) 233-5200. Good diner cheesecake seems a hopeless mission, but the plain cheesecake here — light and airy — merits induction in the Diner Cheesecake Hall of Fame. The chocolate cheesecake is less successful, with its mousse-like chocolate swirled inside.

White Diamond, 1207 Raritan Road, Clark; (732) 574-8053. Renovated diner just off Exit 135 of the Parkway. Inferior meat, mediocre burger, although many swear by them. No-surprise fries and onion rings.

White Rose System, 1301 E. Elizabeth Ave., Linden; (908) 486-9651. Specials written on blue and red construction paper ruffling in the fan-whipped breeze. The Complete — pork roll, egg, cheese and potatoes — a resounding success. The day's best bacon — distinctive, smoky — found here.

Yosh's Linwood Inn, 15 S. Wood Ave., Linden; (908) 862-2334. Best burger of the day, but we never called it "New Jersey's best burger," as the banner out front proclaimed. Neighborhood bar with wide-ranging menu. Burger plump, juicy, nicely char-grilled.

Warren

Best's Fruit Farm, 40 Route 46, Independence; (908) 852-3777. Excellent pies, all with thick, sugary crusts. Blueberry, apple, peach — we couldn't decide which we liked most. "Every blueberry tasted good!" raved one Muncher. Other varieties include apple crumb, fruit berry and coconut custard.

Candy's Country Cafe, 2423 Route 57, Washington; (908) 213-1889. Convivial country cafe. Thick yet light-tasting pancakes, a bit on the dry side. But the French toast is chewy and crunchy, and the waitresses — and Candy — are a fun bunch.

Cara Mia Cafe, 218 Main St., Hackettstown; (908) 684-3801. Gigi and Tommy Wohlrub met at Panevino in Livingston, where they worked. Now they run Cara Mia, Italian fare with a touch of Creole and French. For starters, choose the calamari mala femina or salsiccia con rapini, grilled sweet sausage topped with broccoli rabe and sun-dried tomatoes. Then move on to lombata de vitello saville (veal chops) or the tonno alla alexis (yellowfin tuna topped with sun-dried cranberries, shiitake mushrooms and scallions).

Charlie's Pool Room, 1122 East Blvd., Alpha; (908) 454-1364. The state's oddest/coolest hot dog joint, with its squeaky hardwood floors, one pool table, wooden cash register and one item on the menu — hot dogs, topped with "Grandma's Fencz's secret sauce." Absolutely not to be missed.

Chocolate Shoppe, 22 E. Washington Ave., Washington; (908) 475-1218. Old-fashioned candy store right out of your childhood. Average chocolate overall, although we liked the strawberry cheesecake candies and the chocolate potato chips. Sweetest surprise: the dark chocolate cherries, with a lush, liquidy core.

Hog Hollow Bar-B-Que, 400 Route 57, Lopatcong; (908) 454-4294. Barbecue roadhouse decorated with pig kitsch. Meaty, smoky, tender ribs, beautiful baked beans and irresistible sweet-potato fries.

Hot Dog Johnny's, Route 46, Buttzville; (908) 453-2882. Roadside hot dog shrine overlooking the Pequest River. Many swear by these dogs; we don't.

Jim's Doggie Stand, 7 Union Square, Phillipsburg; (908) 454-2999. A variety of dogs available here, including a slammin' Berks beef and pork with a cheese and jalapeno interior.

Joe's Steak Shop, 274 S. Main St., Phillipsburg. A steak sandwich legend in this part of the state, although we couldn't understand why. The steak sandwich contains a heap of meat, but it's dried out, and the sausage in the sausage sandwich is practically tasteless. Good onion rings, though.

Log Cabin Inn, 47 Route 46, Columbia; (908) 496-4291. Abe Lincoln never slept here, but he would have felt at home in this rambling roadhouse. Old-time beer signs, mounted antlers and a funhouse-like tilted floor add to the appeal. I loved the sausage-and-mushroom pie, but most of the Munchers preferred the plain pie. Great place to spend an afternoon; the Delaware River is right across the street.

Red Wolfe Inn, 130 Route 519, White Twp.; (908) 475-4772. Owner Rudy Walz keeps four friendly wolf hybrids — including one named Chaos — in an enclosure. Where's the beef? Inside. The 24-ounce New York strip Loki, named after one of Walz's former hybrids, is excellent. If you must try one dish, though, make it the rack of lamb.

Runway Cafe, 36 Lambert Road, Blairstown; (908) 362-9170. Many of Jeanne Anderson's customers are pilots; one rigged straps on the plane floor to hold his pies down. Apple pie, with layers of Granny Smith apples and the barest of crusts, is good, but her coconut custard, creamy without being runny, is super.

Sammy's, Route 22 West, across from the Phillipsburg Mall, Pohatcong. Good roadside dogs, excellent milk shakes. Tuesday is classic car night.

Sub Shack, 312 Main St., Hackettstown; (908) 852-6677. You'll like the ambience — cramped quarters, slightly tilted ceiling — although maybe not the cheesesteaks. Philly-style steak came with substandard, overcooked meat. "French- style" cheesesteak, with white American cheese, sauteed mushrooms and an onion sauce, more palatable.

Thisilldous Eatery, 320 Front St., Belvidere; (908) 475-2274. One of the best little luncheonettes around. Creative omelets, including the Farm to Market (tomatoes, broccoli, spinach, mushrooms and other vegetables) and the Firecracker, an eye-opening mix of hot pepper relish, bacon and cheese with nary a hint of grease.

Toby's Cup, 857 Memorial Parkway (Route 22), Lopatcong. Part fast-food joint, part carnival funhouse, with eight-sided structure, grinning clown face and panoramic views of New Jersey's kookiest highway. Big surprise: excellent steak sandwich, on good torpedo roll. Good shakes, too.

THE 10TH ANNIVERSARY RUN

In 2008, the Munchmobile celebrated its gala 10th anniversary with substance, style and the usual great big appetite. We did the standards — ice cream, healthy food, baked goods, Down the Shore, 4th of July picnics — while adding such categories as chowder, curry, real Chinese, and trips concentrated on two highways — Route 46 and Route 206. Several former Giants players accompanied us on our steak sandwich excursion, and seven women marathon runners showed they could really chow down on our fried chicken trip. On our last trip, a group of Newark firemen were guests of the summer's last trip: reader's choice, after which the Big Dog rode off into the sunset, to await 2009 and more roadside food adventures.

BERGEN

The Emerson Hotel, 31 Emerson Plaza East, Emerson; (201) 262-7557. Call this gingerbread hotel across from the railroad tracks Victorian-meets-Bergen County. Wonderfully tender meat in the steak sandwich, but it was too buttery, and the barely-there bread didn't help.

Havana The King of Cuban Steak Sandwiches, 525 Moonachie Road, Wood-Ridge; (201) 933-3111. Cozy little storefront with tiki-hut-thatched front counter. The steak sandwich is good, greasy and garlicky, the latter from the mojito, or Cuban garlic marinade.

Pizza Town USA, 89 Route 46 west, Elmwood Park; (201) 797-6172. First pizzeria in New Jersey to introduce pizza by the slice — or so they say. Decent, straightforward pie; no superlatives, no surprises. But worth a late-night stop if you're on Route 46; it screams Jersey.

CAPE MAY

Bella Vida Cafe on Broadway, 406 N. Broadway, Cape May; (609) 884-6332. Cozy cafe far from the madding Cape May crowd. Creative, though not always successful, takes on breakfast. Recommended: the seafood club, and the Land and Sea burger, topped with crab and shrimp salad.

Crab Cake Hotline, 24th Street and New Jersey Avenue, North Wildwood; (609) 523-2400. Walk-up stand. We were of several minds about the "signature" crab cakes, but several seafood dishes rocked, especially the shrimp scampi and the stuffed flounder. The owner, the crab pendant-wearing Vince Cacio, is a character.

Duffer's, Hildreth and Pacific avenues, Wildwood; (609) 729-1817. Celebrated Wildwood ice cream store offered decent, but not daring, product. The maple walnut ice cream and the Chocolate Storm sundae, with caramel and Heath bar crunch, best of the bunch.

Vanilla Bean Creamery, 958 Route 109, Lower Township. Ramshackle house converted into a cheery ice cream stand. The peach ice cream is sensational; it whispered more than screamed peach. If there's a better chocolate ice cream than the chocolate fudge chip here, I haven't found it.

ESSEX

Jefferson's Cafe, 88-90 Maple Ave., Montclair; (973) 744-2106. Memorable Southern/soul food in plain-Jane storefront. The fried chicken got my vote as the best of our fried chicken trip. The sausage biscuits will brighten your day, or breakfast. And don't forget to try some of Sasha Price's cakes, especially the coconut and carrot ones.

Jimmy Buff's, 60 Washington St., West Orange; (973) 325-9897. You can smell the peppers and onions in the parking lot of this tiny, narrow doggie diner. "Perfect greasy goodness" was one Muncher's analysis of the Italian hot dog. It's still the benchmark for Italian hot dogs.

Hunan Cottage, 14 Route 46 East, Fairfield; (973) 808-8328. I could easily make a meal out of many of the vegetables here, including the scallions in the squid with hot pepper sauce. We loved the conch with basil, with its splendid, complex brown sauce, and the beef with bamboo shoots. Start your meal off with the top-notch soup dumplings.

Island Life Cafe, 307 Irvington Ave., South Orange; (973) 763-7900. Storefront with colorful murals of Jamaican advertising icons. Ask for your jerk chicken spicy; ours was too toned-down. Oxtails tender and tasty, and the chicken curry worth a try. And don't miss the juice bar!

Park Wood Diner Restaurant, 1958 Springfield Ave., Maplewood; (973) 313-3990. Creative, fresh salads. I didn't like the "sliced Roumanian steak" in the steak sandwich; others did. First-rate onion rings.

HUDSON

Chicken Galore, 325 Kearny Ave., Kearny; (201) 998-3034. Crispy, crunchy chicken in 45-year-old chicken joint. A shrine to all things fried: you can get fried Snickers, fried Oreos, fried broccoli, and more. The chicken among the day's best. The ribs are pretty good, too. Subs Galore, its sister shop, is next door.

Dos Amigos, 5300 Bergenline Ave., West New York; (201) 348-2255. Cash only, and pretty much one item on the menu — steak sandwiches. The meat, the thin layer of crispy potatoes and the flaky, chewy roll made for the day's best — and cheapest — steak sandwich, in my opinion.

Helmer's, 1036 Washington St., Hoboken, (201) 963-3333. Casual but classy high-ceilinged haunt. The steak — strips of succulent, juicy top round — is excellent, but the bread is bland. Excellent selection of beers, and a wide-ranging menu.

The Little Food Cafe, 330 Kennedy Blvd., Bayonne; (201) 436-6800. Cute, sun-shiny cafe with plenty of nutritional — and naughty — choices. The taco turkey wrap is marked a "must" on the menu, and it more than qualifies. The roasted breaded eggplant sandwich with fresh mozzarella and homemade pesto is scrumptious. Excellent brownies, fudgy and chewy.

Su Healthy Cuisine, 725 River Road, Edgewater; (201) 840-7988. Healthy Asian-influenced fare served with flair. The eggplant parmigiana the single best dish of our healthy food outing. The nori-wrapped bean curd with baby bok choy: sounds dubious, tastes delicious. Spring rolls and handmade scallion pancakes are recommended appetizers.

MERCER

The Brothers Moon, 7 W. Broad St., Hopewell; (609) 333-1330. Tables to the right, temptation to the left, in the form of a long display case jammed with baked goods, cheeses and prepared foods. The mushroom risotto cakes are marvelous. Loved the red, juicy meat in the roast beef, Gruyere and greens salad, but it deserved better than the bland country bread. Call the chocolate mousse the ultimate chocolate pudding.

Peggy Sue's Ice Cream, 8 Gordon Ave., Lawrenceville; (609) 620-0044. Cute, cozy ice cream shop decorated with pictures of pop culture icons. Solid, though not spectacular, ice cream. My chocolate milk shake could have been better. Tables outside. Hot dogs also on the menu.

MIDDLESEX

George Street Co-Op, 89 Morris St., New Brunswick; (732) 247-8280. One of the state's best-known co-ops. Of the packaged salads and sandwiches, we liked Moshe's Organic Hummus Sandwich and the Sunneen Vegetarian Chicken Deluxe Sandwich. One loser: the Sassy Soy Sandwich. We made S'mores-like treats out of Green & Black's Organic Dark Chocolate.

Wonder Seafood Restaurant, 1984 Route 27, Edison; (732) 287-6328. Busy, frenetic dining room. Many of the dishes are overly salty, but there are several standouts, including the divine, delicious soft shell crab with salt pepper, and the jellyfish with boneless duck feet. Try it, you'll like it.

MONMOUTH

Caputo's, 444 Ocean Blvd., Long Branch; (732) 222-3838. Neighborhood bakery, albeit one located a block from the beach. Nothing special here; the danish — big, chewy, fruity — are the best bet.

The Flaky Tart, 145 First Ave., Atlantic Highlands; (732) 291-2555. Owner Marie Jackson makes limited quantities of high-quality danish, muffins, croissants, scones and, yes, tarts. Her almond danish is near-pastry-perfection. Not everything succeeds — the blueberry muffin seemed short on blueberries, and the pecan sticky bun is not gooey enough.

La Rosa's Pastry Shop, 79 E. Newman Springs Road, Shrewsbury; (732) 842-2592. Call this Cannoli Central; they make 9 million cannoli a year, many for restaurants. The variety is impressive — chocolate truffle cannoli, peanut butter cannoli, and more. Ordinary cream puffs, good sfogliatelle.

Trinity Restaurant, 84 Broad St., Keyport; (732) 888-1998. Church converted into restaurant. Our resident crab expert called the soft shell crab here the best he's ever had. Pork chop monstrous and tender, but lacking flavor. Best dish: the Hukilau Pot, with shrimp, clams, monkfish, stir-fried veggies, sausage and couscous.

MORRIS

Chef 81, 81 N. Beverwyck Road, Lake Hiawatha; (973) 335-9988. Love the decor; call it '50s-airport lounge-meets-Shanghai-noodle house. The braised duck Shanghai style? Call it the best Thanksgiving ever; it's that good. The day's best soup dumplings. The sautéed fresh water eel Shanghai, with scallions and a smooth, silky brown sauce, made for a slithery surprise.

Cliff's Dairy Maid, 1475 Route 46 West, Ledgewood; (973) 584-9721. My vote for the state's best roadside ice cream stand. The double-dark chocolate fudge crunch in a sugar cone — I could live on that alone.

Jamaican James Jerk Pit Restaurant, 1034 Route 46 East, Ledgewood; (973) 252-4339. I couldn't stop eating the curry goat here. The jerk chicken neither savory nor spicy, but we liked the oxtail and the curry chicken.

Kristine's Dessert Works, 1206 Sussex Turnpike, Randolph; (973) 895-9656. Open-kitchen shop; watch owner Kristine Mavraganis spin her sugary spell. The coconut fudge bar is wonderful; the blueberry tart, full of fresh sweet berries, is terrific.

Market Place, 182 Route 206, Mount Olive, (973) 448-1530. Everything you could possibly want under one roof: sandwiches, salads, desserts, meats, gourmet items, even wine and beer. I really liked several salads — the Mediterranean shrimp salad, the San Gennaro pasta salad, and the crunchy wheatberry salad.

M&S II Pizzeria, Route 46 East, Rockaway; (973) 361-9137. Average pizza, at best. Garlic knots are lacking in garlic, and the dipping sauce tasted right out of the jar.

Noodle Chu, 770 Route 46 East, Parsippany; (973) 299-6518. Spare-looking storefront opens into a spacious, high-ceilinged dining room. Ask for the little black-book-like Chinese menu. The sautéed fresh frogs with yellow chives are special, and is the Triple Crown (shrimp, scallops and squid) in chili and special salt.

Pat Thai, 435 N. Beverwyck Road, Lake Hiawatha: (973) 257-1444. Storefront tucked around the side of the local ShopRite. Our favorite curry here: the yellow, with carrot, onion, peas, tomatoes, cumin and turmeric. Perfect ending: the delicious little banana spring rolls.

Saffron, 249 Route 10 East, East Hanover; (973) 599-0700. Dishes artfully constructed; the saffron tikka is ringed by what seems like an endless necklace of cucumber. The goat curry is husky, tender and spellbinding. Also liked the saffron tikka, the lamb jardalo and the Goa shrimp curry.

OCEAN

Olde Corner Deli, 22 Central Ave., Island Heights; (732) 288-9098. Hardwood-floored deli in sleepy little Island Heights. Squishy-good roast beef sloppy Joe, and fresh-tasting vegetables. The prosciutto, mozzarella and roasted red peppers wrap a winner.

Shut Up and Eat!, 213 Route 37 East, Toms River; (732) 349-4544. There's no place quite like it in New Jersey: the waitresses wear pajamas, and there's a ton of 1950s kitsch on the walls. But it's not merely show; the food's quite good, especially the peach pear stuffed French toast, and the omelets.

PASSAIC

Chicken Supreme, 309 Union Ave,. Paterson; (973) 790-6145. The owner told us he sells more chicken than any other single chicken joint in the state. Nice, crackly skin, but the meat nowhere as juicy as others sampled on our trip.

The Hot Grill, 669 Lexington Ave., Clifton; (973) 772-6000. "World's Tastiest Texas wieners" are hardly that. So-so dog and overly-cinnamon-y chili.

Khun Thon, 179 Cahill Cross Road, West Milford; (973) 506-4942. Top-notch Thai and curry at the top of Jersey. Golden curry puffs, delicately fried, one of my favorite dishes of the summer. Fresh Vietnamese rolls, soft shell crab, Singapore noodles and the green curry with pork also standouts.

Libby's, 98 McBride Ave., Paterson; (973) 278-8718. A hot dog with history, though it tastes rather ordinary. Best part about a visit: walking across the street and marveling in the Great Falls' thundering, spellbinding majesty.

Pizza 46, 1188 Route 46 West, Little Falls; (973) 256- 4646. "Quintessential Jersey pie" was one Muncher's apt description of the pizza here. Excellent garlic knots.

Sam I Am Bagels, 225 Route 46 West, Totowa; (973) 785-3399. Highway bagel store claims "the most exotic specialty bagels in the state." Forty kinds in all. Fat, chewy bagels, and fresh, funky spreads.

SOMERSET

Joe's Pizza Restaurant, 856 Route 206, Hillsborough; (908) 874-6661. Better-than-average thin-crust pizza. Toppings-wise, the mushrooms are much better than the sausage.

SUSSEX

Cafe Pierrot, 212 Route 206, Andover; (973) 786-6069. Makes the baked goods for sister restaurant in Sparta. Great — I use that word sparingly — scones. The apple pie is jammed with fresh-tasting apples — what a concept! Excellent muffins, walnut bars and danish. Good luck getting out of here with just an item or two.

Everything Homemade, 68 Olde Lafayette Village, Lafayette; (973) 300-3336. Bakery nestled amid outlet shops and craft stores. Delicious apple strudel, and the berry and apricot star pastries are incomparably flaky. Outstanding carrot cupcake.

Grist Mill Cafe, 4 Lenape Road, Andover; (973) 786-6400. Every town should have a place like this, a book-lined coffeehouse with good, healthy salads and sandwiches. Must-tries: the tarragon chicken salad, the grilled veggie panini, and the blueberry pancakes. There's a jazz brunch on Sundays.

Riviera Maya, 340 Route 206, Branchville; (973) 948-0964. One of the state's most colorfully kitschy restaurants; tables are decorated with bright suns, smiling parrots, hard-working villagers. The mixote, pork tenderloin in a delicious, tangy sauce, a stunner. The cactus steak will satisfy your red-meat fix. Salsa markedly better than the chain-Mexican versions.

UNION

Blackberry's, 500 Watchung Ave., Plainfield; (908) 755-3444. The owner is Shelly Withers, who is making a name for herself in the Queen City. Her fried chicken is fine; the sides are fabulous, including the black-eyed peas and sweet potatoes. Fun place; albums and 45s of soul/R&B artists provide the decor.

Galloping Hill Inn, 325 Chestnut St., Union; (908) 686-2683. Five Points landmark started as a fruit stand 80-plus years ago. The hot dog roll is soft, spacious and wonderfully chewy, and the hot relish is spicy and addictive. Beer on tap.

International Pastry, 73 Westfield Ave., Clark; (732) 381-3570. The day's best croissant, fat, chewy and flaky. The dietary apple strudel is surprisingly good. The puff pastries: wonderfully flaky, but so-so fruit.

Just a Little Healthier, 228 W. Scott Ave., Rahway; (732) 381-5777. Replaced Pat's Cafe. The lunch order took forever to complete, but there was much to like, including the apple walnut salad with grapes in honey-orange lemon juice, and the chipotle chicken sandwich, with lettuce, tomato, vegenaise (vegan mayo) and pepper jack cheese.

Star of India, 496 Boulevard, Kenilworth; (908) 272-6633. Cool, quiet hideaway on Kenilworth's main drag. The curry trip's most fragrant if not overpowering curries; subtlety not spoken here. The lamb vindaloo is the Bombay bomb, with its spicy, tangy, tomatoey sauce.

Sweet Lew's Bakery and Pastry Shoppe, 1348 South Ave., Plain-field; (908) 222-1001. Bakery located in space formerly occupied by Margie's Cake Box. Good danish, but nothing you can't find elsewhere. We loved the apple pocket, with a soft, sugary crust and great filling.

Swiss Pastry Shoppe, 1711 E. Second St., Scotch Plains; (908) 322-4751. Get the rugelach warm out of the oven and be prepared to be transported to pastry paradise. Canned filling, though, in several pastries, and neither the croissants nor the apple strudel made an impression.

WARREN

Golden Skillet, 333 Mountain Ave., Hackettstown; (908) 852-5552. The Munch fried chicken jury split on this one. Several called it the day's best chicken, but I don't think it's anywhere as good as Chicken Galore, Blackberry's or Jefferson's Cafe. A bit too salty and greasy for my taste. Really liked the grouper sandwich, though.

Gunnar's Landing, 487 Route 46 East, White Township; (908) 475-4900. The food (sports bar-worthy, nothing more) takes a back seat to the lovely location, on the Pequest River. Our favorite item: the crackly-good chicken quesadillas.

Hong Kong Palace, 192 Mountain Ave., Hackettstown; (908) 850-4212. The least authentic of the "real Chinese" restaurants visited, but we liked several dishes, including the house special fried rice; the Singapore noodles; and the beef chow ho fun.

Hot Dog Johnny's, Route 46 East, Buttzville; (908) 453-2882. I've never been a fan of this roadside legend, but the dog did taste snap-pier and fresher than on previous occasions. One thing I have not yet steeled myself for: a hot dog with buttermilk.

Smokehouse Barbecue & Tavern, 86 Route 46 West, Indepen-dence; (908) 850-6677. Another place claiming "world famous" food that doesn't deserve the tag. Just-okay ribs, but the monstrous beef ribs are charred and oh-so-chewy. Excellent onion rings and Southern mashed sweet potatoes.

ALPHABETICAL INDEX

F

G

H

I

M

O

P

W

Y

Z

CUISINE INDEX

African

American   *See also Barbecue; Buffet; Cheesesteak; Diner; Southern/Soul*

Asian   *See Chinese; Indian; Japanese; Korean; Sushi; Thai; Vietnamese*

Bagels

Bakeries

227

Barbecue

Breakfast *See also Coffee Shop; Donuts*

Buffet

Caribbean

Cheesesteak

Chinese

Coffee Shop *See also Breakfast; Donuts*

Deli *See also Polish Deli*

Dessert   *See also Ice Cream; Italian Ices*

Diner

Donuts

Drive-ins

European *See German; Greek; Irish; Italian; Italian Ices; Pizzeria; Polish Deli; Portuguese; Spanish*

Fast Food

German

Greek

Health Foods

Hot Dogs

Ice Cream

Indian

Irish

Italian   *See also Pizzeria*

Italian Ices

Japanese   *See also Sushi*

Korean

Lebanese

Mexican

Middle Eastern *See also Turkish*

Pizzeria

Soup

South American

Southern/Soul

Southwestern

Spanish

Sports Bar

Steak House

Sushi

Thai

Turkish

Vegetarian

Vietnamese